The Psychology of Learning
and
Techniques of Teaching

FRONTISPIECE

Which is it – an old woman with chin sunk in wrap, or the heroine of an
early twentieth-century romantic novel, her chin in air?

The Psychology of Learning

and

Techniques of Teaching

JAMES M. THYNE, M.A., Ed.B., F.B.Ps.S.

Principal Lecturer in Psychology
Jordanhill College of Education
Glasgow

UNIVERSITY OF LONDON PRESS LTD

UNIVERSITY OF LONDON PRESS LTD
ST PAULS HOUSE WARWICK LANE LONDON EC4

Printed in Great Britain for the UNIVERSITY OF LONDON PRESS LTD
by NEILL & CO. LTD, Edinburgh

Contents

Preface to the Second Edition

The second edition contains a new chapter, *Teaching by Programming*. That addition has been made not only because the developing interest in programming suggests that that technique should be included but also because an analysis of it serves very well to illustrate, extend, organise and make more precise the principles discussed in the earlier chapters. For that reason, understanding of the new chapter will depend to a large extent upon understanding of the others.

There are also two changes in terminology. Since the programmer's usage of the term 'prompt' is almost the same as my previous usage of the term 'pilot-cue', I have substituted the former in the interest of parsimony. The other substitution is that of 'reinforcer' in place of 'tie'. Until fairly recently the term 'reinforcer' was customarily introduced as a technical term for Reward, and in many texts is still used in that way. More recent accounts, however, have tended to use the term to refer not to any particular sort of item but rather to a *function*, namely the function of increasing the probability of a specified response's being made to a given kind of situation. This latter usage is so close to what was intended by my term 'tie' that here also parsimony of terminology suggests that I should adopt the more widely known term. The basic theoretical concepts themselves nevertheless remain the same; only the names have been changed.

J. M. T.

Preface to the First Edition

This book, intended for student-teachers, aims to show how a knowledge of the nature of learning can give guidance to the act of teaching. If, as I have assumed, the primary purpose of teaching is the promotion of learning, teaching has the peculiar function of satisfying the various conditions learning requires; and the greater one's knowledge of these requirements the more intelligent and efficient one's teaching can be. Such knowledge provides the basis of a rationale of teaching-technique.

In concentrating on the acts of teaching, the book omits many topics properly included in textbooks of educational psychology. But its restriction to issues like Habit-training, Habit-breaking, and Explaining allows a more thorough treatment of teaching-technique than is practicable in texts of a more general kind. Pupils may, of course, learn a great deal without being taught, but it is with the actual business of teaching that this book is concerned. I believe, and shall try to show, that between teaching-technique and the necessarily limited psychological knowledge the student-teacher can be expected to acquire, it is possible to establish a relationship which is both systematic and profitable.

That affirmation may seem unduly optimistic. It is true that the psychology of learning is far from complete, and that the number of well-substantiated findings applicable to human learning is disappointingly small. I am, nevertheless, of the opinion that the paucity of the literature on the teaching-learning relationship is due, in large measure, to our giving insufficient thought to it. The knowledge we do have, small as it may be, is sufficient to make teaching much more effective than it would be without that knowledge – if we organise it in the appropriate way.

Serious thinking is needed, however, not only by the educationist-psychologist but also by the teacher himself, for if the relationship between the psychology of learning and teaching-technique is to be effective, it is within the mind of the teacher that that relationship must hold, and to achieve this he must be prepared to think hard and think straight about the tasks he has to perform. It is, of course, true that in the school of experience one learns lessons that cannot be learnt elsewhere. I have no doubts about that. But a woolly belief in the value of 'experience', or reiteration of faith in the 'personality' of the teacher, is no substitute for professional competence that can be won only by honest thinking and action based on insight. Accordingly, while I shall present what I believe to be the major, relevant, facts of learning, yet I am concerned primarily with the way in which they will be thought about. My underlying purpose is to suggest a way of thinking about learning which will be profitable to those who aim to promote it.

The basic concepts and theses of the book are worked out in Part One; in Part Two these are applied to a variety of teaching techniques. For this reason, and others, the student is advised to read the chapters in the order in which they have been written. The reader with little or no previous knowledge of psychology is invited to ignore the footnotes.

Acknowledgments are due to many people: to colleagues past and present who have discussed the subject-matter of the book with me and suggested improvements; to students who by their questions and comments have helped me clarify my own thinking; to those teachers and lecturers, a generation ahead of me, who kindled my interest in teaching as a skill; to my teachers of psychology who first encouraged me to think imaginatively about psychological problems; to many authors whom I know and respect only by their works. No one of them is likely to agree with the whole book, but for those parts of it which they like they have my sincere thanks.

J. M. T.

PART ONE

WHAT IS LEARNING?

1 · Teaching and Learning

Teaching – The Promotion of Learning

The teacher fills many roles: examiner, vocational adviser, disciplinarian, moralist, administrator, and many more. But all are subsidiary to his chief function, namely to teach. What he teaches will vary from generation to generation, age-group to age-group, culture to culture. It might be reading, writing, and arithmetic. It might be a moral code, citizenship, the elements of a trade, a religious system, or, as in Fagin's school, the art of picking pockets. Yet whatever he teaches the intention is the same, that his pupils will learn it: the primary purpose of all teaching is the promotion of learning.

It follows that the student of teaching must be at the same time a student of learning, for how can he hope to promote it if he is ignorant of it? He must, of course, know other things also: a variety of subjects such as English, arithmetic, and so on; he should know something about Intelligence and its measurement, about Child Development, Personality, and so forth. The view of the teacher as a promoter of learning nevertheless implies that he will study these things, not merely for their own sake, but because a knowledge of them contributes to his chief task of promoting learning. If his pupils are to learn arithmetic, patently he must himself be a competent arithmetician; and the study of (for example) Child Development would help him plan his work in accordance with the capabilities and interests of the age-group he was teaching.

I shall nevertheless put the emphasis on learning itself, for there are certain fundamental principles of learning common to all subjects and all learners, principles which are therefore an appropriate topic of study by all teachers. It could perhaps be objected that in order to promote learning the teacher need not know about learning as such; all he need know are the procedures, methods, techniques, stratagems or dodges which promote it. But that is not enough for the most effective teaching; it requires a knowledge of learning itself.

Learning How to Teach

Since not all procedures promote learning, the teacher must select procedures which do. Despite some truth in the dictum that a teacher is born, not made, he is not born ready armed with a repertoire of effective pedagogical techniques. Somehow he must learn which procedures are the most effective.

He might learn this by trial and error. That way of learning permits a sense of independence, and has the further advantage that he is likely to be most thoroughly convinced of the soundness (or futility) of a teaching method only when he has tried it out for himself and noted the results. On the debit side, the only relevant results are the pupils' learning (or lack of it), and since pupils necessarily take time to learn, the student-teacher may not be with his pupils long enough to make an assessment. And even if his errors are available for inspection, they may not be recognised or admitted; it is more comfortable to suppose that one's class is stupid, or inattentive, than to concede that one's teaching is unsatisfactory. Also, learning to teach by trial and error ignores the skill and knowledge acquired by others. Young teachers tend to assume that the problems they meet are peculiar to themselves, whereas a great many of the difficulties they encounter are familiar to their older colleagues and have already been overcome. Must the pupils' learning suffer for needless errors in their teacher's trials?

A second way of learning to teach is suggested by this last criticism of trial and error. The prospective teacher might learn to teach by imitating the procedures used by teachers of greater experience. This assumes, however, that the student-teacher knows which of his seniors best merit imitation. Even if this difficulty is overcome his imitating may be blind and consequently ineffective: he may try to apply a copied procedure to a learning-situation to which it is in fact inappropriate; or he may not appreciate that what seems to be a novel situation can be tackled by means of a procedure he has already acquired. In copying blindly he may fail to distinguish the 'bones' of the procedure from aspects of it dependent upon the personality of the teacher from whom he copied it, and having very little to do with its efficiency; or from aspects of it peculiar to the particular learning-situation in which he has seen it used.

Much the same criticism applies also to learning to teach by trial and error. There, what the learner does in effect is copy his own previously successful performances; but if he does not see why they were successful he may find that they do not work on occasions which he fails to see are significantly different from those on which he previously achieved success. Likewise, he may fail to apply the previously successful procedures to situations which are essentially but not obviously the same as those involved in the earlier successes.

The crux of the matter is that a teaching-procedure, whatever it may be, works well not just because of what it is in itself (such as speaking slowly, writing notes on a blackboard, making jokes, using illustrations, asking questions in the course of the lesson) but because it meets the requirements of the learning-situation to which it is applied. I doubt if this point can be over-emphasised. A teaching-technique works because it fits. It must therefore be designed for the express purpose of making learning take place; the gears of teaching must be cut so as to engage the cogs of learning. Teaching-techniques cannot be assessed in a vacuum. They are tools; like keys they must be judged not by their intrinsic elegance, nor conformity to contemporary fashion, nor historical interest, but by whether they turn the locks of learning.

The implication of the analogy is that if tools are to be designed to do a particular job, the designer must be thoroughly familiar with the nature of the job they have to do. I appreciate that it could be argued that the teacher need not be the designer, and is only the workman who will use the tools designed for him by someone else. Yet even if we rate the teacher so low, it is nevertheless necessary that the workman should have sufficient insight into the nature of the job to enable him to select appropriately and use effectively the tools provided. If a teaching-technique is good in so far as it meets the requirements of learning, for the most effective teaching the teacher must bear these requirements in mind and so must be familiar in the first place with the nature of learning itself.

This thesis implies a third way of learning to teach, namely by insight into the nature of the learning which has to be promoted. This way will be examined in a moment. First we may note how it relates to imitation and trial and error. It does not imply that the teacher must think out every teaching-technique for himself, never resorting to imitation. What is suspect is not imitation as such, but only imitation that is blind; if, however, the student-teacher has a knowledge of the nature of learning his imitating will not be blind. Shown a procedure he has not thought of for himself, he will see why it is likely to be (or not to be) effective; it will be seen to be (or not to be) in accord with the way in which he now knows learning takes place. With that knowledge he need teach neither with blind trust, nor with equally blind distrust, in his advisers. If he chooses to copy a procedure he recognises as useful, he will be able to adapt it to suit his own special talents, or different subject-matter, or different pupils, because now he will recognise its characteristic features, the features which make it effective. As for trial and error, knowledge of the nature of learning is not yet sufficiently detailed to provide the teacher with every procedure he will need, but his trials can be guided by his knowledge of the *kind* of technique the promotion of learning requires, so that his trials will be nearer the mark and his errors will be less frequent and less serious.

Accordingly, learning to teach by insight into the nature of learning does not preclude one's learning to teach also by trial and error and by imitation. On the contrary, it makes capital of their advantages while at the same time eliminating their major disadvantages. In addition, it allows of the construction of new techniques which are unlikely to be found by trial and error alone and which, being new, are not available for imitation.

Learning about Learning

The main point has been that the teacher will promote learning most effectively if he has insight into the nature of learning; in short, if he can answer the question, 'How does learning take place?' To answer that question is one of the main purposes of this book, and our subsequent task will be simplified if we note first that this is really two questions in one, and make clear what the two questions are.

On the one hand there is the question, 'What makes learning take place?' In more formal language, 'What conditions govern learning?' It is sometimes suggested, for example, that reward of some kind is necessary for learning, or that practice is needed, or that on occasion the learner may have to be punished. Whether these are valid conditions we need not consider just now. The present point is that none of these things – reward, practice, punishment – is itself learning, though they may be things that make it occur. A prize may induce Jack to learn some geometry; but neither the promise nor the award of the prize, nor even the pleasure he has in receiving it, is itself the learning of the geometry. A month's imprisonment may cause Bill to refrain from stealing; but the being locked up, effective as it may be, is not itself the learning not to steal. Such things, even when they do make learning take place, themselves stand outside the learning itself. Like the increase in pressure under which a gas may contract, but which is not itself that contraction, they are (possibly) 'conditions' of learning, but not learning itself. Plainly anything which *makes* learning take place is not itself learning.

This is in no sense to make light of them, for if we are to make learning take place we must know what its conditions are. All I have been emphasising, for a reason about to be given, is that they are not themselves learning.

On the other hand, if we are to discover and make effective use of the conditions governing the event, learning, we must know also what that event is. It would be foolish to look for the causes of an event if we could not recognise the event when it took place, for if we could not recognise it we could never be sure we had made it occur. Also, and particularly relevant to the theme of the following chapters, the more we know about the event itself, the more expeditiously can we discover its conditions of occurrence. To use the same analogy again: if our aim is to turn the lock, we know we need some sort of key; but if we know in detail how that particular lock operates, we can deduce from that knowledge the particular sort of key required. And the more detailed our knowledge of the lock, the greater the guidance we get. It is for this reason that I have spent a considerable amount of time, in the following chapters, in trying to make as clear as possible what learning itself is. It is about this matter that the other aspect of our two-edged question is concerned. In its second sense it is equivalent to, 'Of what events does learning itself consist?', or briefly, 'What *is* learning?'

If he is to promote learning the teacher must be able to answer the first form of the question. To make learning take place is to use procedures providing the conditions which govern learning. He must therefore know what these conditions are. If these conditions are provided, learning will necessarily take place; and so although teaching is popularly envisaged as the using of a number of stock procedures (a view unwittingly caricatured by little girls 'playing school'), any procedure whatsoever merits the name 'teaching' if it does provide the conditions requisite for learning. Two reasons for being able to answer the second form of the question ('What *is* learning?') were given in the last paragraph. Another reason is that the teacher is unlikely to be able to make full use of the conditions of learning unless he sees how they fit in with the learning they govern, sees the peculiar functions they fulfil and how they fulfil them. And to do this he must be familiar with the ways in which learning itself takes place.

If, then, the teacher had a complete knowledge both of what learning is and of its conditions of occurrence, he could work out for himself the essential characteristics of teaching-technique and be completely independent of imitation and trial and error. Here would be teaching par excellence. Unfortunately, no one as yet possesses all the necessary knowledge. What is already known can nevertheless make teaching much more intelligent than it would otherwise be. It is certainly worth asking the two questions – 'What is learning?', and 'What conditions govern learning?'.

How are we to answer them? There are two sources of information, one for each question; and it is of some importance that we should distinguish carefully between them. Only confusion arises if we try to answer one by the means required for the other.

The conditions governing (causing) learning can be discovered in only one way, namely by experiment. If we suspect that a certain circumstance, such as reward, may be a condition of learning, we must compare what happens when that condition holds with what happens when it does not. Such issues are considered in Part Two, where we shall have to examine the circumstances in which habits are formed, in which understanding can take place, in which skills are acquired, and so on.

On the other hand, the answer to 'What *is* learning?' does not depend upon that sort of experiment at all. It poses the same kind of problem as was cited many years ago by William James.[1] A hunter walks in a wide circle round a tree, to try to catch sight of a squirrel which has hidden behind it. But the squirrel has seen him, and as the hunter moves so does the squirrel – round the tree, so that hunter and squirrel always remain face to face, and the same distance apart, but with the tree between them. At last, hunter and hunted return to their original places. Both man and beast have gone round the tree, one in a large and one in a small

[1] And quoted by R. H. Thouless (51).

circle. But has the hunter gone round the squirrel? That apparently simple question can raise heated argument. But what is the argument about? It is not about the events that took place, for these are clear enough. Nor would filming the scene be of any help, for we know already what happened. What is being disputed is not the *event* that took place, but whether it is appropriate to use the *word* 'round' to refer to the event with which we are quite familiar. It is an argument about the use of a word, and involves what is commonly known as a 'verbal problem'.

I am not suggesting that verbal problems are unimportant. On the contrary, in view of the confusion they cause when their nature is not recognised, and they are mistaken for experimental problems, they merit the closest examination. My point is that since they raise questions about the use of words they have to be answered accordingly. 'Did the hunter walk round the squirrel?' is a verbal problem, and the answer depends upon how we define the word 'round'. It is not like the question, 'Was the hunter over six feet tall?', which can be answered by a simple experiment. The question, 'What is learning?' is of the verbal kind, and asks, not for the results of experiments on learning, but for a definition of a word – the word 'learning'.

A way of defining it is exploited in the next chapter, but I should say now that a definition calls not for experiment, but for an assertion. To define a word is to state how one is using it, and a definition is therefore neither right nor wrong. Anyone who defines 'learning' is but indicating the events he means when he uses that word. In effect he is saying 'When I say "learning", I mean this . . .'. The question raised by a verbal problem asks not for an experiment which will add detail to the description of some already specified event, but for a descriptive assertion which will itself specify the event in the first place.

I have stressed this point because few discussions of learning make it explicit, and because I think it is of practical importance. If we try to find out what learning is by performing experiments, we merely become confused and reveal our inability to think clearly about the problem confronting us. But if we appreciate its verbal nature we can exploit the means appropriate to the solution of problems of that kind, and so arrive more directly at a pertinent answer to it.

One final point: if this book is to have its intended effect, it must cause the reader to think, both creatively and critically. But although such thinking may be a prerequisite of good teaching it is not equivalent to it, because teaching is not thinking but acting. The purpose of this book is to help the student-teacher think out what he must do before he begins to do it; to help him to acquire foresight into what he must do in the classroom itself.

2 · What is Learning? –
A Definition

A Method of Defining Learning

The question, 'What is learning?' calls for a definition of the word 'learning', and a definition, as was noted in the last chapter, can be neither correct nor incorrect, for it merely states how a word is being used. Strictly, then, I may define learning in any way I please. I could say, for example, that to learn means to climb a tree, or to have a bath: I should not be wrong, or right, for there is no intrinsic relationship between events and the words used to refer to them. A definition can nevertheless be judged in another way, namely by its usefulness, and on this ground the possible definitions just mentioned would be rejected because no one ever uses the word 'learning' in these ways. These definitions would not be wrong, but they would be out of fashion, so much so as to be worse than useless.

This criterion of usefulness suggests a way of answering the question. My answer to 'What is learning?' is intended to be of use to teachers, and so ought to have regard for what they mean when they use that word. But I cannot simply copy their definition, for the reason that teachers generally do not have occasion to formulate definitions of learning at all. What teachers, and most other people, usually have in mind when they use the word 'learning' is not a formal definition (which I might copy) but a collection of events they regard as 'instances' of learning. Fortunately for my purpose there appears to be a large measure of agreement about these events. Teachers, parents, psychologists, and indeed pupils themselves seem to accept very much the same events as instances of learning. Accordingly, although in everyday speech the word 'learning' has no formal definition, yet this general agreement about events accepted as instances constitutes a common usage in which, as I shall show in a moment, a definition is implicit. This common usage of the word provides the basis of more formal, and at the same time, more useful definition: we can examine a variety of the events generally accepted as instances of learning, and note what they have in common. The assumption behind this procedure is that if the variety of events selected is great enough, what they have in common, but do not share with events not generally accepted as instances of learning, will itself be the learning of which they are said to be instances.[1]

In this chapter, then, I shall examine a variety of events accepted as instances of learning (hereinafter referred to conveniently as 'instances of learning') and note the features they share, but do not share with non-instances. Having abstracted these features I shall then embrace them in a statement which will be as lucid and as concise as I can make it. That statement will be our definition of learning.[2] For the sake of readability, however, I shall introduce exemplary instances as the main argument requires, rather than begin with the long list of instances from

[1] I am rejecting here the notion that there 'really is' a thing called 'learning', lying around somewhere awaiting investigation. I reject it, not on the ground that it is false, or naïve, but on the ground that it is not susceptible of scientific investigation. There is no scientific means of proving that what we observe 'really is' learning. By treating 'What is learning?' as a verbal problem, however, we do have to perform a certain kind of experiment – the kind implied by the procedure just noted in the text, and involving the collection of items characterised by general acceptance, and requiring classification. But this, as I have noted already, is not the same kind of experiment as would be used in answering the question, 'Can week-old infants swim?' See also H. B. English: 'Learning – "They ain't no such animal" ' (11).

[2] Since the number of accepted instances is very large, I can examine only a sample. Also, since learning is usually regarded as being of different kinds (illustrated shortly), a representative rather than a random sample seems to be appropriate. Unfortunately, the various kinds of learning implied by common usage are seldom made explicit and have to be inferred. The argument must therefore be treated critically, though not all apparent exceptions need be exceptions, nor will it be possible to draw attention to every instance likely to be so regarded.

which the argument was in fact derived. Perhaps it should be mentioned also that some non-instances share *some* of the following features; the argument is only that generally accepted instances of learning are characterised by sharing them all.

The Feature of Behaviour

All instances of learning involve the learner in a behaviour of some sort: he learns to *do* something. This feature is obvious in cases described as 'Learning to . . .'. Examples are: learning to drive a car, learning to recite a poem, learning to play the violin. But it is exhibited also, if not obviously, by instances referred to in other ways.

To say that someone is learning a language may not seem to refer to a behaviour; and yet to say so is to imply that he is learning to speak it, write it, and so forth. Were he not learning to *behave* in some such way we should not say he was indeed learning that language. Moreover, did he not behave in some such way we could not know whether he had learned it. Similarly, 'learning a skill' implies that someone is learning to perform some action or system of actions, like riding a bicycle, filleting fish, typing, dancing. 'Learning a game' and 'learning a trick' have the same significance.

The same feature of behaviour is exhibited by instances that could be described as 'Learning to *be* something' – learning to be a teacher, a doctor, a drunkard, a nuisance. A teacher is one who teaches; if he never did any teaching the name 'teacher' would be a misnomer. 'Non-drinking drunkard' is a contradiction in terms. Any name of this sort is a 'functionary' name, referring to someone in terms of the function he performs, naming him by what he does. Conversely, if he does not need to do something to be so named, we do not say he 'learns' to be that named person. We do not speak of 'learning' to be an aunt, or a nephew, or a widow. To learn to be something is at once to learn to do something.

Less clearly exhibiting the feature of behaviour are instances like learning the meaning of a word, learning history, and learning the highway code. These might be called instances of 'Learning to Know'. But if there were no behaviour, we should have no way of ascertaining whether learning had taken place. How, for example, could we judge that a child had learned the meaning of a certain word if he never used it in some way – by providing us with a synonym of it on request, or by using it correctly in context, or by following an instruction couched in terms of it, or something of the sort? I am not denying that there is such a thing as learning to know, or learning to think. I mean only that unless instances of it exhibit the feature of behaviour (which could be the behaviour of speaking), for all practical purposes the instance might as well remain unmentioned, because we should have no way of knowing whether it had taken place.

Instances of 'Learning to Feel' may be treated in the same way. To judge whether someone had in fact learned to enjoy classical music, feel ashamed of telling a lie, like porridge, hate treachery, we should have to observe what he did – speaking being, of course, a form of doing.

There is, however, a class of instances which at first sight might seem to be an exception, namely instances of 'Learning Not to Do Something'. As typical of this class consider the instances, learning not to speak so loudly, and learning not to be cheeky.

The first of these plainly exhibits the feature of behaviour, and not merely the behaviour of speaking loudly, for to learn not to speak so loudly is at once to learn to speak more quietly. (It will be recalled that what I am stating are, not incontrovertible facts, but the implications of common verbal usage). If one stopped speaking altogether, it would be inappropriate to say one had learned not to speak so loudly. That statement implies that one continues to speak, but more quietly. Other examples of this same sort are learning not to be late for school (implying that one learns to arrive in time), learning not to sing out of tune (implying that one learns to sing in tune), and learning not to drive in the middle of the road (implying that one learns to drive at the side of the road). These examples imply, not that the person concerned abandons action, but that he does something else instead.

Even in the second instance – learning not to be cheeky – a new behaviour is implied, though less directly. Cheeky behaviour can occur only in some personal relationship, and when we say that someone has learned not to be cheeky we do not mean that he has become a hermit. Such a step would deprive him of the very opportunity of learning not to do what he has been doing.

We should mean, rather, that on the social occasions on which he used to be cheeky he now behaves in ways that are not cheeky. In this kind of case, however, the form of the new behaviour is very loosely indicated, namely by negation of the form previously engaged in.

So far as instances of learning *not* to do something are concerned, then, the argument is that unless the person behaves in some new way, we cannot know whether he has learned not to behave in the old way.

An example of 'Learning not to Feel' provides a final illustration. To be able to say, with confidence, that a youth had learned not to feel embarrassed when addressed by a young lady, we should have to observe what he now *did* when so addressed. If he did nothing at all, we could not know whether he was aware that she had addressed him; and if his lack of embarrassment could be put down to such unawareness, it would not be customary to say he had now learned not to be embarrassed when so addressed. Usually we should assert such a thing only if we knew that he *was* aware of her; but we should know that he was aware of her only if he reacted in some way to her addressing him. We could assert that he had learned, in this instance, only if behaviour indicative of embarrassment had given place to some other behaviour.

A similar sort of argument applies to instances of 'Learning Not to Think . . .'.

To summarise: in all instances, even those commonly described as 'Learning Not to . . .', someone learns to do something.

The Feature of Change in Behaviour

This second feature has already been mentioned in connection with instances of 'Learning Not to . . .'. In these instances the learner does not merely stop doing what he was doing; he does something else instead. I shall now try to show that this change of behaviour is a feature of other instances also: they involve not only the behaviour said to be learned but also some previous behaviour which is superseded.

Suppose (merely for the sake of argument) that when Jack first sees printed words he reads them correctly. Then if we used the word 'learning' at all to refer to this unusual child, we should have to say he did not need to learn to read. Generally, when someone does something when first given the opportunity of doing it, we do not say he has 'learned' to do it. We do not speak of a child's having to 'learn' to breathe, or to cry. Normal children do these things when first given the chance to do them. We speak of 'learning' to do something only if at the first opportunity, and perhaps at others also, he does not do it. We should usually be entitled to say that a child learns to swim, to read, to speak, to count, because most children, when first in circumstances in which these might be done, do not do them. But not only is the behaviour in question not performed; some other behaviour does appear. The reason for this assertion is the same as that given in the previous section. If the child did nothing at all, we should not know whether learning was necessary. If, for example, he appeared to be unaware of the presence of the printed words, we should not know whether he had learned to read them. We should know that he had still to learn to read if, on being confronted by print, he asked what the words said, or misread them, or told us he could not read, or something of the kind. Likewise, if he never went into water we should not know that he had, or had not, learned to swim. To know that he still had to learn to swim we should have to observe non-swimming behaviour when he went into water deep enough to swim in.

The general principle is that we do not customarily speak of someone's 'learning' to do something unless he previously behaved, in the same circumstances, in a different way. Learning involves the changing of one's behaviour.[1]

The Feature of Situation

A third feature of learning, implicit in all our examples so far, becomes apparent when we observe that in any instance the new behaviour occurs in circumstances of the same sort as those in which the earlier behaviour occurred. For convenience any specified set of circumstances may be called a 'situation'. The point to be made, then, is that in any instance of learning the change of behaviour (noted in the previous section) refers to some particular kind of situation.

In being particular, any kind of situation is restricted. This restriction is imposed in two ways. It is imposed, first, by the nature of the behaviour itself. I cannot learn to swim if there is no water, learn to be a pianist if there is no piano, and so on. Second, the situation is restricted by the circumstances attendant upon learning. No learned behaviour is performed in every kind of situation, even when it is conceivable that it might be. Here is an example.

Tom has learned to answer correctly questions like, 'Six from nine?' and 'Five from twelve?' But the circumstances of his learning could have been such that he does not think of subtracting when confronted by some everyday problem for which subtracting is required. He knows that the distance to his grandmother's house is twelve miles, is told that he has now travelled five miles, and yet asks how far he has still to go. Apparently

---

[1] Of many instances we might say that an old behaviour is 'abandoned' in favour of a new one; but to say this of all instances would exclude cases in which the change entails an *addition* to the old behaviour, and which would generally be accepted as instances of learning. It is therefore more appropriate to speak simply of a change. How great must the change be before we may speak of 'learning'? The answer seems to be that since learning takes place only in specific instances, and since any instance has to be stated before we can argue about it, the nature of the change will be specified by the statement of the instance in question. See also footnote to p. 35.

he has not learned to subtract in this kind of situation. It would therefore be inaccurate, and misleading, to say simply that Tom had 'learned to subtract', if in fact he had learned to subtract only in situations in which he was specifically asked to do so. Likewise, John may seem to have learned to solve simultaneous equations; but it may be that he can solve them only when informed by his teacher or by the page-heading that this is what they are. A child said to have 'learned to be tidy' may be tidy in one kind of situation but not in others. To avoid misunderstanding, therefore, the statement of any instance of learning should contain a reference to the particular kind of situation in which the behaviour occurs.

Nor do we speak of 'learning' unless the old behaviour also was performed in the *same* kind of situation. This point has already been illustrated in another connection. We do not say that a child 'learns' to read unless when first confronted by printed words he does not read, but does something else. The emphasis now, however, is on the point that the non-reading behaviour, like the behaviour of reading, occurs in the same printed-words kind of situation. The new, swimming, behaviour occurs in the same in-the-water kind of situation as did the earlier splashing and spluttering behaviours. In learning to ride a bicycle the earlier behaviours of wobbling about, losing the pedals, and so on, take place in the same on-a-bicycle kind of situation as will the later behaviours of the skilled cyclist. In general, in any instance of learning, the *change* of behaviour relates to some particular kind of situation – the kind of situation varying, of course, from instance to instance.[1]

If, then, Kind of Situation is one of the characterising features of any instance of learning, that feature must be included in any description of it.

[1] I am not asserting that the whole of learning, in any instance, occurs within the situation itself. As William James said, we learn to swim in winter and to skate in summer. My point is simply that any instance of learning exhibits a change of behaviour in the same kind of situation. It is beside the point that this change may be occasioned by events which lie outside that situation. Whatever may happen during the summer, we have not learned to skate until we move skilfully on the ice.

The Feature of Response

In any instance of learning, both the old and the new behaviours occur (in turn) in the same kind of situation. But it is not enough to say only that they take place 'in' the same kind of situation: learning involves a relationship between behaviour and situation more rigorous than the word 'in' implies.

A child has to learn to come indoors when his mother calls him. Suppose now that on several occasions he does come in when so ordered, and that this constitutes a change of behaviour in that kind of situation, for previously he has run away or pretended not to hear. But suppose also that, just as his mother calls, it has begun to rain, or the strains of the introductory music to his favourite TV programme drift from the open window, or he catches sight of his father in the background with an 'or else' look on his face. Then we might doubt whether the child had indeed learned to come in when his mother called him. When we examine the reasons for such a doubt it seems that we should say he had learned, not if he comes in merely *when* (at the time that) his mother calls, but only if he comes in *because* she calls. Coming-in behaviour which is merely coincidental with the mother-calling situation is apparently not enough: the behaviour has to be occasioned, caused, initiated by, has to be a 'response' to, the kind of situation in question.

The statements of other instances have a similar implication. To say that Jim has learned to take off his cap on entering school is to imply, not that he now 'happens' to take off his cap at the time that he is also entering school, but that his cap-doffing behaviour is a result of, is a response to, the entering-school situation. To say that he has learned to read the word 'psychology' is to imply, not that he happens to make the required sound while he happens to be confronted by that printed word, but that what he says is a reaction to, or is occasioned by, or is a response to it. In general, the new behaviour not only has to take place in, but has to be a response to, the kind of situation in question.

While the meaning of this is clear enough, there is a practical difficulty. Even if we accept (as I shall) the psychological axiom that all behaviour is a response to something or other (whether outside or inside the subject), how are we to be sure, in a particular case, that the behaviour we are observing is a response to the particular kind of situation in which we are interested, rather than to something else? How are we to be sure that the child who comes in is indeed responding to his mother's calling? To eliminate the possibility of his behaviour's being a response to something other than the mother's calling, we should have to perform a controlled experiment, observing a series of situations in each of which the mother called him, but which differed one from another in all other features. Complete elimination would, of course, be impossible, because the series would have to be infinite. In practice we must rest content to eliminate other *likely* causes of the child's coming indoors. We might observe what happened on his being called when the TV set was out of order, when his father was at work, when it was not raining, and so on. The greater the number and variety of situations we observed, the more confident could we be that the child's behaviour was indeed a response to his mother's calling, and not to something else.

For all practical purposes, then, we are entitled to say that a certain behaviour is a response to a certain kind of situation only if that behaviour occurs in that kind of situation on a variety of successive occasions.[1]

I have been concentrating on the requirement that the *new* behaviour must be a response to the situation, but the old

---

[1] The number of occasions required for confidence will vary, from case to case, with the number of 'likely' or 'suspected' causes, and so the number of observations required cannot be stated within a general principle. By analogy with the mathematical definition of infinity, or with tests of statistical significance, we might nevertheless say that the number of observations must be at least as great as the critic demands.

From the view expressed in the text it follows that there cannot be a once-only observation of a response (to any *specified* item), because a behaviour's being a response to any specified kind of situation is necessarily a matter of inference from a series of observations. Insistence on a series of observations nevertheless makes it possible to 'cash' the concept of Response in terms of observable events.

behaviour also must have been a response to it. This point has already been made. Unless the learner reacts to the situation we cannot know whether he was indeed aware of it. To know that the child has still to learn to come indoors when called, we must know that the calling has been heard; to know that it has been heard we must observe a response to it; and that response must not be that of coming indoors, for if it were he would not need to learn. Some old response is therefore presupposed. In general, in any instance of learning, there must be a change of *response* to the kind of situation in question.

A Definition of Learning

From a variety of instances of learning four features have been abstracted. In each instance the person concerned learns to do something – the feature of Behaviour. Also, he previously did something different – there is a Change of Behaviour. Further, that change of behaviour occurs in a particular Kind of Situation. Finally, both the old and the new behaviours do not merely 'happen in' the situation: each is occasioned by, or is a Response to it.

In terms of these four features, which appear to characterise learning, any instance of learning may be described as follows. Someone makes one sort of response to a certain kind of situation, and then makes a different sort of response to it. That statement can nevertheless be shortened. Reference to the old response can be made indirectly by our saying that the learner makes a *new* response – the implication being that he previously made a different one. We may let the term 'a situation' do service for 'a kind of situation'. Also, to emphasise the point that 'response' implies a series of behaviours (p. 28), we can use the word 'adopts' in place of the word 'makes'. With these amendments the definition reads thus:

'*To learn is to adopt a new response to a situation.*'

In different sorts of instances of learning, different aspects of the definition will receive emphasis. In the learning of skills, for

B

example, attention is likely to be focused (by the observer) on the complex nature of the response required, rather than upon the kind of situation to which it has to be made.[1] In some instances the new response will be new in only a special sense: saying Thank-you may be a new response by the learner to receiving a compliment, but not a new behaviour for the learner, because she will have said Thank-you before, in response to other situations. In some instances, on the other hand, the response may be new for the learner himself – as in learning to climb a rope. In some instances the response may be simple enough, but the situation may be complex, and attention is likely to be focused on the kind of situation rather than on the response made to it. The relevance (and irrelevance) of these various emphases will be discussed in Part Two.

Some Comments on the Definition

Although the definition just offered has been derived from common usage of the word 'learning', and so does no more than state explicitly what most people presuppose or take for granted when they speak and argue about learning, yet it is not so very different from definitions arrived at in other ways.[2] Some of its implications nevertheless merit comment.

It treats learning as observable, for it is possible to observe the kind of situation present, and also the two series of behaviours constituting the old and the new responses. Popular speech sometimes implies that learning is an activity hidden 'in our heads', or 'in our minds', but it is easier to test hypothetical *conditions* of an event if the event itself is directly observable. For

[1] This example serves to indicate that I am using the term 'response' in a much wider sense than is often implied by exponents of Stimulus-Response theories. It is in accord with what I have been arguing to say that the complex activity of buying a plane ticket, hiring a car, packing one's trunks, and so on, may be a 'response' to an invitation to visit a friend a thousand miles away.

[2] For examples see:
   Yearbook XLI, Part Two, National Society for the Study of Education (35).
   Bugelski: *The Psychology of Learning* (6).
   Hilgard: *Theories of Learning* (21).

that reason I have chosen to define learning as I have done. This does not mean that I think the brain plays no part in learning, or that behaviours never occur out of sight of the interested observer. What the definition does is oblige us to regard these hidden occurrences as conditions *governing* the observable event of learning rather than as part and parcel of that event itself.

As well as excluding reference to brain events, the definition excludes any reference to other events commonly proposed as conditions of learning. For example, to have defined learning as a change in performance as a result of practice would have begged the question (sometimes asked, and presumably worth asking) of whether practice is necessary for learning. With such a definition of learning that question could not be put to the test, because by the definition practice would be presupposed.

Some definitions contain reference to 'Experience'. I have avoided mention of experience for two reasons. For one thing, experience is often equated (sometimes unwittingly) with consciousness, whereas it is obvious that learning (as the term is commonly understood) often occurs without the learner's realising what is happening to him. The formation of some habits illustrates this point. Second, mention both of experience and of response would be redundant. We cannot know that the learner is experiencing some specified thing unless he makes an observable response to it. Conversely, if he does make a response to it (as judged by the 'successive occasions' test noted on p. 28), it would be appropriate to say he must have been experiencing it in one way or another. And since mention of only one of these ('experience', 'response') is enough, mention of the observable event appeared to be the better choice.

The definition eschews value-judgments. For example it does not stipulate that the new response must be better, more efficient, or in any way preferable to the old. That stipulation would have precluded our saying that someone learns to be a thief, or to swear, or to say that six and five are twelve, or to think that Glasgow is the capital of Scotland, or to be careless – except in so far as we were prepared to say that he was now better at doing something bad, or at doing something badly. Since we often do wish to say that someone has learned to be careless, and so on, the exclusion of value-judgments appears to be desirable. For one thing, it saves unnecessary quibbles; for another, it carries the point that there is no *psychological* difference between (say) learning to pronounce 'rough' as 'ruff', and learning to pronounce it as 'roe'.

Further, since change of behaviour, by this definition, is part and parcel of learning, it would be illogical to say that someone changed his behaviour *because* he learned to do so. We might be entitled to use causal terms in referring to conditions *governing* learning. We might say someone changed his behaviour because he was rewarded, or punished, or shown how; but it would be illogical to treat learning as an agency by virtue of which changes in behaviour can be effected. Failure to observe this ostensibly trivial point is not uncommon, and results in howlers like, 'Is this change in behaviour due to learning or to maturation?'[1]

Although the definition refers explicitly to a change of behaviour, yet many instances in school do not exhibit an 'old' behaviour, and so a change of behaviour is not apparent. For example, on first meeting the French word 'vous', the pupil may be told to translate it as 'you'; and here there is no 'old' response to that French word. His being told how to translate it nevertheless presupposes that had he not been told, he would have made a 'wrong' response. An old behaviour is presupposed, even if it is not allowed to occur.

A fundamental implication of the definition is that learning is not some single 'thing': it is, on the contrary, a particular pattern or *Gestalt* of behaviours, in relation to some kind of situation. Any instance of learning can be envisaged as consisting of more basic elements; it is a structure, not an indivisible entity.

Finally, why offer a definition at all? Is it of practical use? In Chapter 1 I answered that question in a rather general way by saying that the more we knew about the lock to be turned, the

---

[1] In accord with the definition offered here, the events commonly referred to in terms of 'maturation' could be proposed as possible *conditions* of learning.

more guidance we got about the kind of key needed to turn it. Now the question can be answered more directly and without resort to analogy. From our initial basic assumption we could infer only that the teacher's job was to promote learning. The inference may be valid, but it is somewhat vague. Now we can be more specific. In any instance, the teacher has to see to it that a new response is made to some specified kind of situation, and so he must decide exactly what form of response he wants and what kind of situation has to elicit it. We can be more specific still. From the definition it is possible to deduce four requirements, no more and no less, which are both necessary and sufficient for learning. The practical value of this exercise in logical deduction is that the requirements so deduced will indicate the *kinds* of conditions we must discover by experiment. These logical requirements specify the peculiar *functions* practical circumstances (conditions) must fulfil, and so give direction to our search for them. They also serve to explain why certain techniques used by the teacher are not fully effective: some of the logically necessary requirements are not met. These four requirements are deduced in the next chapter.

3 · Four Requirements of Learning

The Requirement of Cue

In any instance of learning, the situation must get two responses, an old response and then a new, different response. Further, to ensure that each of these is indeed a response to that situation we must observe a series of behaviours of the kind in question (p. 28). Accordingly, any instance of learning involves a twofold series of behaviours, each beginning in the same kind of situation. If, however, there is to be a series of behaviours, each beginning in the same kind of situation, there must be a series of *situations* of that kind. If, for instance, a child is to learn not to be cheeky, he must participate in a series of social situations in which cheeky and not-cheeky behaviours are possible.

That inference may be obvious, but if the teacher is to promote any instance of learning, he must ensure that the required series of situations occurs; and as I shall illustrate shortly, the matter is not always so simple as it looks. In particular, he must be quite clear about the particular *kind* of situation that has to recur. It is therefore necessary to consider exactly what this requirement means.

The kind of situation involved in any instance is given by the statement of that instance. 'Learning to say Thank-you on getting a present' specifies a getting-a-present kind of situation. 'Learning to swim' specifies (by implication) an in-the-water kind of situation. And so forth.[1] The statement of an instance of learning nevertheless specifies the kind of situation it contains, not by giving a detailed description of a particular situation, but by specifying whatever *feature* makes it the *kind* of situation it is. The expression, 'getting a present', which indicates the kind of situation in the instance, learning to say Thank-you on getting a present, is not a complete description of any particular situation. It is the name of a feature shared by a great variety of situations. The present might be large or small, Christmas or birthday, wrapped or unwrapped, liked or disliked, and so on. The getting-a-present feature is common to, and so characterises the kind constituted by, many otherwise different situations.

Were all instances of learning as simple as those used recently in illustration, the point I have just made would be scarcely worth making, for the characterising feature is obvious. But not all instances are so clearcut; there are many in which the kind-characterising feature is not obvious, and may be very complex. 'Learning to be tactful' is a case in point. The kind of situation calling for a tactful response is often far from simple and not easily recognisable. What does characterise such situations? Many scholastic examples, simple enough at first sight, are in the same case. A child multiplies in trying to solve a problem which calls for division, and is told, 'Surely by now you can recognise a division-problem when you see one?' But by virtue of what feature are such problems to be recognised? What makes them the kind of problem-situations they are? Not all such problems contain in their statements the word 'divide', or 'share' or 'group', or the sign $\div$. And to say that one should divide when one meets a division-problem is sheer tautology – referring to the situation in terms of the sort of response it has to get – when what is required is a statement indicating what the kind of situa-

[1] This presupposes a point already noted (fn. to p. 25), namely that any instance of learning can in fact be stated. I assume that presupposition to be valid on these grounds: if we do not know what the kind of situation is, nor what constitutes the change of response to it, how can we know that what we are considering is indeed an instance of learning? Scholastic instances, of course, are usually stated in advance of their occurrence, and in such cases this argument is unnecessary.

tion is in itself. The most useful statements are those in which the characterising feature is explicitly mentioned. I am not suggesting that the particular problem I have just posed is necessarily a difficult one. It is intended only to illustrate the sort of problem that can arise. Nor am I suggesting that the characterising feature must be named by the pupil. On occasion it might help if he could name it, but there are many cases in which a pupil can recognise a situation yet be unable to put into words the criterion he has used to recognise it. My point refers to the teacher; if the teacher cannot express in words the kind of situation he has to create, his inability to give a description may be a sign that he is not as clear as he should be about the kind of situation that is required.

To return to the main argument: there must be a series of situations of the specified kind. Accordingly, there must be a series of situations each of which exhibits the feature which characterises that kind. If Tom is to learn to say Thank-you on getting a present, patently he must participate in a series of situations in each of which he gets a present. If Mary is to learn to tie her shoelaces, it is a logical necessity that she should be allowed to get into (or be put into) situations in which her shoelaces need tying.

But this requirement, though necessary, is not sufficient. Not only must there be a series of situations each of which exhibits the specified, characterising, feature; strictly, it should be the *only* feature these situations share. If Tom now says Thank-you for all the presents he gets, but all these presents are given to him by his father, we are not entitled to say that Tom has learned to say Thank-you on getting a present. That statement would imply that Tom now says Thank-you for presents generally, whereas the evidence does not warrant such a generalisation. To be confident that Tom has learned to say Thank-you on getting a present, we must have evidence that he now says Thank-you for presents received from many different people, presents which disappoint as well as presents which please, and so on. The presents would have to be given, on some occasions, when his parents were not at hand, and so forth. Strictly, the mere getting of a present should be all that is common to the successive situations. In practice, of course, this logically necessary requirement cannot be met in full; we cannot possibly see to it that the characterising feature is the only feature common to all the situations of the series. We can but judge whether the variety of situations has been great enough to justify our saying that Tom has learned to say Thank-you for presents; but the greater the variety of situations, the more closely the actual instance will approximate to the instance intended.

To this most important feature, the feature characterising the kind of situation in any instance of learning, I propose to give a special name. I shall call it the 'cue'. The cue of any instance of learning, then, is the feature characterising the kind of situation involved in that instance. In the example I have been using, the cue is the 'getting-a-present' feature. In the instance, learning to come indoors when Mother calls, the cue is the 'mother-calling' feature. In learning to read, the cue is the 'printed-words' feature.

I choose this theatrical term ('cue') because if the stated instance is to take place, nothing other than the feature characterising the kind of situation involved will be a reliable cue for the learner's behaving in the specified way. If he has to subtract on meeting a certain kind of problem, he will in fact subtract in *all* problems of that kind (which the instance demands) only if he takes as his cue the feature common to and characterising them all. Any other feature, which might be shared by only some of these problems, would be unreliable. Such a feature, in this instance, might be the word 'from'. It would be appropriate in the problem-statement, 'Take six from ninety-eight', but it does not occur in the question, 'What is the difference between thirty-four and eighty-three?' It would be unreliable, not only because it fails to occur in some appropriate situations, but also because it does occur in situations which are not of the specified kind. 'How often can I take sixteen from ninety-six?', contains the word 'from', but would probably be set with the intention that the pupil should divide. In general, any instance of learning will take place only if the cue to the required behaviour is the feature which characterises the kind of situation in that instance.[1]

With this term I can now state formally and briefly the requirement I have been discussing.

'*In any instance of learning, there must be a series of situations sharing, and sharing only, the cue of that instance.*'

For obvious reasons this will be called the Requirement of Cue.

As I have said, this ideal requirement cannot be fully met in practice, because we cannot ensure that the cue is the only feature common to all the successive situations. And yet, the nearer the teacher gets to fulfilling it, the greater the chances of the instance's taking place. On the other hand, the less well it is met the more narrow will the *actual* instance be. The pupil who subtracts only on the cue of 'from' or 'take away', or 'subtract', has achieved very much less than the pupil who can react to the feature which characterises all, is the cue of, subtraction-problems. The pupil who can 'do simultaneous equations', but only when the page-heading tells him that this is what they are, has learned less than the pupil who spots the kind of problem for which these equations are necessary. And to help the pupil spot such problems, the teacher himself will have to be perfectly clear as to what the characterising feature is. Precisely what is (or should be) the cue for the use of the present subjunctive mood in French, the cue for resorting to the use of logarithm tables, the cue for the use of the ablative absolute construction in Latin, the cue for the use of a tenon, rather than a cross-cut saw? Whatever the cue may be in

[1] This usage of the term 'cue' follows its theatrical usage closely, but is implied also by its use in psychology, in which it is customarily defined, in terms not of a situation, but of the response to which it is said to be a cue. If, however, as the customary psychological usage implies, the cue does elicit the response whenever it appears, the response will be made to all situations exhibiting that cue. And since that cue is the only feature these situations need share, it will be in effect the characterising feature of these situations. A major difference between the two usages, however, is that I do not assume that the cue will of itself get any response at all, and so without self-contradiction I can say that someone 'misses his cue'; whereas if 'cue' is defined (or in effect defined) in terms of response, terms like 'ineffective cue' and 'missed cue' constitute contradictions in terms.

the instance in question, our first requirement makes explicit the point that the teacher has to ensure a series of situations each of which contains the cue – and so far as possible share nothing else.[1]

The Requirement of Force

The Requirement of Cue refers only to the situation, whereas the definition of learning requires not only that there should be a situation of some specified kind but also that responses should be made to it. This latter requirement is twofold because any behaviour has two distinguishable aspects. On the one hand, a behaviour has a form, in being this behaviour rather than that: running rather than chewing, buying a loaf rather than writing a letter. But a behaviour, whatever its form, has also a time of beginning. It begins at this time rather than that: at six fifty-five today rather than at noon yesterday, at the time the whistle blows rather than at the time the clock stops. Any behaviour will, of course, exhibit both these aspects, for a behaviour that has a form, if it is a behaviour at all, must begin some time; and a behaviour that begins must have one form or another. It is nevertheless convenient to *discuss* these aspects separately, and in this section I shall consider only the question of time of beginning, leaving the question of form until the next section of the chapter.[2]

[1] At first sight it might seem that there are occasions on which this theoretical demand runs counter to sound practice. When, for instance, a child is learning to count, it will be easier if the objects to be counted are all rather similar – all pencils, or all little blocks, and so on. Indeed, the very young learner might find difficulty in counting pencils if they differed a great deal in size. The resolution of this ostensible dilemma between theory and practice is nevertheless to be found, not in tampering with a logically consistent theory but in one's being clear-sighted about the practice. The child who can 'count' only when all the objects are very similar – such as yellow pencils all six inches long, cannot strictly be said to have 'learned to count'. We can be confident only that he has learned to count objects which are all yellow pencils, and so on. If, from our knowledge of child development, we know that the child will not be able to count if the objects show very marked differences – like a pencil, a cat, a book, a teacher and a window, we do not try to 'teach him to count'; we restrict the *instance* to be effected at that stage.

[2] The distinction is made on the ground that it is conceivable that the circumstances which determine when a behaviour will begin will not necessarily be the same as those determining what form the behaviour will take. For example, the suddenness of an object's appearance might determine that a response would be made to it; but the form

Although in any instance there is a change in the form of behaviour, yet both the old and the new behaviours are responses, and are responses to the same kind of situation. The difference in form may be more pronounced, but the common aspect – that both are responses to the same kind of situation – is equally important. It runs through the obvious change of form. For example, the behaviour of coming indoors and the behaviour of putting out one's tongue, when mother calls, are very different in form, but both are responses to the same (mother-calling) kind of situation.

This common aspect can be referred to in either of two ways. We can say that the learner must make some sort of response to the situation, or we can say that the situation must elicit some sort of response from him. The two ways of speaking have the same basic meaning, but from the teacher's point of view there is a significant difference. The first puts the responsibility, as it were, on the learner; the response is something 'he must make'. The second puts the onus on the situation: the response is something 'it must elicit'. I choose the latter view because it is only from outside that the teacher can promote the pupil's responses, namely by ensuring that the pupil's environmental situation is such as to evoke a response from him. This has nothing to do with responsibility in the moral sense, or with free-will or otherwise. I am but saying that it is only by influencing the pupil's situation that the teacher can have any influence on the pupil. He can use the medium of sound, by coaxing, arguing, blackmailing, flattering, threatening, banging the pointer on the floor, and so on. He can use the medium of visual objects – words on the blackboard or in books, diagrams, pictures, facial gestures, play-acting, and so forth. But he cannot at any time enter into the pupil and operate him from within. Teaching consists necessarily in manipulating the situation in which the pupil lives. It would be untrue as well as un-grammatical to say that the teacher can 'learn him'. From the

of that response might depend not on the suddenness of the object's appearance but on what the object was. At any rate, the distinction I have drawn leaves the experimental issue open and indicates that such an issue is present.

teacher's viewpoint, then, it is appropriate to think of the situation's having to be such as to elicit, evoke, or initiate a response. It is appropriate because it is only by means of the situation that the teacher can teach.[1]

Within this view, in turn, there are two possibilities, for the situation may evoke a response in either of two sets of circumstances. If the learner is doing nothing, the situation's giving rise to a behaviour consists in rousing him from a state of rest. On the other hand, if he is already active when the situation arises, its initiating a behaviour necessarily consists in making him do something different, diverting him from what he is already doing. To this function of initiating a behaviour, no matter what form the behaviour may take, I propose to give the name 'force': a situation has force for someone when it rouses him from rest or diverts him from the behaviour in which he is engaged.[2]

In any instance of learning, then, the situation must have force. This is merely a short way of saying that the situation must make the learner react, must be such as to elicit a response of some sort from him. The requirement nevertheless can be expressed even more precisely because, as I shall now show, the force of the situation must be exerted by its cue.

[1] This assertion may seem to run counter to the view that the learner can and should decide for himself when he will respond. True, I (the learner) can, of course, decide, in advance of the situation's occurrence, that I will respond to it when it does occur. But to keep my word I must make the implementing of my decision hostage to the occurrence of the situation, and so it may still be said that it is the occurrence of the situation itself which, in the last resort, determines when the behaviour will begin. It may be that a previous decision of this sort is one of the ways in which a situation acquires the power or 'force' to elicit a response, but at the moment I am not concerned with the conditions in which such force is acquired. I am concerned only to state the logical requirement that the situation must indeed have it. How it gets it is beside the present point.

[2] For the sake of emphasis I have used terms like 'evoke', 'elicit', 'give rise to' and 'initiate', all of which (like the term 'force' too) often have an implication of causality. The term 'force' nevertheless can be 'cashed' in terms of observable events, because to say that a situation has force is but to say, less clumsily, that on several successive occasions its occurrence is succeeded by the beginning of a behaviour of some sort. I have borrowed and adapted the term from Newton's first law of motion: A body continues in a state of rest or of uniform motion in a straight line unless acted on by a force. The analogy is not perfect, but no other term seemed as appropriate. See also the footnote to p. 47, and the definition of 'force' offered by English and English (12).

To return to an earlier example: to say Tom has learned to come indoors when his mother calls him is to imply, not just that he now comes indoors because of some situation in which his mother happens to be calling him, but that his coming indoors is a direct response to her calling. The implication is that the response is made to the mother's calling, and not to some other aspect of the situation, such as a shower of rain. Similarly, to say that I have learned to rise when the alarm-clock rings is to imply that I rise in response to the actual ringing, and not to some other feature of the situation, such as the sunlight at my window. To say that Jack has learned to take off his cap on entering school is to imply that his cap-doffing behaviour is a direct response to his entering school, and not (say) to the sight of other boys' cap-doffing behaviour, or to the instructions of a teacher. But the mother's calling, the ringing of the alarm, and the entering school are the *cues* of the instances quoted. The definition of learning implies that, in any instance, the responses are made to a certain *kind* of situation; and as these three examples illustrate, this means that the responses have to be made to the feature which makes the situation the kind of situation it is, namely to the cue. It is the cue, in particular, which has to elicit the response. In other words, it is the cue which must have force.[1] A second requirement of learning may therefore be stated thus:

'*In any instance of learning, the cue must have force.*'

It will be appreciated that on many occasions this requirement is not met. Learning may seem to have taken place, until the situation changes in some way, and it then appears that it is not the cue but some other feature which has been getting the response. A class seems to have learned to bring a certain textbook every Tuesday – until the hockey period is switched to Friday, when it becomes apparent that what many of the pupils have learned is to bring that textbook on the day they bring hockey sticks. A pupil may seem to have learned to cooperate in school activities – until his favourite teacher leaves. Or he may seem to

[1] As is made explicit in Chapter 7, the 'kind' of situation *is* the cue.

have responded to his teacher's exhortations about homework – until his father goes away on business for a month and the homework is neglected. In each of these examples the cue to the response was not the cue of the instance intended. They illustrate the point that it is the cue, and not something else in the situation, which must elicit the response.

The same requirement raises the problem not only of ensuring that the cue is the feature which has force, but also of how a feature which does not have force may acquire it. Are some things intrinsically forceful, as sudden loud noises are often assumed to be? If not, how can a cue be made forceful? This basic question is connected with the issues of Attention, Interest, Perception, and also Understanding. To say that I attend to something is to say, in effect, that it elicits some response from me. If it does not receive my attention at all, it is not eliciting a response; it has no force for me. Similarly, to say that something interests me is equivalent to saying that when it appears it gets a response. Likewise, I cannot perceive everything that is physically before me, but select unconsciously from the environmental scene – noticing perhaps a student's facial expression but ignoring the colour of his hair. And as will be argued in Chapter 7, to understand something is to see the *kind* of thing it is, that is to react to its cue. How does this come about? What causes me to respond to this rather than to that? Questions of this kind will be dealt with in Part Two, though it is of interest to note now that in terms of this basic notion of Force we can see that issues often assumed to be distinct have the same structure and raise the same basic problem. To repeat the main point: unless the cue of the instance to be effected has force, that instance cannot take place.[1]

---

[1] Since 'force' was defined in terms of behaviour as well as of situation, there is no question of a situation's having force if no one is confronted by it. Nor need a feature that has force for one person have force for another. From the background hum of conversation my own name may leap out and have force for me, but leave others unaffected. Also, a feature that has force for me at one time may not have force for me at some other time. Force is a function a feature may or may not subserve, and is not necessarily one of the feature's intrinsic qualities.

The Requirement of Prompt

Although the Requirement of Force ignores the *form* of response made to the cue, a response will of necessity be this response rather than that. Therefore, something in the total situation on any occasion must be determining what form the response takes. If Tom's response to the receipt of a present, on some occasion, takes the form of his throwing the present on the floor, something in that situation must be determining that he does this rather than grabs it in silence, says Thank-you, throws it in the air, or anything else.[1] Although the Requirement of Force says nothing about the response's form, the forceful situation will nevertheless have a form-determiner in it. It is with form-determination that our third requirement is concerned.

If, now, the instance demands that Tom should say Thank-you on getting a present, at some stage in the series of getting-a-present situations there must appear something which will determine that his behaviour takes the form required, namely saying Thank-you. This thing cannot be the cue itself, for had the cue some quality which could ensure that the behaviour would take the specified form, of necessity the behaviour in situations of that kind would always have taken that form, and so learning would be neither necessary nor possible. It would be impossible because (in this instance) Tom would have said Thank-you from the outset and so a *change to* that specified behaviour, demanded by the definition of learning, would be precluded. Of course, the cue itself must eventually get the specified response, and so in some way the cue must *acquire* the function of determining that the response will have the specified form, but the cue cannot of itself effect the

[1] This presupposes that present events have present conditions of occurrence. If yesterday I left my car wheels in full lock, today when I start the car it will begin to move in an arc. In a sense, then, the conditions governing today's wheel-behaviour belong to yesterday. Strictly, however, the car will move in this way today because the wheels are in that position today. Unless the results of what I did yesterday remain until today, yesterday's event will not determine how the car now moves. Although the determiner of a behaviour's form may seem to belong to the past, yet in cases of this kind the actual determiner is the present 'remains' of a past event, namely a set of circumstances present now.

requisite change to it. It follows that at first some other feature must determine that the response to the cue takes the form specified. What this other feature might be is not difficult to imagine. In the instance cited it could be an instruction from Tom's mother, who is standing by. In teaching a child to pronounce some unfamiliar printed word we could pronounce the word for him and make him imitate it. In training a dog to beg on command we could ensure the required behaviour in the first place by holding a titbit above his head. In none of these examples could the change to the new response be effected by the cue itself –receipt of present, printed word, command to beg. Some other feature – verbal instruction to say Thank-you, model pronunciation, titbit above head – would have to be introduced, its function being to ensure that the behaviour will take the specified form in the first place.

A convenient way of referring to this point is to say that the requisite additional feature must already have the required form of behaviour 'connected' to it. Such connection in some cases might be part and parcel of the natural order of things, but in a great many cases the connection which is exploited to effect one instance of learning will itself be the result of some earlier instance of learning.[1] For example, if Tom were obedient to his mother's instruction to say Thank-you, that instruction would have 'Saying Thank-you' connected to it, and could be used to get the Saying-Thank-you behaviour in the getting-a-present situation in the first place. But at some previous time Tom would have had to learn to say Thank-you when told to say so.

This additional feature, to which the specified form of behaviour is already connected, I shall call the 'prompt'. This name has been chosen not only because it continues a useful theatrical analogy but also because its meaning here is very similar to the meaning it already has in Programmed Learning (See Chapter 11). A prompt, then, does *not* have the function of ensuring that the cue *evokes* some sort of response, for that is covered by the Requirement of Force; its function is to ensure that the response which the cue does evoke has the specified *form*.

[1] *Cf*. higher order conditioning.

By the analogy, the person giving the prompt would not chase after the actor who had missed his cue (made no response to it); he would prompt the actor who was in danger of making a *wrong* response to the cue he has in fact taken. Thus, in the illustration used already, the cue is the receipt of a present. That cue is likely to get *some* response. The mother used the prompt, 'Say Thank-you, Tom!' to try to ensure that the response Tom makes is of the required *form*. For some children, 'What do you say?' would have exactly the same prompt-function.[1]

Without recourse to experiment we cannot assert how many times the prompt must appear in the situation. All we can infer from the definition of learning is that it must appear at least once. The Requirement of Prompt may therefore be stated thus:

> '*In any instance of learning, a prompt must appear in one or more of the successive situations.*'

Some possible examples of prompts have already been given. In school, the prompt often takes the form of an instruction

---

[1] Since interest in learning is usually focused on the form of the new (specified) response, I have defined 'prompt' in terms of it; but it is worth noting that the old responses must have had forms too, and that each of these must have had a determiner also. As I said earlier, if Tom threw his present on the floor, something must have determined that he would do that rather than do something else. Each of the earlier situations must have had some feature fulfilling the same *sort* of function as does the prompt. Very often these will not have been inserted by anyone, but they must nevertheless have been present. So-called Trial and Error learning illustrates this point.

What I have called the prompt is similar in some respects to an unconditional stimulus, but I have avoided the latter term for several reasons. For one thing, it customarily refers to something relatively small or simple, such as food in the mouth, or a buzzing sound, or a change in the intensity of illumination; whereas in many instances of learning the prompt will be relatively complex. The prompt for a skilled movement might be a series of complex instructions coupled with a demonstration – as in learning to drive a car. Further, the term 'stimulus' implies a stimulative, initiatory function as well as an orientative one. As I have just argued, however, it is not *logically* necessary that this should be so. It is logically sufficient that the prompt should determine the form of response initiated by the forceful cue. It is not logically necessary to suppose that the thing which determines a behaviour's form must have also the function of making that behaviour begin. Indeed, emphasis on the form-determining, as contrasted with the stimulative, function of the prompt allows us to infer something often assumed to require experiment. If the prompt's function is to give the requisite form to the response elicited by the cue, it is reasonable to deduce that the thing serving as prompt (such as a verbal instruction) should occur very close in time to the cue. See also the chapter on Habit-training.

from the teacher. At first, the problem in the arithmetic textbook does not itself get the required form of response, and that form may have to be determined by the teacher's instruction or hint. In one of our earlier illustrations a page-heading was serving as a prompt. In many cases the teacher will show, rather than tell, the pupils what to do. In such cases the prompt is the content of a demonstration. Further examples, worked out in greater detail, are given in Part Two.

Although all my illustrations of prompt have been taken from instances of learning to do something, yet a prompt is equally necessary in instances of learning not to do something. When the statement of such an instance is taken at its face value, all the teacher need do is provide an inhibitor of the old behaviour. In the instance, learning not to swear when angry, anything which prevents the learner's swearing would be enough, because so long as the cue (being angry) remained forceful, *something* in the situation would determine what form the new behaviour would take, and this 'something' (which would include the inhibitor) would be the actual prompt. There are nevertheless many instances in which the statement implies more than it says. If, instead of swearing, the child were to smash windows, the change would be scarcely acceptable. In general, a purely inhibitory role is rarely sufficient, and it is usually necessary to introduce not merely an inhibitor of the old behaviour but also, or instead, a prompt for some quite specific new behaviour. (See, for example, the chapter on Habit-breaking.)

The practical problem indicated by this third requirement is that of discovering or inventing, in any instance, something which will serve as prompt, that is, will give the response to the cue the form specified.[1]

---

[1] The analogy with physical theory might be extended by our treating the form of behaviour as the directional, as contrasted with the intensive aspect of the vector, Force; but it is probably simpler to keep Force and Prompt as distinct concepts. Nor does it seem profitable, at present, to think of behaviours as varying in intensity, beyond the variation from having intensity (that is, occurring) to having none at all (not occurring). Is sprinting, for example, a more or less intensive behaviour than repairing a watch? What is to be the criterion?

The Requirement of Reinforcement

So long as the cue of each of the successive situations has force (gets a response of some sort), and so long as a prompt remains as a feature of each of these situations, the specified response to the cue will necessarily be given. But so long as the prompt remains, learning is not complete, because by sharing the prompt the situations receiving the new response will not be of the same kind as those which received the old response – and learning requires that the old and new responses are made to situations of the same kind. If Tom's mother is always present and reminds him to say Thank-you when he gets a present (her reminder serving as prompt), the situations receiving the Thank-you-response are not mere getting-a-present situations; they are getting-a-present-and-Mother-reminding-him situations. By sharing not only the cue but also the prompt, the latter situations are less general than the situations which received the old response, and less general than the kind of situation specified by the statement of the instance to be effected. To satisfy the definition of learning, the prompt must eventually disappear.[1]

It is true also, however, that learning will not take place if,

---

[1] For the reader interested in psychological theorising three points merit comment. First, as noted earlier, the cue must be the only feature shared by the successive situations: the present point entails the converse, namely that the kind of situation actually constituted by a series of situations is specified by all that they share. Second: if, as is logically necessary, the item intended as prompt is indeed shaping the response to the *cue* and not getting a response in its own right, it might seem that learning is complete because the cue is now getting a new response.   But the definition of learning implies that the cue must not only initiate a response but also be the determiner of its form, the form specified; and so long as the prompt shapes the response's form, that requirement is not met. It is only when the prompt is dropped that we can know whether the cue has acquired the requisite orientative function. The third point relates to the technique of conditioning. In Pavlovian conditioning it is not always necessary to drop the item serving as prompt (food-powder as a prompt for salivation in response to a buzzer, for instance), because as training proceeds the new response comes closer in time to the conditional stimulus, and eventually precedes the onset of the unconditional stimulus,. There is no contradiction here, however, because whatever other function the food-powder may now serve (reinforcement?), patently it cannot be serving as prompt for a response which has already occurred. The example nevertheless illustrates the point that although we may often have to drop the *item* serving as prompt, yet strictly what has to cease is the *function* the item performs.

when the prompt is dropped, the new form of behaviour ceases too – if, for example, Tom ceases to say Thank-you for presents once his mother ceases to remind him to say so. The prompt must fade out, but the specified form of response must remain, being determined by the cue itself. Eventually, Tom's saying Thank-you must be elicited by the mere getting of a present. In the long run, the cue must determine not only that some sort of response is made to it but also that the response which is made has the specified form. In other words, before learning can be complete the specified *form* of behaviour must become connected to the cue.

What will serve to effect that connection? By its own definition the prompt does not do it, for its peculiar function is to give the response the required form in the first place; it is not defined as being able to do any more than that – such as to transfer its function to the cue. It is, of course, open to investigation that once a response to the cue has taken a certain form, it will continue to have that same form on subsequent occasions even when the prompt is removed, but we are certainly not entitled to suppose that this will be so. Also, many theories of learning presuppose that it will not. It is widely held, for example, that once the required response has been made, a reward of some sort is necessary to connect it, or reinforce its connection, to the cue. And since a behaviour cannot be rewarded until it has occurred, reward (even if it does serve as connector) cannot be also a prompt for that behaviour.[1] Another hypothesis is that if a behaviour can be made to occur several times in the same situation, the sheer repetition will serve to effect the necessary connection. True, a repetition of the response, while learning still proceeds, will necessitate a repetition of the prompt for that response; but even so, the connection is being effected, not by the prompt as such, but at best by its repetition. These and other theories of what constitutes the connector will be examined in Part Two. The immediate point is that *something* must serve this connecting function, and anything which does in fact serve it may be given

---

[1] A *promise* of reward, if coupled with an instruction, nevertheless might be so

the name 'reinforcer'. The event in which a reinforcer operates is usually called 'reinforcement'. The precise function of a reinforcer merits emphasis. That a behaviour of *some* form will be evoked by the cue is covered by the Requirement of Force. That the behaviour evoked by the cue will assume the *specified* form is covered by the Requirement of Prompt. Thus, so long as forceful cue *and* prompt operate, the response will have the specified form. It is the peculiar function of the reinforcer to ensure that, once the prompt is faded out, that *same* form of response persists. Its function is to *connect to the cue* the form of behaviour made available, by the prompt, for such connection. For instance, Tom's response of saying Thank-you, made available for connection while the prompt ('Say Thank-you, Tom!') is present, must be connected to the cue of receiving a present, so that Tom will continue to make that response even after his mother ceases to prompt him.

The fourth requirement of learning, the Requirement of Reinforcement,[1] may therefore be stated thus:

'*In any instance of learning, the specified form of response must be tied to the cue.*'

In order to distinguish the four requirements, each was dealt with separately. But while each is necessary for learning, learning will occur only when all four are fulfilled. We must consider, then, how they fit in, one with another, in a systematic way. That system is outlined in the next chapter.

---

[1] The term 'reinforcement' has not always had this meaning. At one time it was (in effect) defined not, as here, in terms of the *function* of the item said to be a reinforcer, but in terms such as Reward, Punishment, Satisfaction, Drive-reduction, and so forth. When 'reinforcement' was so defined, it was legitimate to ask whether reinforcement was necessary for learning. (Guthrie thought it was not necessary.) In the newer sense, in which *anything* serving the cue-response connection is a reinforcer, and in which reinforcement can be shown (as above) to be a *logically* necessary requirement, that question is improper. But one may of course ask whether *reward* (etc.) is necessary. For a short clear, recent statement of the newer view see Kimble, in Melton (32). The only extension implied by my usage is that the 'strengthening' of the connection may begin at zero strength.

4 · A Theory of Learning

'Theory of Learning' and 'Learning-Theory'

In this chapter the four requirements of learning worked out in Chapter 3 are arranged to form a system. Since I shall refer to the system as a 'theory' of learning I should explain briefly why I have given it that name and how it differs from what is currently called 'learning-theory'.

The system consists of the Requirements of Cue, Force, Prompt, and Reinforcement. These were deduced from the definition of learning; that definition had been deduced from events commonly accepted as instances of learning; and so the system has a practical basis in common experience. But even so, it will not itself tell us how the four requirements constituting it can be fulfilled. It states, for example, that every instance of learning requires a prompt, and so indicates that in any instance a prompt must be sought; but it does not tell us what will serve as prompt in a particular case. It does not even advance hypotheses about how that function might be served. For such a system, which does not itself venture experimentally verifiable hypotheses, the term 'theory' seems to be appropriate.

To call it a theory is not, of course, to decry it. Although purely logical requirements remain of no practical use until we discover some means of fulfilling them, yet we are most likely to find such means once we know what the necessary requirements are.

On the one hand, then, are statements which can be subjected to experimental test – such as that reward or repetition can serve as a reinforcer; verbal instructions can serve as prompts; and so forth. These I shall refer to as 'hypotheses'. On the other hand is a body of requirements which are not susceptible of empirical verification at all. This is the body of requirements I have referred to as a 'theory'. The two things are nevertheless related: since the hypotheses are necessarily hypotheses about the requirements, they must be expressed in terms of them. The theory provides the conceptual framework of the hypotheses.

The sort of theory I have just described differs from what is known as 'learning-theory'. The chief difference is that learning-theories consist, in the main, of statements purporting to be experimentally verifiable hypotheses. They differ among themselves also, of course, in the conceptual systems they presuppose. Some employ the concepts of Stimulus and Response, some employ the concept of Sign, some employ the concept of Gestalt, and so forth; but when different learning-theories are described and compared, attention is usually directed not to the concept-systems ('theories') they involve but to the hypotheses they advance. The theory outlined in this chapter, in contrast, does not advance hypotheses at all. The value of such a theory has been already suggested, is referred to again at the end of this chapter, and is exploited in Part Two.

A Theory of Learning

Basic Postulates

Instances of learning may be classified in various ways – learning to do something, to be something, to think something, to feel something, or learning not to do, be, think, or feel something. Also, within any class of instances the instances will differ one from another. Learning is nevertheless common to them all, and this theory rests on the proposition that whatever is common to all instances of learning (and not found in non-instances) is itself the learning of which they are said to be instances.

On that view, then, in order to state what learning is we must examine a variety of instances of learning and note what they have in common, but do not share with events that are not instances of learning. But if the very purpose of our examination is to discover what learning is, what are we to use as criterion in selecting events as instances of it? The solution offered here is that 'What is learning?' is a verbal problem, a problem of definition, and that if our definition is to be useful we should choose for examination the events generally accepted as instances of learning. If we abstract the features common and peculiar to events customarily accepted as instances of learning, we shall be formulating a definition which serves to make explicit what is already implicit in common thinking.

When such a variety of accepted instances is examined we find four features which, together, characterise them. In every case, no matter how it may have been classified, the learner learns to Do Something. Further, what he learns to do is done in Response to some particular Kind of Situation. Finally, we do not commonly speak of learning unless the kind of situation in question previously elicited a different form of response. Briefly, to learn is to adopt a new response to a situation.

A Theory of Requirements

Once a definitive pattern has been elaborated, it can be broken down again into parts – parts that are not necessarily the same as the items first used to build it. It can be restructured. How this restructuring should be effected will depend upon our purpose. In the present case the purpose is to discover what the teacher must do in order to promote learning, and so the analysis of the definition aims at abstracting the requirements which the promotion of learning imposes. These requirements are four in number.

First, to be sure that any behaviour is a response to the given kind of situation, rather than to another, we must observe that that behaviour is initiated in that kind of situation on a succession of occasions. There must therefore be a succession of *situations* of that kind. (This point is reinforced by the need of a *change* of response to the same kind of situation.) This means, in effect, that there must be a series of situations each of which exhibits the feature which characterises that kind of situation. The feature characterising the kind of situation involved in any instance is called, here, the 'cue' of that instance. For example, in the instance of learning to shut the door on leaving the room, there would have to be a series of situations in each of which the child left the room: the leaving-the-room feature, common to all these successive situations, would be the cue of this instance. Strictly, the situations of the series must share no more than the cue, for a series of situations is characterised by *all* that they share. If, on each occasion the child left the room, his father was sitting looking at him, the situations would be not merely leaving-the-room situations, as stipulated by the statement of the instance, but leaving-the-room-while-father-watches situations.

The requirement just described is called, here, the Requirement of Cue, and may be stated formally as follows:

'In any instance of learning there must be a series of situations sharing, and sharing only, the cue of that instance.'

Ideally, then, the situations in which the child leaves the room should differ one from another in every respect except the leaving-the-room feature – not in order to make learning easier, but to ensure that it is the specified instance which takes place.

Second, while the Requirement of Cue is necessary for learning, it is by no means sufficient, for the situation must not only arise but must evoke a response on each occasion. At some stage the form of response has to change, but more fundamental is the point that both the old and the new behaviours are responses to the same kind of situation. Each of the successive situations must therefore be such as to evoke some sort of response from the prospective learner. More precisely, the response, whatever its form, must be evoked by the cue of the situation and not by any other aspect of it. It must be the leaving of the room, and not (say) the father's presence or the threat of punishment, which evokes a response.

A feature which does evoke a response, either by rousing the learner from rest or by diverting him from what he is already doing, is said, here, to have 'force'. A forceful feature is a feature which, at the time in question, evokes a response of some sort. This definition of 'force' precludes the question of 'degree of force', and intentionally so, because there is no simple way of assessing the intensities of different behaviours. Force, as defined, is an all-or-nothing matter; a feature either has force or has not.

This requirement, called here the Requirement of Force, may be stated formally thus:

'In any instance of learning the cue must have force.'

In our example, some sort of response must be made, not merely *when* the child leaves the room, but *because* of that particular feature of the situation.

The main reason for distinguishing between the situation's initiating some response, any response, and its determining the form of response so initiated, is that it is conceivable that the conditions determining that a response of some sort will be made may not be the same as those determining what form the response will take.

Third, although it is necessary that the cue, each time it appears, must get a response of *some* sort, this is not enough. The definition of learning requires that at some stage in the series of situations the response must take the specified form. At some stage in the series of leaving-the-room situations the cue (leaving the room) must evoke not merely 'any' response but the response of shutting the door. It is logically impossible, however, that the cue itself should effect this change, for if there were something inherent in the cue which could determine that the response would take the specified form, that form of response would have appeared from the outset, and so a change *to* it would be impossible.

Accordingly, if the specified new form of response is to appear, some new feature must appear in the situation, a feature which will ensure that the response to the cue takes the form required. It is emphasised that it is not the function of this new feature to make the response occur; the initiation of responses is covered by the Requirement of Force. Its function is to give the requisite *form* to the response initiated by the cue. It has to be, not an instigator, but a form-determiner. To any feature which does determine that the response to the cue takes the specified form, the name 'prompt' has been given. The prompt is a feature (of the situation) to which the specified form of response is already 'connected'. It is defined as a feature 'of the situation' on the ground that an item which served as a determiner of a specified form of response in one kind of situation might not so serve in another; its function might change with change of context. If the requirements of learning are to be logically rigorous, that point must be incorporated in the definition of 'prompt'.

In the same example, the prompt might be an instruction from someone in the room, or a 'model behaviour' demonstrated by someone the child liked to copy. If, however, the instruction were not obeyed, by definition it would *not* be a prompt. Nor would it be a prompt were it to get a response in its own right, because the function of a prompt (as defined) is to determine the form of a response evoked by the cue.

This requirement, called here the Requirement of Prompt, may be stated formally as follows:

> '*In any instance of learning a prompt must appear in one or more of the successive situations.*'

The phrase 'one or more' is incorporated because without resort to experiment we cannot assert how often the prompt may have to be presented before learning can be effected.

Fourth, if learning is to be completed, the prompt must eventually disappear, because if it remained the kind of situation receiving the new response would not be of the same kind as that which received the old response and was specified by the statement of the instance in question. So long as the child's father continues to remind him to shut the door, the child may continue to shut it (and will in fact do so if that instruction is indeed a prompt), but the situations receiving the door-shutting response will be not leaving-the-room situations but leaving-the-room-and-father-instructing situations. But neither will learning be effected if, when the prompt is dropped, the new form of response disappears too. That form of response must remain, connected to the cue itself. Some sort of circumstance must therefore effect that connection.

Whatever does in fact effect that connection is called a 'reinforcer'.[1]

It is sometimes suggested that reward is a reinforcer, but all that the logical analysis of learning permits us to say is that the function of reinforcement must be served. This requirement, the Requirement of Reinforcement, may be stated formally thus:

'In any instance of learning the specified form of response must be tied to the cue.'

Three points about Reinforcement merit comment. First, it is not logically necessary to state that the prompt must be dropped, because that is presupposed by the Requirement of Reinforcement. Second, what has to be tied to the cue is a *form* of response; that a response of some sort will be evoked is covered by the Requirement of Force. Third, prompt and reinforcement are different functions. Reinforcers cannot fulfil their connective function until the requisite form of behaviour is available for tying, and it is the peculiar function of the prompt to make it available.

Here then is the complete picture of learning. As demanded by the Requirement of Cue, there is a series of situations of the specified kind; that is, situations sharing the cue and only the cue. The child leaves the room on a variety of successive occasions. Each time he does so, he makes a response of some sort – heaves a sigh, runs round the corner, or anything at all: the Requirement of Force is met. At some stage a prompt is introduced, such as an instruction from his father to shut the door. The child now

[1] This definition does not imply that there are special sorts of circumstances serving to connect *cue*-features with *previously specified* forms of behaviour. On the contrary, since the requirement refers to any instance of learning, the implication is that there are circumstances which will serve to connect any form of behaviour to any feature of a situation, because any form could be the form specified, and any feature could be specified as cue.

shuts the door each time he leaves the room – so long as he is instructed to do so. Eventually the prompt is removed, but some circumstance ensures that the door-shutting response continues – the Requirement of Reinforcement is met. The child has adopted a new response, shutting the door, to the leaving of the room. The instance is effected.

Application to Teaching

The value of the theory for the teacher lies in its making explicit the requirements he must fulfil if he is to promote learning. How they may be fulfilled is considered in Part Two, but first it is necessary to be clear as to what are the requirements themselves. A knowledge of the requirements that are both necessary and sufficient for learning is a prerequisite of intelligent teaching.

Each of the four requirements relates to a whole body of problems, and at this stage we may note what some of these problems are, considering each requirement in turn.

If he is to fulfil the Requirement of Cue, patently the teacher must know, for the instance in hand, what the cue is. Ideally the nature of the cue will be specified by the statement of the instance in question – as in the example used above; but not all instances are stated explicitly and sometimes it will be the teacher who has to make the statement himself. To repeat some illustrations given earlier: what should be the cue for division, in arithmetical problems? What should be the cue for the use of the subjunctive mood in French? What should be the cue for resort to logarithm tables or a slide-rule? The answers to such questions are to be found, of course, not in a knowledge of psychology but in a close familiarity with the subject concerned – arithmetic, French, and so on. Very often the choice of cue for an instance will have to be the result of the teacher's own decision – which implies that he must have thought clearly about what he wants to happen, and, made up his mind about the purpose of his teaching. Again, although in practice one can only approximate to the demand that the cue must be the only feature shared by the successive situations, yet the teacher will have to judge, partly from his experience of children and the classroom situation, what features must be eliminated and what features may safely be retained. Even the very event of being in school while learning may make an instance more restricted than was intended; there are skills which children use while they are pupils but cease to use after they leave, though they might with profit be retained.

The Requirement of Force is also concerned with cues. The cue must be such as to get some sort of response. Obviously a cue will fail to get a response from the learner if he cannot perceive it, but the main difficulty usually lies, not in the cue's being imperceptible (like a colour-difference for a colour-blind child), but in its being obscured by some other feature which gets the response instead. Instead of responding to the content of the sentence written on the blackboard, the pupil may react to the form of the handwriting or the colour of the chalk. A student may react to an anecdote used to illustrate some psychological principle, but fail to respond to the principle it was intended to illustrate. The Requirement of Force (that it is the *cue* which must have force) relates to the problems of the psychology of perception, attention, interest and understanding.

The Requirement of Prompt raises the problem of what sorts of things can be used to ensure that the responses take the required form, and how they are best introduced into the situation in question. Everyday experience indicates that this function may be served by verbal instructions and by 'model' behaviours which may be imitated. But when should they be introduced – before the cue, along with it, or after it? Are there any special precautions that must be taken in trying to fulfil this requirement? How can we ensure, for example, that the prompt object does not usurp the proper function of the cue and get responses in its own right?

The Requirement of Reinforcement raises the question of what things or procedures may serve as ties. Will reward be effective for this purpose? If so, will punishment have the opposite effect, and serve to break a connection already established? May not repetition become boring and run counter to the Requirement of Force by leading the learner to lose interest and cease to respond? In dealing with Reinforcement we meet a variety of hypotheses advanced by different learning-theorists – such as that what is effective is a reduction of the intensity of hunger, or thirst, or of some other 'drive' (as suggested by C. L. Hull), or a sense of satisfaction (E. L. Thorndike), or the fulfilment of an expectancy (E. C. Tolman), or the mere contiguity of behaviour and situation (E. R. Guthrie).

How do more or less stereotyped forms of instruction used in the classroom fulfil these four requirements? Indeed, do they fulfil them? If not, why not? What more is needed? Where does Motivation fit in? When the teacher goes out of his way to 'explain' something, what requirement is he trying, in effect, to fulfil? Does rote-memorising serve better than understanding? Serve better for what? And what precisely is the difference between them?

These and other related issues are dealt with in Part Two.

It is apparent that a host of practical problems springs to mind once we begin to think about these theoretical requirements. That is their purpose. In a sense they are 'ideal' requirements, but it is better to strive to fulfil these specific requirements, which are necessary (and sufficient) for learning, than to strive blindly in ignorance of them.

PART TWO

TECHNIQUES OF TEACHING

5 · Teaching as Habit-training

What are Habits?

Habit-training provides a useful beginning for our examination of teaching-techniques because it is relatively simple, it illustrates all four of the Requirements set out in the theory, and it suggests problems we must deal with in more detail when we consider techniques of a more complex kind. First, however, we should be clear as to what a habit itself is.

The question, 'What is a habit?', like the question, 'What is learning?', poses a verbal problem, and I shall answer it in the same way, by making explicit its commonly accepted meaning.

Any habit involves a behaviour of some sort. Indeed, the term 'habit' is often applied to the behaviour itself, as when we say that brushing one's teeth can become a habit. We may assume, however, that no behaviour occurs without cause; it will be occasioned by, that is, be a response to, some kind of situation. Observation of habitual behaviours supports this assumption. People do not brush their teeth all day long, or at quite unpredictable times; they brush them after meals, at bedtime, or something of the sort. (Sometimes, of course, the kind of situation to which the habitual behaviour is a response is internal to the learner, and may be difficult to detect. The behaviour may be a response to an incipient headache, or to signals from the digestive system, and such habits are often very difficult to control, largely because we cannot discover precisely what kind of situation is involved.) To repeat: any habit involves a response to some kind of situation. Moreover, if the response has a built-in connection with the situation, we do not usually call it 'habitual'. Habits are usually regarded as acquired: we are said to 'form' them, or to 'pick them up', or to 'learn them'. The eye-blink which is a response to sudden movement in front of the eye is not usually called a habit. Also, to be sure that the behaviour, in a particular case, had in fact been acquired, we should have to observe that the same kind of situation did not previously elicit that behaviour, but elicited a different behaviour. A habit, apparently, is an instance of learning.

Not all instances of learning are, of course, habits. Habits seem to have four distinguishing features. First, the response has a relatively simple form. If it had not, some other name (such as 'skill') would be more appropriate. Second, once the habit has been established, the response is made more or less automatically, without forethought or intention, as is illustrated by someone's saying he did something 'from habit'.[1] This is in accord with the first point, for a response could scarcely be automatic if it were not simple. Third, the kind of situation involved in a habit is usually relatively simple too. A situation that was not relatively simple could scarcely get the same automatic response each time it arose; we should have to give the situation some consideration, figure it out, puzzle over it, in which case the response would not be automatic. Fourth, before an instance of learning is called a habit it has to occur fairly frequently. If I sometimes scratch my cheek when I am puzzled, it is almost certain that I learned to do this, but if I do it only now and again it would not usually be called a habit.

A habit, then, may be regarded as an instance of learning in which a relatively simple response is made, automatically and fairly frequently, to a relatively simple kind of situation.

Sometimes the term does have another usage, even in popular speech, as when we speak of a habit of politeness or of punctuality, but I mention this merely to point out that this usage is

---

[1] We do, of course, speak of 'habits of thought', but the same point can still be made. The thinking involved *in* the habit is not itself the result of deliberation.

different. In such examples the situation and the response may be far from simple, and the response may not be automatic. The only close resemblance lies in the consistency of the behaviour, and it would be less confusing if we said that so-and-so is usually polite, or can be depended upon to be punctual. In the following account I shall use the term 'habit' as defined in the preceding paragraph.

The Technique of Conditioning

Means of fulfilling the theoretical requirements of learning (Cue, Force, Prompt, and Reinforcement) must be found by experiment, or at least by controlled observation. Most experiments on habit-formation, however, have used not human subjects but animals – dogs, cats, rats, and even worms. I shall begin by quoting one of these experiments, not (I should emphasise) because I believe that what is true of animals in the psychologist's laboratory will necessarily be true of children, but for a quite different reason. Where habits are concerned the *technique of training* is fundamentally the same for human and animal learners, but human behaviour is so complex that if we begin our study with it we may be distracted from the relevant issues. In human behaviour there is so much to see that we may fail to see what we should see. In the (relatively) simple behaviour of animals we may more easily discover the crucial features. I shall, of course, have to show that what we have observed in the animal-experiments is true also of human subjects. I may nevertheless comment that since here we shall be concerned only with habits – involving relatively simple, automatic responses to relatively simple situations, in which human subjects can scarcely be said to be acting in the most characteristically human way, it will not be very surprising if we discover that in this respect animals and human subjects are not very different.

Animal experiments on simple learning fall into two main groups. In one kind the animal is left to learn more or less by itself: the cat has to learn to escape from a box by pushing a lever.

the rat has to learn to run a maze to find food. Nobody helps the animal to do what it has to learn to do. In the other kind the experimenter controls the situation to a much greater extent, and builds into it a device (prompt) to ensure that it will be the required response which is given. In our discussion both types of experiment will be examined. At present, however, we shall concentrate on the latter type, in which it is obvious that the experimenter is going out of his way to ensure that the learner will make the response which is required, and make it to the required cue.

A classic and frequently quoted example is provided by one of the experiments of Pavlov (38) – though the experiment was more subtle both in substance and in intention than this brief reference may suggest. A buzzer is sounded in the presence of the dog which is to be trained. To this the dog responds by a slight tensing of muscles, twitching an ear, or something of the sort. But now, just after the buzzer is sounded, food-powder is puffed into the dog's mouth. The animal salivates. After several of these twin-presentations, buzzer and food, the dog salivates before the food is given. The form of response to the buzzer has changed. It may still include ear-twitching, and so on, but it now includes salivating. The *total* response to the buzzer is certainly not the same as the total response to the food-powder, but it is nevertheless true to say that the dog has learned to salivate when the buzzer sounds.

Since I shall be using this simple instance as a reference in discussing simple learning, I should perhaps remark that in some texts this kind of experiment is not accepted as an instance of learning at all. Learning, it is agreed, involves a change of response to the same kind of situation; but it is sometimes assumed that what we have here is a change of situation for the same response. Instead of the food-powder as an occasioner of salivation, we now have a buzzer. Now this is, of course, partly true, but two points have to be made. For one thing, the salivation-response is not 'switched' from one thing to another: by salivating in response to the buzzer the dog does not cease to salivate in response to food-powder, and so the term 'stimulus-substitution' may be misleading. The second point is that because the buzzer did not previously elicit the response of salivating it is sometimes called a 'neutral' stimulus; but this also may be misleading in suggesting that before the experiment began the buzzer got no response at all. If this were so, of course, this would not be an instance of learning, but the buzzer did get a response – muscle-tensing, ear-twitching, and so forth, and so there was in fact a change of response to the buzzer. The dog had learned to salivate in response to the buzzing sound.

In greater detail, the instance may be described as follows. The cue in this case is the buzzer. (Or the sound of the buzzer, etc., but we need not argue about this here.) The specified response to this cue is the response of salivating. The prompt, which determines that the response will take the specified form in the first place, is the food-powder puffed into the dog's mouth. What serves as reinforcer we have still to discuss. In peda-gogical terms, the aim of the lesson is to teach a dog to salivate at the sound of the buzzer. This kind of experiment nevertheless has its own terminology, which is now described briefly.

In the instance quoted, the food-powder is the 'unconditional stimulus' (US) to the required response; it gets that response unconditionally – so far as the experiment in question is con-cerned. (This proviso is made because something serving as an unconditional stimulus in one experiment might so serve only because of the result of some previous experiment or training. For example, once the buzzer had become a stimulus to salivation in the experiment being described, it might be used as an un-conditional stimulus in a subsequent experiment in which the dog was to learn to salivate in response to a flash of light.) The buzzer, on the other hand, is the 'conditional stimulus' (CS) to the required response; its eliciting that response is conditional upon the training given within the experiment in question. The salivating is an 'unconditional response' (UR) to the food-powder (US), but is known as a 'conditional response' (CR) to the buzzer (CS). The technique of training, still to be described in detail, is called 'conditioning', or strictly 'classical' or 'Pavlovian' conditioning, to distinguish it from the procedure used in the less highly controlled kind of experiment mentioned above – which is called 'instrumental' or 'operant' conditioning.[1]

How do these terms relate to the terms we have been using? From the example it will be apparent that the conditional stimulus (buzzer) is akin to the cue; but there is a difference. The term 'stimulus' implies that the item so described will in fact stimulate, that is, get a response, whereas a cue will do so only if it has force. A stimulus is apparently a forceful cue. Also, the term 'stimulus' customarily refers to something relatively small or simple, like a buzzing sound, a flash of light, a touch, whereas a cue may be very complex – though in connection with habits this latter difference is of no great importance. The unconditional stimulus, the food-powder in our example, is akin to the prompt for it gets the specified form of response (salivating) in the first place. But here again there is a difference. By definition, the prompt is merely a form-determiner: it gives the required form to the response elicited by the cue; whereas an unconditional stimulus itself elicits a response. It will be apparent, therefore, that an unconditional stimulus may not serve the function of prompt, but may get a response in its own right instead of shaping the response elicited by the forceful cue. Another difference is that an unconditional stimulus is, by customary usage of the term, a relatively simple thing, whereas a prompt may be complex – like a verbal instruction. My reason for working out here the relations between the two sets of terms is that if we use only the terms associated with conditioning we may fail to see how conditioning fits into the general scheme of learning.

Now it is obvious that the *content* of this experiment, and of

---

[1] The account just given is an oversimplification, because the conditional and unconditional responses are not in fact identical. For example, in response to the buzzer the dog not only salivates but also twitches an ear, or something of the sort; and in response to food-in-the-mouth the dog makes tongue-movements, and so forth, which eventually do not appear in response to the buzzer. See also p. 263, l. 33ff.

In many texts the term 'conditioned' appears, instead of the term 'conditional'. I prefer the latter, not just because it seems to be a better translation of Pavlov's intention, but mainly because the significance of the term is plainer.

many others like it, has little if any bearing on the work of the parent or teacher. As I shall argue in a moment, however, the very same *technique* – the Meat and Bell Technique, as Overstreet (37) has called it, applies to the training of human subjects.[1] From this sort of experiment we can pinpoint the details of what the habit-trainer has to do. The following seem to be the main points – though for the present I am still talking about animals.

First, the CS (buzzer) and the US (food) have to be presented very close together in time. Call this the Condition of Contiguity. The longer the interval between CS and US, the less likely it is that the habit will be formed.

Second, success is very much more likely (and in many instances possible only) if the CS and US are presented in that time-order – that is, CS followed by US. Call this the Condition of Sequence.

Third, in most instances the twin-presentation of CS and US (in contiguity and in that sequence) has to be made several times. Call this the Condition of Repetition.

The number of repetitions may be much reduced, however, if the following conditions also hold.

Fourth, success with the dog was achieved more expeditiously when it was trained in a soundproof laboratory. Until this arrangement was made possible, Pavlov found that the dog sometimes learned the wrong thing – such as to salivate at the sound of the experimenter's approaching footsteps. Since the effect of soundproofing appears to be that of preventing the dog's being distracted by irrelevant matters, call this the Condition of Distraction-Removal.

Fifth, success is much more likely if the dog is allowed to become accustomed, 'habituated', to the circumstances of the laboratory, such as the harness in which it has to be strapped, the various pieces of apparatus required, and so forth. Call this the Condition of Habituation.

Since what we have to demonstrate is the relevance of these

---

[1] In using this descriptive term, Overstreet is by no means decrying the technique. On the contrary, he takes the view that it constitutes one of psychology's major contributions to the control of human behaviour – for good or evil.

conditions to the training of human subjects, we may summarise them in the form of a set of instructions:

1. Before training proper begins, the subject should be habituated to the place of training, and all likely distractions should be removed.
2. The cue and the pilot-cue should be presented close together in time, and in that order.
3. The procedure of 2 should be repeated.

I shall now try to show that these same conditions apply to the training of human subjects.

Human Habits

Some human habits are very similar to the habits animals acquire. We may not learn to salivate at the sound of a buzzer, but we may learn to salivate at the sound of meal-preparing in the kitchen. Disgust at the substance of some anecdote may become a response to the person who related it. Human subjects can be trained to blink an eye in response to a musical note – if it has been presented contiguously with a puff of air delivered to the eyelid. Sweat-responses in the skin, which can be recorded electrically, and constitute the so-called psycho-galvanic response (PGR), normally are given to certain 'emotional' stimuli, but by the technique of conditioning can become attached to stimuli which previously were emotionally neutral. These, and similar examples, are equivalent to the Pavlovian example already quoted. Human habits are, of course, much more varied. They embrace not only obvious habits like learning to rinse out the wash-basin after using it, learning to shut the door on leaving the room, and learning to say Thank-you when handed something, but also a great many instances that are not always called or even recognised as being habits. For the child or anyone else who has learned to read, attention is given to what the words mean, and not to their pronunciation. The sounding of the words on the page, either aloud or in so-called inner speech, is eventually done automatically. (Few adults can remember what if felt like to look at 'box' and not to hear the word or imagine some sort of a box; or to see the symbol '7' and not hear 'seven' or think of whatever that symbol was intended to mean. The habits pupils have still to acquire are so clearly automatic that we are in danger of forgetting their acquisition is necessary). Answering questions like 'Eight times three?' becomes habitual; we get 'Twenty-four' before we have time to think. Another example is the writing down of figures to dictation: when someone reads out 'Six three two four', we do not have to think how to write it down. Equally automatic, for many adults, is the closing of a written sentence with a full stop, the writing of a word they have thought of, or even the coming-to-mind of a mathematical formula.

I have quoted a variety of human habits here because habits are often envisaged as rather trivial things, appropriate enough for very young children (*e.g.* toilet-training), but somewhat lacking in intellectual respectability. Nevertheless, although we may on occasion become 'slaves' to a habit, unless a great many of our actions, even in scholastic matters, became habitual we should be unable to give the necessary attention to matters of even greater importance. Probably some of the educational disapproval of habits derives from the observation that a habit may be acquired without the learner's having much idea of what he is doing or why he is doing it, but with such issues I am not concerned at the moment. It is sufficient if we agree that *some* habits are worth acquiring, even if we do not take time to discuss just what they should be; and that once the teacher has decided which habits are worth acquiring, he will wish to use the most efficient means of training that are available.

There is, of course, one obvious difference between salivating, ear-twitching, and the like, and many of the behaviours involved in human habits. The former (in the main) are 'involuntary', whereas the latter in the initial stages may not be. To perform what is required of him the human learner may have to be 'motivated', or 'want' to perform. This is a point we shall have to consider later.

Habit-training by Verbal Instruction

When Pavlov wanted the dog to salivate, he introduced a prompt (or unconditional stimulus) for salivation, namely food-powder. When an experimenter wishes a rat to avoid a certain part of the cage, he arranges that the animal will receive an electric shock whenever it goes there. In few cases, however, will the teacher have occasion to use such primitive devices. In a great many instances the role of prompt (to get the required form of response in the first place) may be taken by a verbal instruction. When the teacher wishes children to behave in a certain way she does not offer food, or ring an electric bell, but simply tells them to behave in that way – 'Stand up!', 'Sit down!', 'Take off your coats!' Such instructions are patently intended to fulfil exactly the same function as was fulfilled by the food-powder in the dog's mouth: to determine that the response that is made will be the response that is required; they are (or are intended to be) prompts. Then should verbal instructions be subject to the conditions made explicit in the account of conditioning?

Here there are few carefully controlled experiments to which we can refer, but observation of human behaviour suggests strongly that the answer is Yes. The following example will serve to illustrate the point.

Tom has to acquire the habit of rinsing out the washbasin after he has used it. The response required is that of rinsing out the basin. The cue, as specified by the statement of the instance, is 'After using the basin'. (As I shall suggest later, the statement may be improved upon, so that the cue is less abstract, but for the moment it will suffice.) The intended prompt is a verbal instruction, given (say) by Tom's mother: 'Rinse the basin, Tom!' Do the conditions of Habituation, Distraction-Removal, Contiguity, Sequence, and Repetition apply?

Consider first the condition of Contiguity – of cue and intended prompt. If the instruction (the intended prompt) is given some time before Tom has finished using the basin (the cue), Tom may forget; and the longer the interval between the issuing of the instruction and the time it has to be obeyed, the more likely forgetting will be. On the other hand, if the instruction is given a considerable time after Tom has finished with the basin, it will be too late to affect the form of his response to finishing with the basin. It might, of course, affect the response on the next occasion he finishes with the basin, but this takes us back to the first point, namely that in the interval he may forget. Observation of many examples of this sort suggests very strongly that if an instruction is to determine the form of a response, it is most likely to do so if it is given at the time the response has to be made. Perhaps I should emphasise that I am dealing here not with whether the habit will continue, but with the getting of the required form of response to the cue at the outset – with getting the habit started. To take another example: if Tom has to learn to wipe his feet on the mat on entering the house, and a verbal instruction is to be used for this purpose, when is the optimum time for giving the instruction – so as to get the required form of response to entering the house? It is obvious, I think, that the instruction should be given at the very moment the child is entering the house. The condition of Contiguity apparently is relevant.

In much human learning the condition of Sequence may be of less importance so long as the condition of Contiguity is observed. For example, if Tom has to learn to rinse out the basin when he has finished washing, it does not matter very much whether he is given the instruction immediately after or immediately before he finishes. A more relevant way of expressing the point would be to say that the instruction should be given at the very moment when that instruction has to be obeyed. (Experiment indicates, however, that where the response approximates to a 'reflex', the condition of Sequence is important.)

The relevance of the condition of Distraction will be, I think, obvious. Teachers who have to work in classrooms bombarded by the noises of passing trains, lorries, pneumatic drills, and milk bottles clanking in the corridor, may well envy Pavlov his sound-proof laboratory. Many distractions are, of course, within the teacher's control. He would not issue a verbal instruction, intended as prompt, when the class was noisy, and a word written on a blackboard already nearly covered with print may be lost in the jumble. If Tom's mother's instruction to rinse the basin is given in the middle of a long harangue on the virtues of tidiness, that instruction may be swallowed up in the verbal context and be quite ineffective. Likewise, if as Tom finished washing there was a crash of crockery from the kitchen, that most distracting event might replace the cue (finishing washing) as the initiator of a response.

One special case of distraction deserves attention. Sometimes the verbal instruction, intended as prompt, itself distracts from the cue. If Tom's mother shouts at him in a rage, demanding in unambiguous language that he rinse out the basin, Tom may jump to obey. But the very intensity of that instruction may defeat its own ends. It may put the cue (finishing-washing) into the shade, so that Tom's reaction is made to the instruction and not at all to the cue itself. It is as if the actor were responding entirely to the prompter, and giving no attention whatsoever to the stage situation (cue) to which he should have responded. When this happens, the instruction is not serving as prompt, because the function of a prompt is to give the required form to the response elicited by the cue – and in this case there is no such response. This danger is always present when the thing intended as prompt is also a stimulus: the unconditional stimulus may prevent the cue (or conditional stimulus) from getting a response. In everyday language, the instruction issued by Tom's mother should not be such as to take his attention from the event of finishing washing. For this reason a quietly authoritative remark is more likely to be effective than is a downright command. (Indeed the bossy command might not even get the required response for itself; it might get a show of resistance.) A further improvement might be introduced: in addition to keeping the remark quietly authoritative, the mother might add the phrase, '. . . now you've finished washing', which could have the effect of drawing attention to the cue itself.

Another form of distraction, not always recognised as such, is an explanation – if given in the middle of training. Even if we agree that children should know why they are asked to do things, see the sense of them, and so forth, an explanation introduced into the training procedure may serve merely as a distraction. Akin to this distraction is the learner's own thinking. It will be helpful if the child thinks *of* the cue, in the sense of making it the sole object of his thought; but his thinking *about it*, in the sense of thinking also of other things associated with it, may merely introduce grounds for distraction. 'Think what you're doing!' is sometimes good advice if our aim is habit-*breaking*, but for this very reason may be worse than useless in habit-*training*.

Distraction-Removal is nevertheless not quite so straight-forward a matter as the foregoing account might suggest. True, there is ample evidence that the removal of distractions has the effect of speeding up learning, but there is another side to the picture. The more distractions we remove, the more similar are the successive situations likely to become; and so we may decrease the likelihood of fulfilling the Requirement of Cue, particularly that aspect of the requirement which states that the cue must be the *only* feature the successive situations share. For example, if we remove all noise, the dog is not strictly learning to salivate in a buzzer-sounding sort of situation; it is learning to salivate in a buzzer-sounding-amid-silence situation. And without resort to further experiment we cannot know whether the dog will salivate in response to the buzzer when there is background noise. In fact there is some evidence[1] that the more highly we control the learning-situation in this way, for human subjects, the faster is the learning but the poorer is the retention. The student who has become accustomed to studying in silence may be unable to study effectively when there is noise. Likewise the lecturer who has had

[1] For a brief discussion of this issue (variability of the learning-situation from trial to trial) see Lawson (27), particularly the references to the experiments of Voeks (54) and Mackintosh (29).

to put up with the sounds of children at play while he is in his study may be unable to study when the family go on holiday. The moral seems to be that the teacher should eliminate gross distractions, but gradually acclimatize the learner to more and more varied situations. (See in this connection the Method of Small Doses, in the following chapter.)

The relevance of the condition of Habituation to human habit-training will be apparent to teachers who work with very young children. Until the school beginners have become accustomed to their new surroundings, and to the teacher herself, there is little point in trying to teach them anything else.

As for the condition of Repetition, it is rarely in school-learning that one telling is enough. In a great many instances the pupil has to be told what to do, on several occasions, before he will do it without having to be told. The condition of Repetition seems to be as relevant to the training of children as it is to the training of dogs in psychological laboratories. In each case, however, it is worth emphasising precisely *what* has to be repeated. It is not just the instruction, or good advice, or demonstration, but the instruction (etc.) in *contiguity with the forceful cue*.

These illustrations do not, of course, provide a rigorous proof of the point that the circumstances found necessary for classical conditioning are appropriate also for the development of human habits, but I believe that if the reader carefully examines examples of his own choosing, and better still, tries to train someone (who might well be himself) in a habit, he will find that these same conditions are applicable. Indeed, now that they have been stated explicitly, their relevance may seem so clear that they scarcely merit the trouble I have taken in making them explicit; but discussions with students and others who have not given much thought to the matter suggest that even these relatively simple conditions do not always come to mind uninvited. The main practical difficulty, however, lies not in the teacher's knowing what conditions must be fulfilled but in his realising, in the class-room itself, that here and now is an occasion when he must fulfil them. A student may be able to answer the examination question, 'In using an instruction as pilot-cue, what conditions should be borne in mind?', yet fail to consider these conditions when a child has to be trained to take off his cap on entering school, to knock at the door before entering another classroom, and so forth. It may be easier, but it is less effective, to say,'You should have knocked at the door!', than to make the child start out again, and knock when he reaches the door. This difficulty cannot be dealt with adequately in a book; all I can suggest here is that the student should make a point of looking for occasions on which he can make use of these various conditions.

I have not yet tried to explain why, or how, these conditions operate. Why is Repetition effective? How does it come about that Contiguity is necessary? What of the learner's motivation – or lack of it? For convenience these and similar questions may be postponed until we have looked at another means of habit-training.

Habit-training by the Demonstration of a Model

In many instances it is less convenient to tell the pupil what he has to do than it is to show him what is required. Instead of giving him a verbal instruction, which in effect points to or describes the form of response required, we ourselves may perform that response and make the pupil imitate the behaviour we have shown him. This latter technique may be called 'demonstrating', in contrast with 'instructing verbally'. The term 'demonstration' is nevertheless somewhat ambiguous, and the term 'model' is used often to refer specifically to that particular content of the demonstration which has to be imitated. In other words the model is whatever is demonstrated for imitation.

For example, one might contrive to teach a child to pronounce a certain word by instructing him how to place his tongue, lips, and so forth, but it is usually simpler merely to say the word ourselves and ask him to say it after us. One might describe, in words, a simple action, but here again it may be more convenient to perform the action, while he watches us, and make him copy what we have done.

Even from these two simple examples it will be apparent that the function of a model, in habit-training, is exactly the same as that of a verbal instruction, namely the function of prompt. The purpose of a model, for imitation, is to get the required form of response in the first place. The use of models as prompts nevertheless raises special difficulties. In many cases the model will be visual – as in showing a child how to hold a pencil, a knife, or a cricket bat; and if the child faces the demonstrator, what the demonstrator does with his right hand the child may do with his left, because to the young learner his action may seem to be a perfect copy of what he has seen. This difficulty, once its possibility is realised, can be overcome easily enough: the demonstrator may stand or sit alongside, or even work from behind, the pupil. Another special difficulty is that the perceiving of the model, by eyes or ears, is by no means the same thing as performing the action which is a reproduction of it. I can move my left ear (without touching it), and the movement is large enough to be perceived clearly by my class, but the student who can see perfectly well what he has to do may have no idea how to do it. His muscles do not know, as it were, what to do in order to reproduce what his eyes have seen. Likewise, there are people who can recognise the final sound in the Scots word 'loch', but who are nevertheless unable to copy it, either in that word or in speaking Spanish or Russian. Also relevant to school-learning are certain vowel sounds and intonations in French and German. (When a pupil cannot follow a demonstrated action it is tempting to 'put him through the motions'; but this may be almost useless, because the 'feel' of having a hand moved is not the same as actually moving it oneself.) Patently anything intended as a model must be such that the pupil can in fact imitate it. Belief in an 'instinct of imitation', justified or not, does not override that simple fact.

These are not the only difficulties associated with the use of models, but most of the others are essentially the same as those discussed in connection with the use of verbal instructions; they are difficulties in using prompts generally. Just as a verbal instruction may become lost in the context of chatter, exhortation, threats, and so forth, in which verbal instructions are sometimes given, so also a model may be obscured by some irrelevant, but nevertheless distracting aspect of the demonstration-situation. The pupil who should be listening to the French vowel may be much too interested in his teacher's facial contortions. The small boy who is being shown, on his own exercise book, how to make a certain letter, may be almost overwhelmed by this large strange hand before his eyes.

That the conditions found effective in conditioning apply also to habit-training by the demonstration of models need not be worked out again in detail. Only the condition of Contiguity appears to merit exemplification. Suppose that the habit to be acquired is the habit of saying (making the sound) 'Cat!' when the printed word 'Cat' is shown. Then the model prompt in this instance could be the teacher's own saying of that word. If, now, the teacher's model pronunciation is given some time before the printed word appears, and the pupil imitates at once, the model is not acting as a prompt at all, because no response to the *cue* (printed word) has yet been made, and so cannot be given the required form. And if the imitation (but not the demonstration) is postponed until the printed word does appear, the pupil may have forgotten exactly what he was to imitate – especially if other spoken words intervene. On the other hand, if the model-pronunciation were not given until after the cue (printed word) had disappeared, it could not affect the response made to the printed word, because any response it did get would already have been made. Nor would it be wise to assume that the reader-beginner could remember what the printed word looked like. In fact, no teacher would resort to any of these procedures. I have used this particular example, not because anyone is likely to need guidance in it, but to illustrate the point that Contiguity is a necessary condition of the effective use of models. The teacher would, of course, give the required pronunciation while the child was looking at the printed word. Better still, she would try to arrange that the model was given at the moment the printed word appeared, because even if the pupil could be made to stare at the word for some seconds, it might begin to get the wrong response, or even fail to get a response at all.

The relevance of the other conditions to the use of models is, I think, fairly clear. A demonstration, like a verbal instruction, usually has to be given more than once (Repetition). The condition of Distraction has already been illustrated in connection with the model itself – the large strange hand in front of the small boy, and the teacher's facial contortions. And, of course, a distraction may prevent the cue's getting a response in this case just as in the other. Also, a model, like a verbal instruction, may itself distract from the cue and itself elicit a response instead of merely giving the required form to the response elicited by the cue. The pupil's attention may be switched entirely to the model, so that for him the cue scarcely exists; the demonstrated action may be so interesting that he forgets all about the cue to which that action has to be a response. For example, the young reader may be so busy copying what the teacher is saying that he cannot look properly at the printed word. The condition of Sequence may be more relevant here than it was with verbal instructions; the model may be less likely to obscure the cue if the model is not presented until the response to the cue is just beginning to be made.

Interpretation

If we are to make use of these various conditions in a number of instances we must know not merely what they are but also how they work, and we must recognise the particular functions they fulfil. In other words, we must see how they fulfil the four basic requirements of learning – Cue, Force, Prompt, and Reinforcement.

About the Requirement of Cue (that there must be a series of situations sharing only the cue of the instance) experiment tells us nothing we do not already know, because that requirement does not call for experiment at all. It is enough to note that in the examples cited there is a series of buzzer-sounding situations, a series of finishing-washing situations, and so forth. If there is insufficient variety in the series, the response may (for all we know) become attached to something other than the cue. The child who has to learn to brush his teeth after meals may learn only to brush his teeth after rising from the table in a particular room, so that when he goes on holiday the habit disappears. In such a case the cue of the instance intended (namely after-meals) is not the cue of the instance that actually occurs (namely rising-from-this-particular-table).

Reference to the Requirement of Force is made in conditioning experiments by the term 'stimulus'. As was noted earlier, a stimulus is a (simple) cue with force. But some so-called stimuli sometimes fail to stimulate, and it is probably wiser not to lump together these two requirements (Cue and Force) as the language of conditioning implies, but to insist that the cue must be such as to get a response. It will be shown in Chapter 7 that there are ways of giving force to a cue which has none, but for the present it is relevant to suggest that it is often simpler to choose, in the first place, a cue which is known to be forceful. Even within the statement of any particular instance, such a choice is often possible. For example, in introducing the instance of learning to rinse out the wash-basin after using it, I remarked that the cue (after-using-it) might be improved upon. What I had in mind was that this particular cue is not likely to be outstanding, attention-getting, forceful, for a child. A feature more likely to get some sort of response would be his own action of pulling out the stopper, or the sight and sound of the water beginning to run away. Such a feature is not incompatible with the statement of the instance. Rinsing out the basin as the stopper is pulled out is in effect the same as rinsing out the basin when one has finished washing. Likewise, Mary may be required to tidy away her toys every night at seven o'clock; but seven o'clock, as such, is not likely to get any response at all. On the other hand, were we to choose as cue 'the clock's-striking-seven', we should now have a feature likely to get some sort of reaction.

One simple way of attempting to fulfil the Requirement of Force, then, is to *choose* as cue something already known to be capable of eliciting a response. I said 'attempting', because an item which has force in one sort of situation may not have force in another, but the wider the variety of situations in which the feature is forceful, the more likely it is that it will be forceful in the situation in question. Another difficulty, in this same connection, is that some other feature of the situation may overwhelm the cue, outshine it, so that the cue does not get a response. It is to this possibility that the conditions of Distraction and Habituation are particularly relevant, because a distraction is something which should not get a response, but does; and the effect of habituation, apparently, is to reduce the attention-getting capacities of items which would otherwise get responses. If, then, the subject could become habituated to all items which should not get a response, and if new items – which might get a response – are eliminated, only the cue would be left capable of eliciting responses. The conditions of Habituation and Distraction-removal appear to be means of fulfilling the Requirement of Force, namely of ensuring that it is the cue of the situation to which the responses are made.

These two conditions relate also to the Requirement of Prompt. A verbal instruction, intended as prompt, may have no effect if other children distract by calling from the garden outside. The mother may get a response, but it may take the form of a refusal to obey. Permanent aspects of the situation may have a similar effect unless the child gets used to them.

To fulfil the Requirement of Prompt, then, it is not enough to choose some item which will usually give the response the required form; we should also strive to eliminate all other 'misleading' prompts.

Also under the head of Prompt come the conditions of Contiguity and Sequence. It is only when the verbal instruction or model is very close in time to the cue that it is likely to shape the cue's response in the required way. Indeed, the condition of Contiguity might be deduced from theory: if something is to determine the form of a response, it is reasonable to postulate that that thing itself must occur just as the response begins to be made. Also if, by a change in the sequence of cue and verbal instruction, the instruction is not obeyed, it is not then serving as a prompt.

There still remains for interpretation the condition of Repetition. What is its peculiar function? A popular view is that if we do something often enough, in the same kind of situation, eventually the arising of that situation will evoke that behaviour; in other words, that repetition serves as a reinforcer; a behaviour which has been concomitant on several occasions with a particular situation will eventually be evoked by that situation. This is, in effect, an expression of the old Law of Frequency. But while it is empirically true, we may doubt whether the matter is quite as simple as it looks. A more subtle view is that the behaviour-form becomes tied to the cue, not by the repetition as such, but by other circumstances which repetition merely makes possible. By analogy, I may have to toss three coins a great many times before all land heads, but it is not the repetition which makes them land in that way. All the repetition does is allow the occurrence of other conditions over which I have no control: the angle at which the coin leaves my hand, the height to which it is thrown, the quality of the surface on which it lands, and so on. It is conceivable, and I believe profitable, to consider that repetition in learning may be having the same sort of effect.

Then what are these 'other conditions' which repetition may allow to occur? An attractive and very simple answer has been offered by Guthrie (17). His view is that *whenever* some behaviour occurs in some situation, an attachment is made – but to only one or two of the features of that situation. The attachment formed in one situation, however, may not show on the next occasion, because no two successive situations are ever exactly alike; the features to which the behaviour was attached on the first occasion may not appear on the second occasion, and so on. Accordingly, learning will become apparent only after the behaviour has become attached to a great many of the features likely to arise in the kind of situation in question. And to effect such a multiplicity of connections we must create a multiplicity of situations in which that behaviour is performed.

With this view I have considerable sympathy – particularly the point that the behaviour-form is connected to *some* feature or other on any occasion. Observation of human learners suggests, not that there are occasions when they learn nothing, but that there are occasions when what they do learn is the wrong thing. The logical analysis of learning in Part One nevertheless indicates that a multiplicity of connections is not necessary, and that even a host of such connections may be insufficient. If any instance of learning is to take place, it is necessary and sufficient that the response-form should be connected to one thing and one thing only, namely the cue – the feature, often complex, which characterises the kind of situation involved. An alternative interpretation of the observed need of repetition in many cases may therefore be that several presentations may be required before it is the cue, rather than some other feature, to which the response-form is connected.

This latter view seems to explain more satisfactorily why learning sometimes occurs without repetition at all. If, for some reason yet to be examined, it is to the cue that the response-form is attached on the first occasion, repetition becomes unnecessary; a multiplicity of connections is not required. The same view explains in a quite simple way some other interesting observations. Instances in which the cue is relatively complex usually call for more repetition than do instances in which the cue is relatively simple. In other words, difficult instances usually need more repetition than do easy ones. Why? Almost by definition, 'complex' cues are more difficult to 'see'; they call for a higher degree of abstraction; it is easier to put all red objects into the one class than it is to recognise all applicants over forty years old. And as I shall argue in Chapter 7, to say that one 'sees' a certain feature or aspect of a situation is equivalent to saying that it is that feature or aspect which is getting a response, having force. But if the cue is complex, difficult to 'see', and does not evoke a response, patently the object intended as prompt cannot be effective; it cannot shape a response which is not there to be shaped. In such cases repetition may have the effect of eventually letting the learner 'see' the cue, partly because his chances of seeing it are increased, but also because the repetition of the cue in a series of otherwise different situations may have the effect of 'over-stamping' it – in contrast with the other features which by their very variety may result in a 'blur'. (For example, the people I learn to know by sight on my way to work tend to be those I see every day. The very repetition seems to make them more emphatic.) Here again, then, repetition may serve, not to strengthen some connection which has already been made, nor even increase the total number of connections, but to allow the cue to become forceful and so to allow the prompt-object to do its job. The same thesis would explain why repetition may be reduced, or even made unnecessary, when the material in question is understood rather than dealt with in a blind trial-and-error fashion. To understand something (Chapter 7) is in effect to see its cue; when something is understood, it is its cue which gets the response, becomes forceful. Accordingly, if the cue of the situation is clear and forceful, *before* the prompt is introduced, there will be no need to resort to repetition to make it forceful. One other support for the thesis is worth mentioning at this stage. As I noted earlier, the number of repetitions can be reduced if the subject is habituated to the situation, and if distractions are removed. But the effect of fulfilling these conditions, I argued, is to increase the likelihood that it will be the cue which gets the response. From this finding it is therefore reasonable to suppose that repetition does have the effect (or at least can have the effect) of allowing the cue to become forceful.

The argument is, then, that repetition does not have the function popularly ascribed to it, namely that of 'strengthening' a connection which has been 'slightly' established. (Indeed it is common knowledge that repetition may have the opposite effect. Enforced repetition may cause us to grow weary, and give up.) Moreover, the argument is that repetition as such does not even establish connections in the first place, not even tenuous ones. What it does is provide opportunity for the forming of the *requisite* connection, namely between the specified form of response and the cue. It does this either by increasing the chances of the cue's being seen and having force; or by actually giving force to the cue by its successive reappearances in an otherwise changing situation. But in neither case is repetition directly serving as reinforcer. On the contrary, repetition appears to be related to the Requirement of Force (that it must be the *cue* which evokes a response), and to the Requirement of Prompt (that it must be the response to the *cue* which is given the requisite form.)[1]

Then if repetition does not serve as reinforcer, what does? A hint of one possibility is given by an extension of the Pavlov experiment referred to earlier. If, after the dog has learned to salivate at the sound of the buzzer, the buzzer is sounded very frequently and at short intervals *without* the food-powder, the salivary response to the buzzer eventually disappears. One explanation of this finding is that the response-form is tied to the cue by some sort of 'reward' or 'satisfaction'; and if the reward disappears, or the response ceases to be satisfying, the response fades. This is the essence of the thesis usually coupled with the name of E. L. Thorndike (50), and expressed in his Law of Effect. It says, essentially, that if some response, in a certain situation, results in a satisfying state of affairs for the subject, the recurrence of that situation is likely to entail the recurrence of that response. A more modern statement of the function of Reward has been given by B. F. Skinner. (See Chapter 11.)

A second major thesis, proposed by E. C. Tolman (53), is that the effective agent is the Fulfilment of Expectancy. Tolman's view has been widely criticised on the ground that it is insufficiently precise, but it is easy enough to see, in a general way, what he intended. If food-powder frequently follows the buzzer (as it does during the training-period), the dog comes to 'expect' it after the buzzer sounds. And if this expectancy is fulfilled on

---

[1] Another way of saying that repetition allows the cue to become the forceful feature is that repetition allows of the requisite discrimination.

several occasions, the salivary response to the buzzer is learned. Indeed, 'expectancy-fulfilment' may perhaps be regarded as a special case of 'satisfaction', so that Tolman's thesis may be envisaged as a special case of Thorndike's. In neither case, however, is it clear why the same response should continue (as in many habits it does) long after expectancy ceases to be fulfilled or satisfaction has ceased. Many human habits, which may have brought satisfaction at one time, continue long after they have ceased to be rewarding in any way at all, an observation which lends support to the 'Inertia' thesis cited shortly.

A third well-known view is that of C. L. Hull (22). His theory is an extremely complex one, but its central tenet is that the effective factor is Drive-reduction. If, when a certain behaviour occurs in a certain situation, some drive (such as hunger or thirst) is reduced in strength, the recurrence of that situation is likely to entail the recurrence of that same behaviour. (It is not necessary that the reduction in drive should be a direct effect of the response; it could be engineered in a quite arbitrary way by the experimenter – such as feeding the rat when it sniffs a certain object in the cage.) A fair comment on this thesis is that human subjects do *not* learn very well when they are hungry or thirsty – unless what they are learning is related to these states, such as how to open a can of beans without a can-opener. Also, Hebb (20) has pointed out that there are occasions when drive-increase can have the same effect.

In the same connection might be cited also the old Laws of Association – the Laws of Frequency, Recency, Primacy, Vividness, and so forth. The Law of Frequency (Repetition) has already been noted: I suggested that it might relate, not to the Requirement of Tie but to the Requirements of Force and Prompt. (The Laws of Recency and Primacy seem less relevant, because learning requires also a *change* in the form of response.) The Law of Vividness, however, does appear to have a bearing on the present issue. To say that something is 'vivid' is equivalent to saying that it gets attention, is dominant, or in effect is the item which gets a response, that is, is forceful; or at least is not over-shadowed by something else. This law, therefore, seems to be a positive version of the statement of the conditions of Distraction and Habituation.

As I have already argued, the cue must not be overwhelmed or cluttered by irrelevant aspects of the situation; and this might be said also by saying that the cue must be 'vivid'.

At this stage I do not propose to analyse these various theses – Reward or Satisfaction, Expectancy-fulfilment, Drive-reduction, and so on, in order to discover just how these alleged conditions operate. For our purpose here it is sufficient to note that each of them does apply to a wide range of instances. Without stating explicitly how Reward reinforces, we can assert with considerable confidence that in fact it often does; and similarly for the other conditions.

For practical purposes, then, the teacher may do best by trying to fulfil all of these conditions in each instance, as suggested in the summary on p. 91. I shall add but one comment here. Observation of much human behaviour suggests that there are many occasions when no one of these conditions holds at all. Many human habits appear to be formed without reward, or satisfaction, or expectancy-fulfilment, or drive-reduction, or even repetition; and one is tempted to suggest that many habitual behaviours persist merely because it would be more troublesome to change them than it is to leave them alone. They proceed, as it were, by their own inertia; or, to use a metaphor allying this view with Allport's concept of Functional Autonomy (2), they proceed under their own steam without the need of other motivation. Or, as D. K. Adams (1) suggested, behaviour exhibits a principle of Parsimony.

To put the matter in still another way, as Guthrie has done, the same response tends to be given to the same situation unless something interferes with it. On this view the conditions referred to above would be cited in a negative way: the same response will continue *unless* the consequence is *dis*satisfying, or *fails* to fulfil what expectancy there was, or results in a *greater* state of drive, and so forth. (But see also p. 261 ff.)

The Learner's Motivation

The various conditions we have been discussing seem to be necessary for habit-training, but will they be sufficient? Unlike the reflexes which can be induced by appropriate stimuli in animal-experiments, the behaviours called for in school are usually voluntary in kind, and the pupil may be *un*willing to perform. This type of problem is usually discussed in terms of 'motivation'. It is widely held that learning will not occur unless the learner is 'motivated', or 'wants' to do what is required. A thorough examination of this issue is far beyond the scope and purpose of this book. I shall refer only to some of the main points, stressing those that have a direct bearing on practice. Because of the relative simplicity of the responses called for in habit-training, the problem of motivation is less pressing there than it is in some of the other techniques considered later, but for convenience of presentation we may look at it now in a general way, and refer back to this account when further details have to be raised.

Although wants, motives, urges, and the like are popularly assumed to be internal causes of behaviour, yet they have to be inferred from behaviour itself. If we say that Mary 'wants' to learn to read, and are asked for the evidence, we could point out that she cooperates with her teacher, follows instructions, persists despite setbacks, goes out of her way to get extra practice, shows pleasure at even small intermediate successes, continues to read after external pressure has been removed, and the like. (Conversely, if behaviours like these seldom or never occurred, we might say that the motivation was low or that the pupil apparently did 'not want' to learn.) Now as I have said, in much popular thinking such behaviours are envisaged as evidence of an inner want; but from both a scientific and a purely practical view-point the citing of causative wants is unnecessary.[1] We know

---

[1] The scientific objection to the citing of such wants is that if a want is inferred only from certain behaviours, and there is no other way of establishing the want's presence, the thesis that these behaviours are caused by the want is unverifiable. A similar objection is brought against Faculty Theory in a later chapter (p. 157). Indeed, the view criticised above could be regarded as a particular instance of that theory.

from our experience of pupils generally that those who *behave* in the ways just listed are more likely to succeed than are those who do not. From the very behaviours popularly cited as evidence of an inner want we can go straight to the prediction of the likelihood of the occurrence of the required ultimate performance.[1]

Why success should be more likely when these behaviours occur is not difficult to see: they have the effect of permitting the fulfilment of the basic requirements of learning. When the learner persists (a major piece of 'evidence' of a want), he thereby facilitates the occurrence of a series of situations containing the cue, and also gives the cue the opportunity of being or becoming the forceful feature. When he complies with instructions he facilitates the introduction of a prompt. And when he shows pleasure in success he exemplifies one of the circumstances known to serve as a reinforcer.

A fundamental practical implication of this very brief analysis is that if we are to use the word 'want' at all we should be wiser to use it, not as the name of a supposed inner cause of behaviour, but to refer to the syndrome of behaviours from which inner wants are popularly inferred. In effect, to say that Mary wants to learn to read is to say that she already behaves in ways like those we have been considering. This way of using the word has the advantage of concentrating our attention on something we can deal with at first hand – namely the pupil's behaviour. In particular, reference to the absence of a want to learn something will mean, not the absence of some internal cause over which we can have no control, but the absence of behaviours of a quite specific kind. And that in turn suggests the form the teacher's task must take. By one means or another he must see to it that the learner does persist, does comply with instructions, does have pleasure in intermediate success, does continue when external pressure is

---

[1] Moreover, although we may assume that our prediction of subsequent performance is based on the inner want we think we have discovered, yet (as was implied in the text) its validity is in fact based on a previously established concomitance between ultimate performance and the behaviours customarily cited as evidence of a want. Its basis, in short, is statistical.

removed, and so forth. For all practical purposes, to create a want to learn means to induce these very behaviours.[1]

The motivation problem, as it affects the teacher, can now be stated clearly and unambiguously. By what means can the teacher induce behaviours of the kind we have been discussing?

Here again it would be out of place to produce a full-scale argument. All I shall do is state a general principle and provide illustrations of it. The answer, in motivational terms, is that a new want has usually to be created by our exploiting some other want which is already present. In behavioural terms, the required behaviour usually has to be fitted into and made part of a pattern of behaviour which is already established. Here are two examples.

A class of semi-literate men, in a military detention barracks, who knew little or nothing of vulgar fractions, learned remarkably quickly to manipulate fractions once the topic had been presented in a context of betting-odds. In the same institution was an illiterate man who was also surly, aggressive, no respecter of persons, and showed no wish to learn to read and write. From the scanty conversation in which I was able to engage him, however, I deduced that he was strongly attached to his widowed mother; and when I offered to help him, privately, to write letters to her, the offer was gladly accepted and indeed bore fruit. Of each case it could, of course, be said that I had discovered a want to which I could appeal, but all I knew for certain were the behaviours I was able to exploit – in the first case betting, and in the other a mode of behaviour which might be called 'doing things which pleased his mother'. True, it might have been interesting to know *why* these men behaved in these particular ways; but for my purely practical purpose it was sufficient to know that these actual modes of behaviour were established.

Though the details of these two examples scarcely apply to school, the principle they illustrate is widely employed. In recent years curricula have tended to be based more and more on the activities in which pupils actually engage. Measurement is linked

[1] To the objection that there might be a want even in the absence of such behaviours the reply is simple: were there no such behaviours the alleged want would be useless.

with the lay-out of sports grounds, music with school concerts, mechanics with motor cars, and so on. In all these cases the teacher is exploiting an established mode of behaviour. The means of exploiting it can be expressed in a variety of ways. Sometimes it is sufficient to show the pupil that the new behaviour is a way of achieving an end he has not yet been able to reach, or a more efficient way of achieving an end he can now reach only with considerable difficulty. Other occasions call for more subtle engineering, and some of these are considered in subsequent chapters. This present account may be concluded by our looking, if only briefly, at a mode of behaviour which is particularly relevant to habit-training. (See also pp. 119, 149, 176, 196, 261.)

Many of the teacher's instructions are complied with, not because they link up with the pupil's extracurricular activities, but because the teacher has given them. Complying with reasonable requests from the teacher can itself become a habit; and that habit can be exploited in the interests of others. I am not referring here to punishment or the threat of punishment, or to the promise of rewards. On occasion these may be means of obtaining obedience in the first place, but here I am referring to the obedience itself. I mean that the pupil has been so trained that normal requests from his teacher will be acted upon without fear or fuss, almost without the pupil's noticing that he is in fact complying. It is in accord with this mode of behaviour that intended prompts like 'Shut the door, Tom!' and 'Hold your pencil like this!' are likely to serve their purpose. Such a pattern of behaviour is, of course, open to abuse; but unless it is established the procedures of habit-training will become so complex as to be almost impossible. All I need add is that if the teacher is to exploit this mode of behaviour he must ensure that it is indeed established.

Summary

Since the aim of this chapter is to provide guidance to the teacher in habit-training, the summary is expressed as a set of instructions.

To train someone in a habit:

1. Specify (to yourself) as clearly as possible the form of response required. Phrases like 'being tidy' are much too vague. If you cannot state exactly what you wish the pupil to do, it is unlikely that you will be able to discover means of making him do it. 'To hang up his coat in the hall' or 'To put his books in the cupboard' are much more useful specifications.

2. Specify (to yourself) as clearly as possible the cue to which the specified response has to be made. Success is unlikely if one refers vaguely to 'things of this sort', or to 'that kind of thing'. *What* kind? The kind, the cue, must be stated clearly and unambiguously. Also, where there is a choice of cue (and usually there is if we look hard enough), select something known to be capable of getting a response of *some* sort, though preferably a response which is not incompatible with the form of response ultimately required. The clock's striking seven is preferable to the mere time, seven o'clock, and leaving the table is preferable to the mere event of finishing a meal.

3. Discover or invent a prompt for the required form of response. In many instances this will be a verbal instruction, or a model, or a combination of these. A verbal instruction which was not obeyed, or a model which was not imitated, would, of course, fail to serve as prompt. It might fail in so far as the learner was incapable of following it, or misunderstood it, or did not want to follow it. Accordingly, in framing an instruction or demonstration make sure that the pupil can in fact cope with it, try to eliminate ambiguity, and present it in a context which promises his cooperation. For many purposes the last of these demands will be met if you have trained your class to obey reasonable requests, but on occasion the request may have to be linked up with some other previously established mode of behaviour – doing things which increase his prestige, being one of a group, saving time, and the like.

4. Ensure that the place of training does not contain so many novelties that the pupil may be distracted from the relevant items, namely the cue and prompt. Do not clutter up the verbal

instruction or model with harangues, exaggerated gestures, patently unfulfillable threats or promises, or even explanations. There is a place for explanation, but its place is rarely in the middle of a habit-training session. Keep in mind that, even for the adult, understanding why something should be done is by no means the same as learning to do it.

5. Introduce cue and prompt very close together in time, preferably in that order. The instruction to rinse out the wash-basin, for example, would be given just as the child was in the act of finishing washing, and not five minutes sooner or later. A very frequent breach of the condition of Contiguity consists of the trainer's telling the learner, some time afterwards, what he ought to have done before – the assumption being, presumably, that he will remember what to do on the next occasion. But the validity of that assumption is highly suspect.

6. Repeat 5, trying to ensure that during training the cue is not allowed to appear without the prompt, for otherwise some 'wrong' prompt may intervene and lead to a 'wrong' instance of learning.

7. Try to ensure that the response, once it is made, results in a sense of satisfaction (for the learner, and not just for the teacher), and is in accord with his expectations. The latter condition can, of course, be met by the teacher's ensuring that the learner has the relevant expectations in the first place. Further, the response is likely to become habitual if, during training, it reduces an unwelcome state of tension or drive – for example, if it enables him to do something he has wanted to do but so far has been unable to accomplish, or if it enhances his status. Equally relevant is the avoidance of negative results, such as feelings of disappoint-ment, or increased anxiety, or dissatisfaction. Ideally it should be easier, less troublesome, for the learner to perform the required behaviour than not to perform it. This is most likely to be achieved if the new behaviour can be fitted smoothly into the context of his other actions.

D

6 · Teaching as Habit-breaking

Habit-breaking – A Special Case of Habit-training

If little Charles screams whenever his light is put out at bedtime, we could eliminate this bad habit by the simple expedient of leaving his light on. In general, we may stop a habit by not allowing its cue to occur. There are cases for which this would be a reasonable solution. If Pamela habitually complains of a headache whenever she is asked to recite a certain poem to visitors, it might be wise to drop the project altogether. But this kind of solution cannot be used in every case, and our first example could probably be considered a case in point. If the light is left on, Charles may not go to sleep for a very long time, or someone else may be inconvenienced, or something of the sort. Also, in many instances we may not be able to ensure that the cue never occurs; when a child leaves our immediate control, even temporarily, he may be confronted by the very cue we have been keeping from him. For many practical purposes the removal of the cue is not likely to be a very profitable approach.

If, however, the cue remains, it is almost certain to get a response of some kind. And since it is not to get the old, unwanted response, it must get a new one. Consequently to break an old habit is at once to promote an instance of learning. The new instance will not necessarily be a habit, but since it often will be I shall assume that it is. The main argument will not be affected.

Although habit-breaking is at the same time habit-training, it is nevertheless a special case, because the new response must not contain the old. In the Pavlov experiment it did not matter that

94

the salivary response was accompanied by the old response of ear-twitching; but now we are concerned with instances of learning *not* to do something – as if the dog were to learn *not* to twitch an ear at the sound of the buzzer. The new response must exclude the old.

For most educational purposes, indeed, we should be even more specific. Strictly, to learn not to scream when the light is put out means only that the child must make *any* other response to the same cue, but we should scarcely acknowledge success if he tore the sheets or banged on the wall instead. Commonsense indicates that we should specify not only the response to be eliminated, but also the new response that is to replace it. This does not raise difficulties different in kind from those considered in the last chapter; we have but to find a prompt for the response required, and follow the procedure appropriate to any instance of habit-training. The problem of habit-breaking lies in *finding* prompts, because in any instance of habit-breaking the prompt must have the effect of eliminating the old form of response as well as introducing a new one. One aspect of this problem is that the learner may not 'want' to give up the old habit, may lack 'motivation'; a piece of advice, which might otherwise serve as prompt for a new response, may not be taken. It is with difficulties of this kind that the following sections are concerned.

The Method of Small Doses

An illustration of this method is provided by the case of a child, Peter, about three years old, who had a fear of furry objects – rabbits, fur coat, fur rug, and so on. In this respect Peter was similar to Albert, in the well-known example reported by J. B. Watson, except that Albert had been trained to fear furry things, while Peter's fear-reaction to them had been acquired without help. (For a short account of both cases see Sandiford (42).) The method of habit-breaking illustrated by the case of Peter may be summarised as follows.

While Peter was seated comfortably, and eating his lunch, a

rabbit was introduced, but at a considerable distance and only for a very short time, so that the child's eating was not disturbed. Next day the rabbit was brought closer and closer until it seemed that Peter was about to cry. The spot was marked, and for several days the rabbit was brought no nearer. Finally it could be brought right up to him without recurrence of the fear-reaction.

It is plain that in this example use was made of 'small doses'. But doses of what? They were not, I need scarcely remark, doses of rabbit, for the whole rabbit was present on every occasion. As will be explained more fully in a moment, they were doses of nearness and time-duration of rabbit. But might not the trainer have used doses of something else, such as doses of size – beginning with a very tiny rabbit beside the child, and gradually introducing larger and larger rabbits? This is an important kind of question, because if we are to use this technique, and the doses must be doses of this rather than of that, we must know what they are to be doses of. What is the principle?

Consider first not the nature of the doses but the state of affairs from which the doses begin; in particular, the way in which it differs from the original fear-producing situation. In our example the doses begin with the rabbit's appearing for a very short time at a considerable distance. The difference between this state and the fear-producing situation is one of distance and duration of appearance. And the significance of that difference is that this new state of affairs does not get a fear-response. By removing the nearness and duration of the rabbit the trainer has at once removed the old response. If, on the other hand, he had removed, or reduced, the rabbit's size this effect would not have been achieved, because (it was known) Peter responded fearfully to even tiny pieces of fur. Nor would it have been effective to remove the 'alive' aspect of the situation, because (it was known) the child gave a fear-response not only to living furry things but also to fur rugs and fur coats. The purpose of the new state of affairs, apparently, is to get rid of the old response; and so it would be pointless to remove something which had nothing to do with the making of that response. Cutting down the rabbit's size, for example, would have been as futile as removing a picture from the wall, because the fear-response to the rabbit was made irrespective of its size. What has to be removed is something which *does* determine the form the old response takes.

Now in any established instance of learning (of which Peter's fear of the rabbit is an example) the determiner of the response's form is, of course, the cue. And in the present case the cue seems to have been furry-object-at-close-quarters-for-some-time. Whether the object was alive, or was a rabbit or a rug, or was large, was apparently irrelevant. *Any* nearby, persisting, furry object triggered off Peter's fear. Accordingly, the fear-response could have been eliminated by the removal of the cue; but in fact only a *part* of the cue was removed, probably because the less we remove the less we have to replace later. The result is nevertheless the same, for the *effective* cue is eliminated.[1]

Although the creating of the new state of affairs, the starting point for the small doses, entails our taking something out of the original situation, it involves also the addition of a new element: when the rabbit appeared, at a considerable distance, for a very short time, Peter was sitting eating – and presumably enjoying what he was doing. This latter device, apparently, serves as a prompt for a new response to the curtailed cue. When the rabbit makes its brief appearance, Peter is mildly interested, so let us call the new response 'mild interest'. To repeat: curtailing the cue removes the old response; the eating-situation provides a prompt for the new response.

The second step consists in reintroducing the aspect (of the cue) which has been removed. Clearly, this must be done, for otherwise the situation which is now receiving the new response (mild interest) will not be of the same kind as received the old response (fear). If the child is to learn not to be afraid of the rabbit, rugs, and so on, the cue must be restored. The 'dodge' of this particular technique is to reintroduce the previously removed aspect of the

---

[1] Although I have used only one example, the principle it illustrates is deducible from theory. If a cue consists of several features, removal of even one of these will be at once the elimination of the cue, and hence the elimination of the response to it.

cue in such a way that the *same* new form of response (mild interest) continues to be made. How it comes about that re-introduction in small doses can have the required effect may be explained as follows.

My hair grows every day, but it grows so little in one day that my reaction to it in the mirror on Tuesday is almost the same as it was on Monday – and so on, for many days. We may suppose, however, that if my hair were to grow as much overnight as it usually grows in a fortnight, my reaction next morning would be very different. Other examples could be one's reaction to balding, a child's reaction to his own increasing size or to the tightening of his shoes as his feet grow. The general principle here is that a change which would be noticeable if it took place in one large lump may not be noticeable if it occurs, over a longer period of time, in very small amounts. More precisely, the response made at the end of a series of very small changes (increases or decreases) is often the same as the response made at the beginning, even if the total change is quite large.[1]

To this interpretation there is an obvious objection. To revert to the analogy, why do I ever get my hair cut at all? The answer is, of course, that my decision to have my hair cut does not derive from a noticeable difference from the day before. It derives from extraneous circumstances such as the recollection of what my hair ought to look like, or a broad hint from my wife, or my catching sight of the sign, 'Hairdresser'. The moral for habit-*breaking* seems to be that such extraneous circumstances should not be allowed to interfere. For example, in the case of Peter, the trainer would *not* point out that the rabbit is now much closer than it was three days ago, because such a comment, though understandably expressive of the trainer's pride of

[1] This explanation differs from the traditional explanation in terms of 'stimulus-threshold'. My suggestion is, in effect, not that the rabbit (at a distance) ceases to get a response, but that by moving it to a distance we get a *different* response, and that by the device of small doses we contrive to maintain that different response even when the rabbit is brought near. The explanation offered here can be based on the accepted principles of conditioning, with the addition of the principle described in the above paragraph, a principle easy enough to validate. It would be more difficult to explain why an item which gets no response should, for that reason, eventually get a different response.

achievement, might well destroy the chain of not-noticeable differences.

The significant features of this method are summarised, below, in the form of a set of instructions.

Summary of the Small Doses Method

1. Examine the cue of the habit to be broken until it can be seen not as one single item but as a complex of features. In the example, three such parts of the cue were nearness, duration of appearance, and furriness. In many cases it may be difficult to discover just what features are indeed cue-features, and on occasion it may be necessary to try removing a succession of suspected items until the removal of one of them results in the cessation of the unwanted response.

2. Remove a part of the cue, preferably a part which can be conveniently reintroduced in small doses over a period of time. In the example, the feature of furriness might have been removed, but it would be impracticable (to say the least) to produce a series of rabbits differing by slight amounts of fur; the features of nearness and duration are more easily controlled.

3. Reintroduce the removed part in small doses. Some experimentation may be required before the optimum dose is discovered, but it is obviously better to make the doses smaller in size, and greater in number, than might seem necessary, than to make them larger and risk failure.

4. If, during the training, it seems that the child is likely to regress, stay at the same point for some time. Also, try to prevent the child's being able to make inappropriate comparisons. Don't remind him, for instance, that he used to cry when the rabbit was as near as it is now.

The application of this method to the case of our fictitious child Charles, who screamed when the light was put out, is left to the reader. I shall but suggest that the extinguishing of the light may not be the whole cue, and that an equally significant aspect could be the mother's leaving the bedroom. If so, it would be more convenient to use small doses of mother's absence than to play about with lamps of different wattage. The method implies, of course, that the mother should leave the room while the child is still awake, with the promise (which must be kept) that she will return (on the first occasion) in a minute. It would also help if the retraining were begun on an occasion when the child was very sleepy.

Should this method seem slow and troublesome, the answer is that in using any method the time and trouble it entails must be balanced against the time and trouble caused by the bad habit. There are, of course, habits for which this method is less suitable than are other methods, described in the following sections.

The Method of Fatiguing the Response

This second method consists in the trainer's tiring out the undesirable response, so that when the cue is presented, the occurrence of a different response will be facilitated.

This procedure is similar in some ways to a laboratory technique known as 'experimental extinction'; but since the two methods need not be the same, and because the laboratory technique is often cited in this connection, I shall now describe that technique very briefly.

Once more Pavlov provides a relevant example. After several twin-presentations of buzzer and food-powder, it will be recalled, the dog salivated before the food was given. At this stage, however, in a further experiment, Pavlov repeatedly sounded the buzzer at very short intervals, without presenting food. The salivary response gradually weakened (as measured by quantity and rate of flow of saliva) and eventually disappeared. Whether that response was fatigued in a physiological sense we need not discuss here. I shall use the phrase, 'fatiguing the response' to refer to *any* procedure in which a response is made to occur over and over again, at very short intervals, until it ceases to occur.

This kind of method is sometimes cited to justify the following sort of treatment. Charles is left to scream (at bedtime), on the ground that he will tire himself out and go to sleep. But this treatment of Charles is not in accord with the Pavlovian technique. Where are the short intervals? Charles is not put to bed over and over again, at intervals of a few seconds, and allowed to scream on every one of these occasions. (Whether this latter procedure would work is beside the point; there are better ways of dealing with this case. See the previous section.) A further objection is that this method would almost certainly defeat its own ends. The point of the fatiguing method, as noted at the beginning of this section, is to facilitate the making of some other response to the same kind of situation. But if Charles is allowed to scream for a long time, and does eventually fall asleep, the falling-asleep response is being made, not to the going-to-bed situation, but to the state terminating a long period of screaming. Nor does the story of experimental extinction end here. If, after the extinction-training, the dog is allowed a period in which the buzzer does not sound at all, the buzzer may eventually elicit the salivary response once more. And the apparent extinction may be undone by the introduction of a new stimulus. My purpose in quoting these additional details is to suggest that experimental extinction does not provide such a simple model as it is sometimes believed to do. It nevertheless suggests a way out of the difficulty.

If the unwanted response could be fatigued, not by frequent repetitions of the cue (or conditional stimulus), but by some other means, *before* the forceful cue was introduced, the difficulty illustrated by the case of little Charles need not arise. If he could grow tired of screaming *before* he was put to bed, it is likely that the going-to-bed situation, if it arose immediately afterwards, would get a response of some other form.[1] A particularly relevant illustration is reported by Guthrie (17).

Here again the undesirable behaviour is screaming. A little girl who screamed whenever a cat came near her was treated as follows. After rapport with the psychologist had been established (which meant, among other things, that she was now more likely

---

[1] More precisely, if the response is fatigued by repeated presentations of the cue itself at very short intervals, the cue may cease to get any response at all; it may lose its stimulus-function altogether, lose force. If so, it will not get any other response, and will fail to satisfy the very purpose of the method.

to comply with his requests and suggestions), she was asked to show him how she screamed when she saw a cat. The child obliged, and on request gave that demonstration frequently within a short time. When it seemed that she was tired of screaming she was taken to the door of a room in which the psychologist's experimental cats were kept in cages, and was invited to look at them from the doorway. She then accepted his invitation to accompany him into the room. After looking at the caged cats for some time she was invited to open the cages and let the cats out. Once more the girl did as she was asked. Eventually, when invited to lift one of the cats and take it to show to her mother, the child again complied and lifted the cat without a recurrence of the screaming. Guthrie's report suggests that the habit was now broken. One of the significant aspects of the method illustrated by this case, as I noted above, is that the unwanted response is fatigued, not by repeated presentations of the cue (cats) which is to get a new response, but by repeated presentations of something else (invitation to scream). The advantage seems to be that the cue is left capable of eliciting responses – though not, of course, the particular response which has just been fatigued. It is noteworthy also that the cue was presented immediately after the unwanted response had been fatigued – before it had time to recover. At the same time a prompt for the new response was presented – in this case the psychologist's invitations. It may be relevant to note also that, as this case illustrates, child-psychologists usually strive to establish a good personal relationship with the learner before therapy begins; and that such a relationship relates to motivation. If the child likes and trusts the therapist, the therapist's invitations or suggestions are more likely to be accepted; that is, to become prompts.

It appears, however, that Guthrie here made use not only of the method of fatiguing the response but also of the method of small doses. Strictly, the cue to screaming was not a cat; it was a nearby cat; and it is probably significant that the child was introduced to cats immediately after the fatiguing-session, not by having a cat suddenly thrust in her face, but by a series of approaches. The 'nearby' aspect was introduced in small doses – beginning at the door, followed by nearness while the cats were caged, and so on. It is reasonable to suppose that a procedure based on two methods may be better than a procedure based on only one.

Summary of the Fatiguing Method

1. Specify (to yourself) the particular response which has to be eliminated. We cannot hope to fatigue a response unless we know precisely what it is.

2. Discover, and specify (to yourself), as precisely as possible, the cue to that response. This is necessary because the cue has to be introduced immediately after the response has been fatigued; we cannot arrange to introduce the cue in this way if we do not know what it is.

3. By some means other than the cue itself cause the undesirable response to occur over and over again at short intervals until it ceases. The reason for not using the cue as a fatiguing agent is that the use of the cue for this purpose may deprive the cue of force, so that it gets no response at all – and will not be able to get any new response, which is the aim of the method.

4. Immediately afterwards, introduce the cue accompanied by a prompt for some desired replacement-response. Guthrie's view is that a once-only use of this method may be sufficient, but one might play safe here and introduce the prompt on a succession of occasions, as indicated in the last chapter. One would, of course, avoid frequent repetitions at short intervals, because this could have the effect of fatiguing the new response also. A further safe-guard may be used, namely the incorporation of the method of small doses.

As I noted earlier in this chapter, my use of the term 'fatigue' is not intended to imply that the response is fatigued in a physio-logical sense. So far as habit-breaking is concerned, it is sufficient that the learner becomes disinclined to make that response, sufficient that he grows 'tired *of* it'. The purpose of the fatiguing-procedure is simply to make the occurrence of the unwanted response highly unlikely. But of course, the same purpose could be achieved in other ways. Sometimes a show of disapproval is enough. And sometimes a child will give up an apparently intractable habit if his schoolmates make fun of it, or mimic him. (Punishment is discussed in a later section.) It is worth emphasising, I think, that since the efficacy of the fatiguing-method depends upon the introduction of the cue immediately after the old response has been fatigued, this method is unlikely to be applicable to habits in which the cue is unknown. Unless we know what makes a child suck his thumb at the time he does suck it, fatiguing the thumb-sucking behaviour by ordering him to perform it over and over again may be useless, unless, of course, the habit is so frequent that the cue is almost certain to turn up anyway. A further difficulty is that in fatiguing the specified, old, response, we may unwittingly fatigue more than we intend; we may fatigue also a set of other responses similar to it. Fatiguing the behaviour of screaming is unlikely to result in a fatiguing of the behaviour of picking up a cat; but it might result in unwillingness to sing – in so far as what was fatigued was the use of the voice. For this reason I should have grave doubts about the advisability of using this method in cases where the bad habit might be described in terms of poor discrimination. If the child does not appreciate the difference between the unwanted response and the response that is to replace it, the fatiguing of the one may well be at once the fatiguing of the other. Spelling, pronunciation, intonation, colour-differences, may be cases in point. The moral appears to be that the fatiguing-method should be restricted to those habits in which the old and the new responses are very different.

The Method of Replication

As far as I am aware, the method made explicit in this section does not already have a name, and so I have named it myself. By 'replication' I mean the making of a replica. It may be illustrated by an ingenious example reported by Guthrie (17).

A young lady with the regrettable habit of responding to the ringing alarm-clock by ignoring it, or even by reaching out half-asleep and turning it off, was advised as follows. Tonight, prepare for bed as usual, but just before you get into bed set the alarm to ring fifteen minutes after you get into bed. When it rings, get out of bed at once, switch it off, and reset it for the morning. Then get back to bed. She was asked also to report the result, and reported that next morning she found herself standing on the floor, without quite realising how she had got there.

The situation in the evening, when the alarm rang, was very similar to the situation next morning. In each case the girl is in bed; the alarm-clock is in its accustomed place and makes the same sort of sound; she is in the same sort of physical situation as she will be next morning; and so on. There are, of course, certain differences. For one thing, it *is* the evening, not the morning. Also, the girl is awake when the alarm rings at night, whereas in the morning she will be asleep. I mention these details because at first sight it might seem that the evening-situation is mere pretence, and if it seems so, it is difficult to see how the method could work. But whether or not we choose to call it a pretence, there is a psychological sense in which this kind of situation is just as good as, or even better than, the real situation. If the pretence-situation *functions* in exactly the same way as the real situation, that is, has the same effect on the subject's behaviour, the judgment that it is only a pretence is beside the point. For this reason I have used the term 'replica' rather than 'pretence'. The training-situation (in the evening, in our example) may be 'only' a pretence, but so far as the subject's behaviour is concerned it is indeed a replica of the real situation.

The less pretence there is in the situation, of course, the more likely it is that it will work. In our example the girl was not asked to pretend that she had undressed for bed, or to pretend that she was in bed, or to pretend that the alarm had rung, or to pretend to get up. All these things really happened. Most significantly, in the replica-situation her getting up was made dependent, not upon her own decision or whim, but upon the ringing of the alarm itself. (See also fn. 1 to p. 41.) The crucial difference between the two situations is that it is easier to find a prompt for rising in the evening-situation. Indeed, the replica-situation should be designed with this point as criterion: the replica-situation should be as similar as possible to the real situation, the cue being contained by both, the basic difference relating to ease of introduction of a prompt for the behaviour required.

In our example that demand was met as follows. The two situations were very similar: each contained the ringing alarm, and so on. The prompt was an instruction, given by the psychologist and accepted by the girl herself. That instruction (to get up when the alarm rings) could scarcely be implemented in the real, morning, situation, because at that time the girl is asleep and unlikely to be thinking about it; but in the evening she is awake, and so the instruction can be effective. That the girl did indeed act on it may be interpreted in terms of her 'motivation'. That she 'wanted' to break her bad habit may be inferred from her taking the trouble to consult a psychologist in the first place. (In contrast, one of my students, hearing of this method in a lecture but being sceptical about its effectiveness in her case, tried it out and reported with some surprise that it worked. She found, however, that the replica-situation had to be created each evening. The difference may be one of motivation. I suspect that she used the method, not primarily to break the habit but to see if it worked; though why there should be this particular difference in result is too complex a question to be discussed here in detail. But see also p. 123.)

As I have just noted, motivation is of considerable importance, but another point also deserves mention. The girl (in Guthrie's account) was motivated to break the habit *before* she was given the advice, but without the technique this was ineffective. Motivation, though necessary, may be insufficient. The man who lies in bed, giving himself reason after reason for getting up at once, may be thoroughly sincere – but he is still in bed. As the example illustrates, good intentions may be needed, but they may not serve as substitutes for techniques based upon the relevant knowledge.

Since the method of replication seems to be particularly relevant to the breaking of human habits, here is another example. My car has an electric heater built into the water system, and connected to a plug in the dashboard, so that by connecting that plug to a socket in the garage I can keep the engine warm on frosty nights. But, of course, I have to remember to plug it in in the evening before I leave the garage – and this I frequently forgot to do. What I had to do was to break myself of the habit of walking straight out of the garage after leaving the car – or, which comes to the same thing, train myself in the habit of plugging in as soon as I got out of the car. The procedure adopted made use of the *morning*-situation as a replica of the evening-situation. In the morning, in the garage, I am seated in my car in exactly the same way as I am when I return in the evening; the view (of the work-bench, the garage wall, and so forth) is exactly the same on the two occasions. The crucial difference is that, because the car is noticeably cold in the morning, I am reminded of the heater and so can introduce a prompt in the form of a verbal instruction to myself. But I do not merely blame myself for my forgetfulness the previous evening, nor do I decide that I must remember when I get home tonight. I have to *train* myself, put myself in the role of learner, and apply to myself the technique I would apply to learners generally. I therefore made a movement as if I were going to get out of the car, muttering to myself, 'Heater plug!' (To ensure that the replica-situation would contain the cue, namely the movement of getting out of the car, I had to watch myself getting out of the car and then copy what I usually did.) The performance was repeated three or four times – all within a few seconds. The method worked. When I returned in the evening I was surprised to hear my own voice (in my imagination) tell me to plug in the heater.

Summary of the Replication Method

1. Make explicit the cue of the instance (*e.g.* ringing alarm-clock, or action of getting out of car.)

2. Make explicit the particular response required (*e.g.* rising from bed, or plugging in heater).

3. Devise a situation which is a replica of the real situation – that is, devise a situation which contains the cue (which may be very complex), but which nevertheless allows of the introduction of a prompt for the response required. (In the first example the prompt was the psychologist's instruction, as the girl remembered it; in the second the prompt was my own instruction to myself.)

4. Introduce the prompt-feature into the replica-situation, so as to get the required response to the cue. That it would be the response to the *cue* which was given the requisite form was ensured in the first example by making the rising dependent upon the ringing, even in the replica-situation; in the second by my saying 'Heater!' when beginning to leave the car.

5. In Guthrie's example the replica-situation occurred only once. In my own example I went through the motions several times. Where the case allows of repetition it probably provides an extra safeguard.

The Method of the Incompatible Response

A small boy, who had been showing a tendency to use his left hand to hold his spoon, but was otherwise almost ambidextrous, was trained as follows. Just before he was given his plate of food, and spoon, he was offered a small toy. The preferred left hand reached out and took it. Immediately afterwards food and spoon were given. Apparently because he had no wish to give up the toy, the right hand reached out for the spoon. After a few repetitions, over several meals, the spoon was taken in the right hand if offered to it, and not switched to the left hand as formerly.

The principle here is that the cue is presented, or allowed to occur, at a time when the learner's behaviour is incompatible with the unwanted response and is likely to continue. In a sense, we make the learner himself prevent himself making the response that is to be eliminated. In using this method it is, of course, necessary to ensure that the cue will remain forceful (*e.g.* that the child will pay attention to the spoon, notice it when it is offered); and that there is a prompt for the response we want (*e.g.* that the child is ready to eat and the spoon is offered to the disengaged hand).

It is doubtful if a dodge like this would work with older children or adults; they would almost certainly see through it. They would discriminate between the simple offered-a-spoon situation and the contrived offered-a-spoon-when-this-hand-is-busy situation. Simple conditioning usually works best when the subject does not think about what is going on. It seems likely, then, that this method will be most successful either with reflex actions of which the subject is not aware or with young children who do not notice the contrivance the method entails. On the other hand, I believe (and know from first-hand experience) that the method *can* work when the subject is prepared to cooperate. As the illustration of the car-heater exemplifies (p. 107), one's 'seeing through' a contrivance does not necessarily invalidate it.

Since this method is simple I need not provide a summary.

The Method of Feed-back

All the methods suggested so far have entailed the trainer's having knowledge and control of the cue. But sometimes it is very difficult, in practice, to gain control over the cue of a habit. We may not know it has occurred until the bad behaviour itself occurs – and very often such knowledge comes too late to be useful. In such cases it is sometimes possible to make the bad response itself provide the means of its own elimination. Because of the obvious analogy with self-governing machines, the term 'feed-back' seems to be an appropriate name. (For example, as steam-pressure increases, that very increase operates a valve which reduces the pressure. A thermostat illustrates the same principle.) Here is a well-known example.

In the condition known as 'enuresis' (incontinence of urine, during sleep, far beyond the age at which continence is usually achieved), the unwanted response is bed-wetting. Strictly, of course, the response is simply urinating, because the bed's being at the receiving end of a behaviour is not itself part of the behaviour.

At any rate, what is usually required is that the child should not urinate in bed, but should instead wake up and visit the water-closet. But when? In response to what cue? If we do not know what 'makes' him urinate when he is asleep, how can we arrange to get a new response to it? (Perhaps I should remark that cutting down the child's intake of fluid before bedtime often makes little or no difference.) A practical and ingenious solution is offered by the use of a specially prepared mat, placed below the child in bed, which operates an electric bell as soon as it is wet. The child sleeps on the mat, and as soon as he urinates the bell rings, and the child wakens. He is also trained to go to the water-closet on wakening, even if at this stage his journey seems scarcely necessary.

The principle behind this procedure is the principle of conditioning. The old response is urinating; the required new response is waking. The prompt is the bell, which gets the required form of behaviour in the first place. Precisely what the cue is does not matter, because (we may assume) whatever it is, it will occur just before the child urinates; and the sequence of events is in accord with the conditioning technique. One possible cause of mis-understanding of this example is that the child must wet the bed before he is wakened – so that it might seem that the wakening will be too late. But it is characteristic of conditioning that the new response gradually moves nearer in time to the conditional stimulus, until it is made before the unconditional stimulus is presented. (In the Pavlov experiment cited earlier, the dog eventually salivated before the food-powder was presented. In this same connection it should be noted that in the Pavlov experiment the bell was the *conditional* stimulus to the required response, whereas in the present case the bell is the *unconditional* stimulus.) The result of the conditioning procedure is that the response to the unknown cue becomes waking instead of, as before, urinating. (Should the reader wish to work out the details of the technique in this case, with a named cue, he might assume that the cue is bladder-tension.)

The immediately relevant point, however, is that the unwanted response is used to eliminate itself. It is by urinating in his sleep (and setting off a bell) that the child is trained to waken in response to the cue which previously got the response of urinating.

Another example is provided by the case of a little girl who talked, then shouted, in her sleep, and then rose from bed and walked about the house without waking. In this case the child was trained to waken in response to her own shouting. Since the shouting wakened her parents, they could then waken the child. In this case the feed-back mechanism included the parents rather than a piece of apparatus, but the principle is exactly the same.[1]

Summary of the Feed-back Method

1. Specify the response required (*e.g.* waking and going to the water-closet).

2. Discover or invent a prompt for (the required response) which can be triggered off by the old response itself. Or if that is not possible, at least discover or invent a prompt for *any* behaviour which is incompatible with the old behaviour, and which can be triggered off by that old behaviour. If the new behaviour is not incompatible with the required response also, a further pilot-cue can be introduced.

It will be apparent that this method calls for considerable ingenuity on the part of the trainer – as well as for considerable knowledge of training generally. It is nevertheless worth mentioning, partly because of its intrinsic interest, and partly because these few examples may induce the reader to devise similar procedures for himself.

The Method of Punishment

It is widely believed that bad habits can be broken by the use of punishment, but before we examine this belief we must first ask what punishment itself is. Part of the difficulty is that what serves as punishment for one person may not be a punishment

---

[1] A suggested improvement on this procedure was that a microphone and amplifier might be fitted at the child's bedside; but while this would have benefited the parents, it was scrapped on the ground that the cue to waking, namely the child's *own*, unamplified, voice, would not have been present at all.

for another. For the child who prefers to be alone, removal from the group could scarcely be called a punishment; some children do not like to be singled out for praise; and there are even perverse characters who take a delight in being beaten. This seems to imply that a punishment, for any one person, is something he dislikes. Yet even if we accept this not uncommon view, how are we to be sure that the thing in question is disliked? What is the criterion?

One answer, suggested by Thorndike, and made the basis of much of his theorising (50), is that dislike (or dissatisfaction, as he called it) may be defined in terms of avoidance. A dissatisfying state of affairs is one which the organism avoids or strives to avoid. This is very much in accord with the way in which the word 'punishment' is used in everyday speech. If a pupil did nothing to avoid corporal punishment, it would be scarcely regarded as a punishment for him. Of course, many things that are avoided are painful or at least unpleasant, but on Thorndike's thesis they would be called punishments, not because of their painfulness or unpleasantness, but because they were in fact avoided. That view has the merit of dealing with something that can be observed, namely the subject's behaviour, and since it seems to be in accord with popular usage I shall adopt it here.

This definition of punishment (as anything which the subject avoids) is nevertheless wider than popular speech sometimes implies. If a child puts his hand in the fire, and is burned, he will there and then avoid the flames; but we should not usually refer in this case to 'punishment', because that term implies usually a dissatisfying state of affairs deliberately engineered by someone else (or 'fate') with a retributive intention. The *effect* may nevertheless be exactly the same, and I shall use the term 'punishment' to refer to anything the learner avoids, whether or not it has been deliberately introduced, and irrespective of whether it could be said to have 'served him right'.

I can now ask, with less likelihood of ambiguity, why punishments should be effective in breaking habits.

A child touches an electric socket and receives a slight shock.

His hand is withdrawn at once. The shock at the socket is therefore a punishment. It will also be an effective punishment for
learning if, when subsequently the socket appears nearby, the
child avoids it. Here is an instance of learning. The cue is the sight
of the nearby socket. It previously evoked a touching-response.
Now it evokes an avoidance-response. And the punishment
(shock in this instance) has plainly filled the roll of prompt: it
was instrumental in getting an avoidance-response to the socket
in the first place.

As the example illustrates, we do not need a special theory of
how a punishment may serve to break a habit. Punishments are
simply prompts, just as verbal instructions, models, and food-
powder are. The only thing peculiar to the prompt of punishment is its restriction to the determining of avoidance-responses.
Habit-breaking by means of punishment is a case of habit-
training, of conditioning. Compared with the view that punishment 'stamps out' the bad response, the view of punishment as
a special case of conditioning is more explicit. The old response
ceases to appear in so far as the cue acquires the capacity to evoke
an avoidance-response instead. (An avoidance-response can of
course be complex—such as attending a meeting on the evening
when boring friends are expected at home.)

Once habit-breaking by punishment is envisaged as a special
case of conditioning, we can make use of the conditions already
known to apply to habit-training generally. In particular, the
prompting object – punishment in this case – must be introduced
very close in time to, and preferably immediately after, the cue to
the reprehensible behaviour; and it will sometimes have to be so
introduced on a succession of occasions. Since the fulfilment of
these conditions has already been illustrated, we may now
consider briefly what may happen when they are not fulfilled.
Here are two illustrations.

A little girl is punished for using an unladylike word, but later
in the evening she overhears the incident being related to visitors
– with obvious amusement on her parents' part. Next day the
little girl uses the word again.

The incident, as overheard in the relating, is in effect a 'replica' of the actual incident. In listening to the tale, the child is 'going through it all again' – but in this case there is laughter instead of punishment, so that in effect she is being rewarded for the very action which was previously punished. The punishment is being undone. This example illustrates, by omission, the condition that the inculcation of a habit may require a *succession* of occasions on which there is a prompt for avoidance. (See p. 113). A popular explanation would be 'lack of consistency', but what I have just said seems to put the point more precisely.

The second example: a little boy who has helped himself to a sweet from the toffee-tin on the sideboard is not observed doing so; but when he goes into the kitchen his mother smells the toffee he is eating and punishes him there and then. What the boy learns, however, is not what was intended. What he learns is to avoid his mother after he has helped himself to a forbidden sweet.

For the moment let us suppose that he is not very bright, being incapable of 'thinking out' the possible results of his actions. Then the explanation of the failure of the punishment is straightforward. He failed to avoid the toffee-tin (which was the intention) simply because the punishment was not awarded at the right time, namely when the tin was getting the response of taking a sweet. The condition of Contiguity (of cue and prompt) was not fulfilled. But by reference to this same condition we can explain something else, namely why he learned what he did learn – to avoid his mother when he was eating a stolen sweet. The punishment acts as prompt in respect of whatever feature of the punishment-situation *was* its forceful feature. The child learns to avoid the forceful feature in contiguity with which the punishment was in fact awarded, namely the feature of the mother-seeing-me-eat-a-stolen-sweet. The laws of conditioning will work, so to speak, irrespective of the trainer's intentions.

It could be and sometimes is objected, however, that this sort of argument treats the learner as if he were an unthinking animal. Surely a great many children would 'see through' this sort of procedure. If the child had any sense, he would keep away from his mother until he had finished eating, and thereby avoid punishment. This seems to be a perfectly fair comment – but it is not an objection to the principle at issue. True, the brighter child knows, without having to be punished; and he contrives to avoid the punishment and yet get the sweet. For him, the 'thought'of what is likely to happen is sufficient. But this 'thought' leads to exactly the same form of avoidance-behaviour as would actual punishment in the same situation. The foreseeing child imagines the situation in which he will be punished – and avoids that situation in fact, just as does the duller child who really is punished in it. In each case the child avoids the situation in which the punishment is (or would be) given. The basic principle is the same in the two cases. For the intelligently imaginative child the 'thought' of the punishment fulfils the same prompt-function in the 'replica' (imagined) situation as does the actual punishment for the other child in the actual situation. The concepts (thoughts) of the foreseeing child fit into the same conditioning-pattern as do the percepts (actual experience) of the duller child.[1]

Examples like these are only too familiar, and it is common knowledge that the punishment should follow swiftly upon the crime. What the principles of conditioning imply, however, is not quite the same: the punishment should be given in the presence of the *cue* to the reprehensible behaviour, so that it will be to the cue, the occasioner of that behaviour, that the avoidance-response will be made. Also, the cue should be not only present but also the *forceful* feature of the punishment-situation. This raises a difficulty, because punishments usually take over that function, and the subject may not learn a new response to the *cue*. These points have already been illustrated by our two

---

[1] This example raises the important question of differences between one child and another. The mere 'thought' of punishment, for some children, is as effective as is actual punishment for other children. As hinted in the Preface, however, the discussion of Individual Differences is not part of the function of this book. The reader who wishes a short, succinct, readable account of differences in 'conditionability' is referred to Eysenck (14). The last sentence of the text, above, indicates that while this book adheres, in many ways, to the principles of conditioning, it departs from a purely behaviouristic standpoint in assuming that 'thoughts' fit into the conditioning pattern.

examples, but they may be illustrated further by our noting their implications for improvement.

Punishments which are intrinsic to the approach to the cue (or seem to the learner to be so) are usually much more effective than punishments awarded by external agencies like parents and teachers. Even a relatively mild shock from an electric socket may be much more effective, for subsequent avoidance, than a severe thrashing from a parent. One reason is that such 'built-in' punishments will be thoroughly consistent. (Cf. the example of the little girl whose parents related her unladylike behaviour with amusement.) Another reason is that punishment by human agencies usually entails the presence of the punisher, or will arise only when the delinquent is caught. And if the forceful feature of the situation is the being caught (rather than the cue to the misdemeanour), or is the punisher himself, the delinquent may learn to avoid only being caught, or the punisher, but not the cue to the reprehensible behaviour. The punishment will act as a prompt, but for the wrong thing. The delinquent may seem to have abandoned his old ways – until the punisher departs. The moral seems to be that the trainer should do his utmost to ensure that it is approach to the cue which is consistently punished, and that he himself should try to keep in the background when the punishment is awarded. Ideally, it should seem to the learner that the punishment stems directly from his reprehensible approach to the cue.

Here again it could be argued that the brighter learner will 'see through' what is no more than a dodge. This may be so, but if the intended punishment is indeed a punishment (an avoidance-determiner), it does not matter that the learner realises that the punishment is being contrived by someone – so long as he fails to discover how to get round the contrivance. It does not matter in so far as the only way of avoiding the punishment is to avoid the cue which always accompanies it. The intention may be reinforced if the trainer acts as punisher *only* when the cue is approached, and at no other times.

A particular example of this principle, especially in connection with younger children, is provided by the teacher who uses punishment to 'get his own back'. Such a teacher is likely to wax indignant, be aggressive, perhaps exult in triumph, and have the effect of stealing the scene from the cue itself. Whether such behaviour is morally justified, or appropriate to a mature adult, is beside the present point. All I wish to suggest is that punishment is more likely to be effective if it seems, to the learner, to stem from the cue itself.

In the examples used so far, the subject learned less than was intended, but in some instances he learns too much. The child who is shocked when he pokes a finger into the electric socket may learn, not just to avoid the socket, but also to avoid electric fittings generally, so that he cannot be persuaded to switch on a light or plug in a radio. (Examples of this from adult behaviour are too common to need illustration.)

This kind of case is often described in terms of Discrimination. The learner fails to see the difference between the intended cue and some similar item. Patently, if there is no objection to this spread of avoidance, punishment will do no harm.

But if it is desired that he should make a different response (not avoidance) to these similar items it would be foolish to punish him if it is known that he is unlikely to discriminate between them. (A system of carefully planned rewards and punishments can nevertheless be used to increase discrimination; but it has to be so carefully planned that I should have doubts about recommending the method for general use.[1]) If a pupil cannot distinguish two colours, or hear the difference between two vowel sounds (perhaps in a foreign language), or between two slightly different musical tones, punishment for the wrong response is likely to lead, not to increased discrimination, but to avoidance of the whole topic.

Summary of the Punishment Method

1. Discover, as accurately as possible, the cue to the unwanted response.

[1] See, for example, Miller and Dollard (33).

2. Discover something which is in fact a punishment for the offender – that is, something he almost always avoids. It might be physical punishment, a reprimand, teasing, isolation, being deprived of something he likes, and so forth.

3. Apply the chosen punishment in the presence of the cue, ensuring that it is the cue which is the forceful feature of the situation. To effect this, one may have to keep oneself in the background, but at the same time make sure that the punishment is in fact given. On occasion the cue-as-remembered (telling the pupil why he is being punished) may be just as effective as the cue itself.

4. The punishment may have to be repeated, the number of awards probably varying with the severity of the punishment, but it is worth noting that it need be no more severe than is required to result in an avoidance-response to the cue.

5. If the new response to the cue has to be something more complex than mere avoidance, it must, of course, be not incompatible with avoidance. A further prompt (in addition to the punishment) may nevertheless be necessary. Punishment of itself results only in avoidance of the cue; it does not itself ensure any specified response to anything else. Moreover, if the punishment is effective, it will result in an avoidance-response not only to the cue but also to other items which the learner cannot distinguish from it.

6. Punishment is most likely to meet one's requirements when the new response has to be a straightforward avoidance-response, and when the learner is not called upon to make fine distinctions between the to-be-avoided cue and other things similar to it. Otherwise he may learn to avoid much more than was intended, even to the extent of steering clear of a whole topic, or subject, or school-work generally. Even when the required response is not a straightforward avoidance-response punishment may, of course, be effective in so far as the performing of the required response is the only way in which the learner can escape the punishment; but it is rarely possible to contrive the circumstances so that this demand can be met.

Motivation in Habit-breaking

So far in this chapter I have made only a few comments about the learner's motivation. It is generally agreed, however, that the breaking of a habit depends to a large extent on the subject's wish to be rid of it. For the subject who wishes to be rid of his stammer or lisp or facial tic the prognosis is usually more optimistic than it is for the smoker or drunkard who clings to his habit and refuses offers of help. This matter will now be examined.

In our previous discussion of motivation (p. 88) I suggested that motivational issues might be approached more profitably by our concentrating on the subject's actual behaviour than by our postulating wants or motives hidden within his mind. In particular, I suggested that wants always have to be inferred from observed behaviour, and that the types of behaviour from which wants are customarily inferred are the very types of behaviour known to correlate with successful ultimate performance. One such behaviour is seeking help and complying with the advice given; such behaviour permits of the introduction of a prompt. Another behaviour is showing satisfaction at even small successes, which permits of the fulfilment of the Requirement of Reinforcement. In general, the behaviours from which the relevant want is customarily inferred are the very behaviours which facilitate the fulfilment of the basic requirements of learning and therefore permit of effective treatment.[1]

Exactly the same principle applies to habit-breaking. We should be confident that the subject 'wanted' to be rid of his habit only in so far as he behaved in certain ways – like seeking help, acting on the advice given, showing pleasure at even small improvements and dissatisfaction when he fell back into the old ways, yet persisting with his treatment in spite of set-backs, and so forth. Conversely, if behaviours like these never appeared we should usually say he had no wish to be cured.

---

[1] From what has just been said it will be apparent that motivation is not something additional to the four requirements (Cue, Force, Prompt, and Reinforcement) but is embraced by them.

When the matter is expressed in this way it becomes obvious why the prognosis is more optimistic when the subject 'wants' to be cured. As noted a moment ago, to 'want' to be cured is in effect to manifest behaviours which permit of effective treatment, whereas to lack such a want is to fail to behave in these ways. Indeed, on occasion we may have to cope not merely with the absence of the relevant want but with the presence of a contradictory want. The subject may 'cling' to his habit – which would mean, in behavioural terms, that he would listen not to those intent on reforming him but to those who encouraged him in his old ways; take delight in behaving in these ways; and so on. By behaving in such ways he permits of the introduction of 'wrong' prompts, gives himself more practice in the wrong thing, fulfils the Requirement of Reinforcement in respect of the wrong response, and so forth.

Irrespective of the category to which the subject belongs, however, the general form of treatment remains the same. As was noted earlier, we must discover in his repertoire some established mode of behaviour which can be exploited in the interest of training. In dealing with the illiterate soldier I was able to discover and exploit his behaviour of doing things to please his mother; and in teaching fractions I was able to make use of the established activity of betting. As the second of these examples illustrates, the mode of behaviour brought into service need not be eminently virtuous. Had my illiterate student not exhibited the socially approved behaviour of pleasing his mother, it might have been possible to induce him to write scurrilous letters to some of the many people against whom he bore grudges. Where we are concerned with the subject's total education and not merely with technical proficiency it may nevertheless be difficult to discover a mode of behaviour which is at once susceptible of exploitation and in accord with our educational philosophy. Difficult or not, however, the discovery and exploitation of just such a behaviour seem to be a prerequisite of training. In motivation terms, we must find one want which can be played off against another, and arrange a match.

That thesis, in principle at least, is widely accepted. The teacher, when he aims to eliminate some undesirable behaviour, often appeals to some other behaviour which runs counter to it. 'A boy like you, who can put such good material into essays, should take more trouble with handwriting!' 'A prefect should show an example to the younger pupils!' 'If you really do want to be a doctor you will have to work harder at science!' Although admonishments of this sort sometimes work, very often they do not. The pupil may accept the logic of the argument but his behaviour is unaffected: the exhortation does not result in action. A reason for the failure is not difficult to find. The match between the opposing wants must actually be played, and not merely referred to as a possibility. Mere mention of an exploitable mode of behaviour is not necessarily the exploiting of it. Our discovery of a dark horse in the pupil's stable is only part of the solution; the animal must be harnessed and put to work.

It is in this latter connection that the sample of methods described earlier in this chapter can provide guidance to the teacher, for they exemplify a variety of ways in which opposing wants can be put on the field and played off one against the other. In particular, in all the different methods an established mode of behaviour is actually used; it is made to occur, and not merely talked about. Not only this; it is made to occur at the very time when the undesirable behaviour is about to occur. The one mode of behaviour is in fact put into opposition to the other. This is achieved by the trainer's contriving to have the *cue* to the old behaviour present at, or very near, the time when the to-be-exploited behaviour is occurring. Since these methods have already been described in some detail, all we need do now is note how they cover the main points we have been discussing in this section.

Probably the exploiting of an existing want is illustrated most clearly by the method of the Incompatible Response (p. 108). The child's 'want' to keep the toy is played off against his 'want' to hold the spoon. As for knowing which 'want' will be the stronger, only an empirical test will decide; but from our knowledge of the child we can usually select some object which he will want (continue) to hold. The method illustrates very clearly the point that the to-be-exploited mode of behaviour (holding a toy in the preferred hand) has to occur at a time when the old behaviour is about to begin. The *cue* to the old behaviour (the cue here being our offering the child the spoon) is introduced when the other mode of behaviour is in operation. The trainer has to strike, as it were, when *both* irons are hot; and he contrives to do this by going out of his way to heat them at the same time.

In the two illustrations of the method of Replication (p. 104) the behaviours of the subjects (the young lady with the alarm-clock, and myself with my car-heater) indicated that they 'wanted' to behave in a certain way (to rise when the alarm rang, and to plug in the heater in the evening). In the former case the subject was told what to do in the evening – a time at which the 'want' to rise with the alarm was likely to be manifested; and since the two situations shared the same cue, the new mode of behaviour was made to occur in contiguity with the cue to the old behaviour. In my own case too the situations shared the same cue, though in the morning-situation the want to have the heater working was present, and so could be utilised for training. The similarity of the two situations (their sharing the cue) allowed me to strike while the want was hot and also while the cue was present.

The other methods, I think, need not be examined again. Each is, in effect, a means of getting the to-be-exploited behaviour to occur at the time when the old behaviour would otherwise occur, so that the one can be played off against the other. Since the old behaviour would begin when its cue appears, the problem these methods attempt to solve is the problem of getting the to-be-exploited behaviour to occur at about the same time as the cue. The method of Small Doses (p. 95) does this by rebuilding the cue while the new behaviour is occurring; the method of Fatiguing the Response (p. 100) does it by making the learner 'not want' to perform in the old way when the cue is present and so makes him more receptive to suggestions made at that time; the method of Punishment (p. 111) does it by ensuring the occurrence of an avoidance-response when the cue is present; and the method of Feed-back (p. 109) does it by making the old response (itself made when the cue appears) induce the new behaviour very close in time to the cue.

There is nevertheless one respect in which some of these methods may prove ineffective. It was noted that the behaviours from which wants are customarily inferred relate to the four basic requirements of learning. The learner's persistence, for example, relates to the Requirements of Cue and Force; and his seeking help and acting on advice relate to the Requirement of Prompt. But while the continued presence of the trainer may serve to fulfil these requirements, it may not fulfil the Requirement of Reinforcement. It is one thing to induce, persuade, or otherwise cause the learner to go through the necessary motions, but it is another thing to ensure that he derives satisfaction from their consequences. (One of the behaviours usually taken as evidence of a 'want', it will be recalled, is the learner's showing satisfaction with his accomplishment.) I was pleased to find that I remembered to plug in my car heater: it was my car, and I had to start it in the morning. Whether the method would have worked with someone else, who was not particularly interested in the car's readiness in the morning, is at least doubtful. The student who tried out the method of training oneself to rise in the morning (p. 106) but found it only partly successful, may have been in that category. Indeed, a critic who used the method in order to show that it would *not* work, even once, and found that it did, might well have feelings of *dis*-satisfaction.

The practical implication is, apparently, that the new behaviour should be made a part of some established activity which does bring satisfaction or at least is carried along by its own inertia. In some cases that established behaviour may also be the behaviour exploited in the actual training, as in the cases of the illiterate soldier and the backward arithmeticians. In the former case it was my offer to help him learn to write letters to his mother which served as prompt; but had he not derived satisfaction from what he accomplished it is unlikely that the writing would have continued without external prompting – or even with it. In the other case the men's own actions demonstrated that calculating the odds could be done more efficiently by means of fractions, and so their actions were satisfying. Generally, the new response, once it is induced, ought to be 'better', in some way, than was the old response – better, that is, within the learner's own experience, and not merely 'better for him' in the teacher's opinion. And this may be achieved by fitting it into the context of behaviours in which he already engages. In everyday language, it should fulfil some need, or aid his purposes, or raise his status, or increase his self-respect, or go some way to satisfy an ambition. I do not suggest that this demand is easily met. Often it is very difficult to find, within the learner's repertoire, an appropriate pattern of behaviour into which the new habit can be fitted. What I do suggest is that the search has to be made.[1]

Summary

On examination, habit-breaking appears as a case of habit-training – but as a special case in so far as the new response must not contain the old. Habit-breaking must therefore follow the general principles applicable to habit-training, but in the majority of instances special attention has to be given to the problem of ensuring that the old form of response is eliminated. Several procedures were described: *The Method of Small Doses*, in which the old response is eliminated by the removal of some aspect of the cue, so that what remains of the cue gets a different response. The cue is then restored to its original state, albeit in such small doses that the new response remains. *The Method of Fatiguing the Response*, in which the trainer causes the learner to make the unwanted response over and over again at short intervals,

---

[1] In this chapter I have made no reference to the view that in treating the behaviour we may be ignoring its underlying cause and so leaving the way open for some other undesirable effect of it. To attempt even to summarise that view, and the answers to it, would be beyond the scope of this book. All I shall say is that even if that view, on occasion, is empirically justified (and often it is not), few of the habits likely to be treated by the teacher in school are likely to come within its scope.

until he is so tired of making it that a prompt for some new response can be designed. *The Method of Replication*, in which the trainer creates a replica of the actual situation evocative of the unwanted response, but which differs from the latter situation in allowing the introduction of a prompt for some new response. *The Method of the Incompatible Response*, in which the cue is presented or allowed to occur at a time when the learner's own behaviour is incompatible with the unwanted response and will continue despite the introduction of the cue, thus allowing a new response to the forcetul cue. *The Method of Feed-back*, in which the old response is itself made to serve as a means of introducing a prompt for some different response. *The Method of Punishment*, in which a punishment is awarded in contiguity with the cue so that an avoidance-response is subsequently made to the cue itself.

Not all attempts to use these methods are successful; but it is of interest to note that as they have been described in this summary they are indeed logically sufficient for learning. Two examples, the first and the last method, will suffice in illustration. *If* what is removed is part of the cue, and *if* what remains is still forceful and does get a new response, and *if* the cue is restored in such small doses that that new response does not alter its form, the cue will get a new response. Likewise, *if* what purports to be punishment does effect an avoidance-response, and *if* that punishment serves as prompt in that an avoidance-response is made to the cue itself, and *if* that response continues, the method has worked. True, there are a great many 'ifs', so many that my reference to the sufficiency of these methods may seem unrealistic. And yet, as I have argued before, it is better because more realistic to try to fulfil specific requirements which, though difficult, are necessary and sufficient, than not to know what the requirements are. My intention in this chapter was not to suggest that habit-breaking is easy. On the contrary, the application of methods like those described and the fulfilling of the motivational requirements discussed in the last section call for considerable ingenuity and patience. My intention was, rather, to indicate ways in which the teacher might profitably attempt to meet these difficulties.

E

7 · Teaching as Explaining

Explaining – The Promoting of Understanding

The last two chapters were concerned with training in relatively simple instances of learning, with automatic responses to simple cues. This chapter examines a form of teaching regarded often as standing at the other extreme, namely Explaining.

What is Explaining? Like 'What is learning?', this question poses a verbal problem; and although popular usage of the term does not put the issue quite so bluntly, it implies that to explain is to do something which results in understanding. If the teacher really has explained something to his class, they will understand it; and if they do not understand it, despite his efforts what purported to be an explanation was not an explanation after all. I shall use the term in that way: explaining is any procedure which results in understanding.

It follows that explaining need not take the form of talking. If understanding is effected by the teacher's showing the pupil a diagram, or making manual gestures, for instance, these actions constitute explanations. If we wonder why someone is not acceding to a request, and a friend points to his own ears, the problem is resolved; we now realise that the person in question is deaf. The gesture was an explanation.

Equally important, it follows that not all talking is explaining. The teacher who speaks with an air of infinite patience, slowly moves his upturned hands outwards towards his class, and raises his eyebrows at the ends of his sentences, *may* be explaining; but on the other hand, he may be doing no more than going through the motions conventionally associated with it. Any alleged explanation has to be judged, not by what it looks or sounds like, but only by its effects – namely the promotion of understanding.

This view of explaining raises, of course, a further problem. Explaining is any procedure which promotes understanding, bus in what does understanding itself consist? The answer to that question cannot be given so briefly, but neither is it so mysteriout as some references to it suggest.

What is Understanding?

This question also raises a verbal problem, and I shall tackle it in the way already used in dealing with 'What is learning?' I shall examine some events customarily accepted as 'cases' of understanding, and note their characteristic features.

One stormy winter evening my neighbour was puzzled by a strange low humming sound which seemed to come out of the walls of his house. After much searching he traced it to a draught-excluder on his front door – a device consisting of a wooden strip to which was attached a long rubber tube. He now understood. (If the reader has not, no harm is done. An explanation is given later in more detail.)

A colleague, asked if he has fixed his summer holiday, replies, 'Not yet, but I expect we'll be in Manchester for a few days anyway!' I am puzzled. Had he said simply that he was going to Manchester I should not have had the same difficulty. But why does he say also, 'Not yet', and 'expect' and 'anyway'? Then I recall that he once told me that his wife's mother lives in Manchester, and I understand.

A day or two after I have put a biscuit tin on top of the kitchen cabinet, the tin has moved forward and is about to fall off, although no one has touched it. Then I remember that two of the doors of the cabinet are difficult to shut, and have to be slammed. I now understand why the tin has moved.

A child brings me a book, to show me that the word 'color' has no 'u' in it. I find that the book is published in the U.S.A. – which explains the spelling to me. But when I tell the child this, he is still puzzled and apparently expects me to continue.

What do these different examples have in common?

Previous Knowledge

In each case the understanding is dependent upon something that is already known. My neighbour understands the eerie noise, not just because he now perceives that it comes from the draught excluder – for that in itself could be puzzling, but because he knows that an air current across the end of a pipe produces this sort of sound. I understand my colleague's reference to Manchester, not just because I remember that his wife's mother lives there, but because I know also that wives who live quite a long way from their mothers often visit them during vacations. I understand the movement of the biscuit tin, not just because I recall that two cabinet doors have to be slammed shut, but because I know that if one smooth-topped object suddenly moves back, a smooth-based object lying on top of it will slide forward. I understand the spelling 'color', not just because I find that the book is an American one (for the child now knows this too, and he still fails to understand), but because I know that this is the customary American spelling of words of this kind. In each case understanding does not take place in a vacuum: it depends upon certain relevant knowledge.

In the same way, the outsider often fails to understand 'family jokes', not because he is stupid or has no sense of humour, but because he lacks the necessary knowledge of previous events. Political cartoons in newspapers, which draw a smile from the politically conscious reader, are not understood by the person who has not been acquainting himself with current affairs. The demonstrated solution of a problem in geometry will not make sense to the pupil who is ignorant of the theorems on which the solution depends.

Particular Instance of Previous Knowledge

We can nevertheless be more specific, by making explicit the nature of the relation between the thing to be understood and the knowledge required for its understanding. In each case understanding occurs when the thing to be understood is seen as a particular instance of what is already known. Take the same examples again.

When my noise-haunted neighbour understands, it is not just because he appreciates that air is blowing across this particular tube and making this particular sound. If that were all he knew, he would, of course, know where the noise was coming from, but he would scarcely be said to have 'understood' it. If that were all he knew, he might as well have discovered that the noise was coming from a piece of cheese in his pantry, for the one thing would make no more sense than the other. He understands the noise only in so far as he knows that an air current passing over the end of any pipe produces some sort of musical note, and *sees this particular thing as an instance of that general principle.* I understand the spelling 'color' in so far as I know that this type of spelling is customary in American books. (The child does not know this, and so fails to understand.) I understand the movement of the biscuit tin when I see it as a particular instance of a general physical principle. In each of these three cases the term 'principle' is appropriate, but in the fourth case, and many others, that term is too restricted in meaning. The fact that during vacations wives tend to visit their seldom-seen mothers could scarcely be called a 'principle'. We may therefore say simply that understanding occurs in so far as the thing to be understood is seen as a particular instance of something more general, something already known.[1]

Understanding and Misunderstanding

Even this refinement, however, is insufficiently precise for educational purposes, because all that has been said so far about understanding could have been said of *mis*understanding. If my neighbour had interpreted the sound as a noise in the water-pipes below the floor, and knew that water-pipes do sometimes make noises of that sort, here also he would have been appreciating the thing to be understood as a particular instance of something more general, something already known. As further investigation would have shown, that interpretation would in fact have

[1] This general knowledge need not be present in advance of one's meeting the thing to be understood. My point is that it must precede the understanding.

been wrong; but he would nevertheless have been engaging in exactly the same sort of mental activity as he did when (as in our original example) he was right. In a purely psychological sense understanding and misunderstanding are the same. We must nevertheless distinguish them here, because for educational purposes the thing in question has to be understood rather than misunderstood. It must therefore be seen as a particular instance of something which is true, or correct, or generally accepted, or for some other reason has been specified by the educator. This very limitation, however, has the advantage of allowing a more succinct description, and also of relating understanding to what we already know about learning.

A 'particular instance' is a member of a class of instances. It is an instance of a certain kind. And to be one of a certain kind it must exhibit the criterion-feature, the feature which characterises that kind. But if, as in our present context, that kind has to be specified, the criterion-feature is, of course, the cue – the feature which, by definition, characterises the kind specified. To be an instance of any specified kind, then, the thing in question must exhibit the cue, the feature which characterises the specified kind of thing.

In the great majority of educational instances, this in itself raises no difficulty, because if the pupil is required to understand something, the feature which makes it of the kind intended will be exhibited. If an arithmetical problem is to be understood as a problem in profit and loss, usually the problem will really be of that kind; it will exhibit the cue-feature which characterises that kind of problem. If a statement is to be understood as exemplifying a certain figure of speech or grammatical construction, it will usually be an instance of that figure or construction; it will exhibit the relevant cue. The pedagogical problem usually lies, not in ensuring that the thing to be understood does exhibit the cue, is indeed of the kind intended, but in the pupil's seeing it as such. The pupil will understand, not merely in so far as the thing in question *is* of the intended kind, but only in so far as he *sees* that it is.

Here, then, is the crucial issue. Exactly what, in any instance, does the pupil have to see?

Understanding as Cue-recognition

As I have just said, a thing is of a certain kind in so far as it exhibits the feature which characterises that kind.[1] But the kind characterised by a certain feature is not something additional to the feature which characterises it. On the contrary, the characterising feature is itself the kind. The cover of my typewriter, the book on my desk, the background of the wallpaper in my study, all are of the one kind, Grey; but that kind is itself no more than the feature, grey, which characterises that kind. The kind or class to which the instances belong is itself no more than what the instances have in common; and the totality of what they have in common is the characterising feature, the cue. The cue does not merely 'indicate' the kind; the cue itself *is* the kind. Consequently, we can state quite simply what the learner has to see. Since the cue is itself the kind, what the learner has to see is the cue, and he has to see it within the instance confronting him. In illustration we may use the same examples once more.

What my neighbour had to see in the humming-noise situation was not just a particular wood-and-rubber draught-excluder with a cold wind blowing over it, and making a queer noise, but what is characteristic of 'such' instances, namely an air current passing over the end of a pipe and producing a musical note. To understand my colleague's reference to Manchester I have to see, not just this particular man and his wife going to that particular place where a particular elderly lady lives, but what is characteristic of all instances of 'this' kind, namely wife and husband visiting, during vacation, her seldom-seen mother. To understand the spelling 'color', I have to see not just this particular word, but what makes it an instance of a more general kind, namely a word ending in '-or' and lacking the 'u' in the American

---

[1] One thing will, of course, have a great many features, and so at the same time may be of many different kinds, that is, ambiguous.

fashion. To understand the moving biscuit tin, I have to see, not just that round red tin perched on top of our brown kitchen cabinet, and so forth, but one body suddenly moving, and having an effect on another body on top of it. In each case I have to ignore many aspects of the situation which are relevant enough for other purposes, and see the cue, the kind-characterising feature, within the thing to be understood.

The issue can now be stated very briefly. Instead of saying that the pupil has to understand the material in question, or that he has to see it as an instance of some specified kind, we may say simply that within it he must see the cue.

There are nevertheless two important provisos. The first has already been mentioned: if understanding is to take place, not only must the learner see the cue, and see it within the material to be understood, but he must already be familiar with the cue – he must already know it. The cue he has to see in this particular material must be something he will *recognise* once he does see it. The second proviso is now made explicit.

If my neighbour heard the same humming noise again a week later, and had not forgotten in the meantime what happened the week before, he would, of course, recognise the cue again on this later occasion, and very probably on many subsequent occasions also. Recognising the cue could, and often would, continue. If, then, we defined understanding simply as 'recognising the cue within the material', it would be in order to say that understanding took place also on these later occasions. But this is not the way in which the term 'understanding' is customarily used. If on (say) the fifth of these occasions we were to ask the man, 'Do you understand that noise?', he might well reply that he had understood it weeks ago, on the occasion on which the noise was first heard. It is customary to distinguish between the initial event of understanding (on the first occasion) and what happens on the later occasions. We might perhaps say that on the later occasions he 'still understands' the noise, but in so far as he does not forget what happened before, he does not now have to 'go through the business' of understanding; he does not have to 'understand it all over again', or 'do' any understanding. All he has to do now is *remember* what he understood the first time. I am not suggesting that once something is understood it will always be remembered; certainly there will be instances in which what was understood will be forgotten, and the learner will have to go through the business of understanding once more. What I am suggesting is that *when* what has been understood does in fact remain, as in our illustration, the subject is no longer involved in the event of 'understanding', and that the psychology of these later occasions is the psychology, not of understanding, but of remembering. I am suggesting that understanding, as an event, is characterised by something peculiar to the first occasion. And what is peculiar to, and characteristic of, the first occasion is that the learner begins there by misunderstanding, or by being puzzled, and then the cue emerges – he recognises it. On the subsequent occasions, on the other hand, he does not begin by misunderstanding or by being puzzled: he recognises the cue at once. When, on some later occasion, my neighbour hears the same noise (and has not forgotten what happened before), he knows at once what it is. The crucial aspect of the event of understanding is this *change*, on the first occasion, from misunderstanding or puzzlement to recognition of the cue.

This is, of course, a verbal argument, about the meaning to be given to the word 'understanding', but I think that what I have just said is in accord with educational usage. When teachers speak of the need to understand, they refer, very often, to what must happen if the pupil is to 'come to understand', to 'see the light', or if the thing has to 'dawn on him', or 'make sense' for him. At any rate, it is useful to have different words for the initial 'dawning' and the subsequent 'retaining' of what dawned some time before; and in the following discussion I shall use the word 'understand' to refer to the change-over from misunderstanding or puzzlement, and speak of the retention in terms of 'remembering'.

A description of 'understanding' as 'recognising the cue' is therefore too wide. What we need is a description which takes into account the crucial change-over from misunderstanding or puzzlement.

Understanding as a Shift of Force

To misunderstand something is to see it as an instance of the wrong kind. By the same sort of argument as has already been used, when I misunderstand something I see not the cue but some other feature – the feature characterising the wrong kind. Accordingly, the change-over from misunderstanding to understanding entails the cue's appearing (to the learner) in place of some other feature. Likewise, when I am puzzled by the material, I see *some* feature of it, for otherwise I should not be seeing the material at all and so could not be puzzled by it. But the feature which I do see is not the cue, for if it were I should not be puzzled. (I should be puzzled if the cue seen were unfamiliar, but I am assuming that the first proviso is met, and that the cue is susceptible of recognition.) Here again the change-over entails the cue's appearing in place of some other feature.

We may say, then, that to understand something is to see its cue in place of some other feature previously seen in it. Or, to include the first proviso about the familiarity of the cue, we may say that the understanding of any given material consists of a shift from seeing some irrelevant feature to a recognition of its cue.

I have, of course, been using the word 'see' in a popular sense. Terms like 'perceive', 'conceive', or 'appreciate' would have been more accurate. Indeed, for practical purposes we have to be even more precise. We cannot just *know* that a pupil has now perceived, conceived, or otherwise recognised the cue. We can judge that he has done so only in so far as he makes some *response*, a response of such a kind as to indicate that it was the cue, and not anything else, which elicited it. He might describe in words, or by a drawing, what he now sees; or from his actions we might deduce that unless he was now seeing the cue he would not act in these ways. The listener's comment on a joke, for example, will often indicate whether he has seen its point.

The implication of that refinement is discussed in more detail in the next section, but it may be said now that 'seeing the cue' means in effect that it is the cue which is now the forceful feature of the situation. And the shift, from seeing some irrelevant feature to seeing the cue, is in effect a *shift of force to the cue*. As was argued, however, understanding involves not only one's seeing, but one's recognising, the cue; which implies that the cue was forceful on some previous occasion. We may say, then, that the understanding of any given piece of material consists of some irrelevant feature's losing force, the force of the situation being *r*eacquired by the cue.[1]

I have taken some time to discuss the nature of understanding because, as that discussion was intended to show, understanding is not so mysterious as some accounts of it would have us believe. In other words, understanding is itself susceptible of being understood, and can be described in terms of other, simpler, things. By this I do not mean, of course, that understanding actually takes place without difficulty, or that explaining is always easy. I mean, rather, that it is not difficult to *state* in a simple and clearcut way precisely what has to happen if someone is to understand. And the more clearly and simply we can state this, the greater the

---

[1] From this definition it follows that understanding is not a single, unanalysable event. It involves *two* 'seeings', seeing this and then in place of it seeing that. Also, in presupposing a distinction between understanding and misunderstanding, it implies a judgment, on the observer's part, of the relevance of what is seen. And the term 'recognition' implies also past familiarity with what is now seen.

Since 'understanding' is sometimes defined in terms of 'seeing relationships', I may add two further points. First, relationship is implied by my saying that understanding involves seeing the thing to be understood as a 'particular instance' of something already known; all instances of understanding share the relationship between the thing to be understood and the other thing of which it is a particular instance. But second, as reference to the same four examples will illustrate, although all instances of understanding may be said to *involve* that relationship, yet not all instances demand that that relationship be the *subject-matter* of what is seen. The only instances in which the relationship as such must be seen will be those in which the relationship is itself the cue. For example, my neighbour does not have to say, make explicit, that the draught excluder event is a particular instance of the physical principle; it is enough that he should see the principle within that event. His understanding of that event does not necessitate his working through a syllogism. On the other hand, if the *reader* of that account were puzzled by the example, I might have to make explicit the relationship between it and the physical principle, in so far as the cue of this new instance was that relationship itself.

guidance we get in promoting his understanding. In particular, the basic task of the explainer is now plain: his task is to help the learner react to the cue.

Understanding and Learning

Before we begin to analyse explaining we should first consider its relation to teaching generally. To teach is to promote learning; to explain is to promote understanding. What then is the relation between understanding and learning? Is understanding a special sort of learning? Or is it a part of learning? Or is it something quite different? In this section I shall try to show that although understanding is often necessary in learning, yet it is itself only part of learning, because it does not fulfil all four of learning's basic requirements.

A child has to learn to run certain little errands for his mother: to go to the dairy to get three pints of milk, to take a note to Mrs Smith at number 46 The Crescent, and so on. His understanding of the instructions in such cases would be indicated by his learning to perform as requested. In general, the response specified for the instance in question (such as actually taking the note to Mrs Smith at number 46 The Crescent) would serve as a criterion-response for understanding. Actually doing what he was intended to do would indicate that the instruction had been understood. But many other responses could serve the same function equally well. If the child said, 'Is that the house with the ivy round the door – and a big brown dog? Is that where I've to take your letter?', that verbal response could indicate that the request had been understood. But that verbal response is not itself the response required by the instance in question, namely the response of actually delivering the letter to the required address. Indeed, that verbal response would still serve as a criterion of understanding even if it were followed up by a downright refusal to go.

In general, *any* response which is in fact made to the cue is an adequate criterion of the cue's having been seen. Accordingly, understanding does not in itself guarantee that the response which is made to the cue will be the response specified for the instance of learning in question. The change-over from puzzlement or misunderstanding, to recognition of the cue – as shown by a response to the cue – does not necessarily take the form of a change-over to the form of response required by the instance in question. Understanding therefore does not necessarily fulfil the Requirement of Prompt. Moreover, if the Requirement of Prompt is not met, so that the required form of response does not appear, the Requirement of Reinforcement cannot be fulfilled. The only requirements understanding necessarily fulfils are the Requirements of Cue and Force. To understand something is to make *any* response to its cue; the material is understood in so far as it is its cue which evokes *some* response, and this is, of course, the essence of the Requirement of Force. But since understanding entails a change-over from seeing some other feature of the given material, understanding presupposes that the cue was present also on the earlier occasions but was not seen, and so presupposes a succession of situations of the specified kind. That is understanding presupposes the fulfilment of the Requirement of Cue.

Consequently, even if our attempts at explaining are completely successful, explaining is not itself a complete technique of teaching, because it need fulfil only two of the four basic requirements of learning. It does not of itself ensure that the response which is made will be required response, nor, of course, that the response-form will be tied to the cue. This is not to detract from the value of understanding or of the explaining which promotes it. What the argument does, on the contrary, is to focus attention on the crucial issue, namely that the function of explanation is to ensure that the force of the situation is exerted by the cue. Understanding consists essentially of a shift of force, a shift of force from some other feature to the cue itself. When the learner comes to understand, 'does his understanding' of the material, he reacts to the cue instead of, as formerly, to some irrelevant feature of it.

An educationally relevant implication of the above argument is that the popular antithesis between learning by understanding and learning by being conditioned is improper. (See also p. 162.) It is often alleged that learning by understanding is in some way 'better' than learning by being conditioned; but while the two things are different, they are different in a way which precludes such a simple judgment. Conditioning is concerned with relatively simple instances of learning in which understanding is rarely if ever necessary; the cue is the forceful feature from the outset, and a shift of force is not required.[1] Also, when conditioning is completely successful, all four requirements of learning are fulfilled. Understanding, on the other hand, is concerned with instances involving relatively complex situations, but at best it can fulfil only two of the four basic requirements, Cue and Force. It would therefore be inappropriate to ask which is the better: to fulfil all four requirements in relatively simple instances or to fulfil only two in instances that are relatively complex? There will be many instances in which understanding is *necessary* for learning (in ensuring, in particular, that the Requirement of Force is fulfilled), but in no case will understanding of itself be *sufficient* for learning, because the Requirements of Prompt and Reinforcement have to be fulfilled also.

One further point: in the sense in which I have been using the term 'understand' it would be improper to say that a pupil had 'misunderstood' on the ground that he had given a wrong response. For example, if in his account of an experiment he uses the term 'pipette', when 'burette' would have been appropriate, and on being asked to show what he means points to a burette, he is merely making a wrong (verbal) response to the right thing. Misunderstanding is characterised, not by a wrong response to the right thing, but by some (right or wrong) response to the wrong thing. On the other hand, if in analysing the sentence, 'This is the place where I was born', he called the subordinate

---

[1] It would nevertheless be in accord with the definition of understanding given above to say that the dog which salivated in response to the sound of the experimenter's footsteps had 'misunderstood' the situation.

clause an adverbial clause of place, on the ground that it began with 'where', this would be a case of misunderstanding. The cue here should be the *function* of the subordinate clause in relation to the principal clause, and not the mere word 'where'. In this case he has made a response to the wrong thing, and so could be said to have misunderstood. It is of practical importance to distinguish between making a *wrong response* to the right cue – which calls for a prompt, and making a response to the *wrong cue* – which calls for an explanation, a shift of force to the correct cue. In the former example all we need do is tell the boy, 'That is a *burette*!'. In the latter we should have to find a way of letting him see the grammatical relation.

Having considered the question of what understanding is, we can now ask how it comes about. In what ways can the crucial shift of force to the cue be effected?

The Concept of Structure, or Gestalt [1]

In the last section I described the occurrence of understanding in two rather different ways: the learner recognises the cue; there is a shift of force to the cue from some other feature. In a sense these two descriptions are the same, but the first puts the emphasis on the pupil's own act of 'seeing', whereas the second puts the emphasis on the material. On the first view the task of the explainer is to help the learner to see the cue, whereas on the second his task is to effect a shift of force. Here again the two views are fundamentally alike, but the second offers a more practical approach. The teacher cannot directly control the pupil's act of seeing; he cannot manipulate, as it were, the pupil's seeing-apparatus. But he can manipulate, arrange, and otherwise control the material to be understood. On this view, the explainer's task consists of his presenting the material in such a way that irrelevant

[1] For accounts of Gestalt psychology and some of its applications see Ellis (10), and Katz (24). A more formal treatment is given by Koffka (26), and a critical account by Petermann (40). For an interesting application of Gestalt theory to teaching, particularly to the teaching of mathematics, see Wertheimer (55).

features lose their force, their power to evoke reactions, and fade into the background; and the cue becomes the dominant, response-evoking feature. Just how this may be done will be discussed shortly; the immediate point is that if understanding is to take place it will be more profitable for the teacher to think, not of ways in which pupils see, but of ways in which material can be presented.

A more general way of making the same basic point is to say that the teacher can control the 'structure' of the material to be understood. This is more general because change of structure does not necessarily involve a physical rearrangement. For example, the picture in the frontispiece can change its form, pattern, or structure, without any physical change in the picture itself. One aspect, the face of an old woman, can fade into the background, being replaced by another feature – the face of a young woman. (Or, of course, conversely. If the reader has not experienced the change just referred to, his understanding of this section will be enhanced if he stares at the picture until the change takes place – or gets someone else to help him, to explain it.) Here is another simple, well-known example (Fig. 1). Without any physical change in the picture, it may change from being a white vase, with a black ground, to being a pair of black faces, on a white ground – or the converse.

Fig. 1

We may, of course, assume that this sort of change would not take place if no one looked at the picture; the change is a change *for* someone whom the material confronts. But when someone does look at it, there is nevertheless a quite apparent change *in* it. Its 'structure' alters. Fig. 2 illustrates a similar phenomenon. The dots will group themselves in different patterns – rows, or columns, or diagonal lines, or domino fives, and so on. The structure alters. And that alteration is a change in the aspect or feature which is seen, the dominant or forceful feature.

The term 'Gestalt' is more or less synonymous with 'pattern', 'form' and 'structure'; and Gestalt psychology has given considerable attention to the manner in which structures can change their character.

These three examples illustrate points we shall meet again in the following sections. First, the material is *ambiguous*: it can be seen in different ways and can assume different structures. Second, the examples illustrate what may be called *psychological events in the material* (as contrasted with mental acts perpetrated inside the learner's head.) The changes that take place can be envisaged by the teacher, not as things the pupil does with his eyes or ears or brain (though these will, of course, be involved), but as 'happenings' in what we look at or listen to. Third, they illustrate *the shift of force* which is the basis of understanding: we pay attention to this aspect of the material rather than to that. In these examples it did not matter, of course, which feature we saw, because the pictures were intended to be ambiguous, but this is no criticism of them, for all material is potentially, if not always patently, ambiguous.

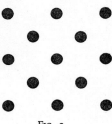

FIG. 2

To repeat the main point: understanding entails a shift of force to the cue, and this shift can be envisaged by the teacher as a change in the structure of the given material. Explaining therefore entails the teacher's restructuring the material to be understood, so that the cue becomes the dominant feature. We may now consider some of the ways in which restructuring can be effected.

Restructuring as Fluctuation of Figure and Ground

The type of restructuring exemplified by the vase-and-faces picture (Fig. 1) is often described as 'fluctuation of figure and ground'. Were it intended that the observer should see the vase, understanding would occur when the material fluctuated so that the vase was the figure and the black area was no more than an undifferentiated ground. A similar phenomenon sometimes occurs when we look at a black-and-white map. In the map in Fig. 3, which of the large areas is seen as land will depend (for the landsman at any rate) upon which area is the figure rather

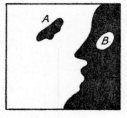

FIG. 3

than the ground. The same point applies to areas *A* and *B*. Which is island, which is lake?

Like the examples already used, Fig. 3 is intentionally ambiguous (indeed it may appear as a face looking at a small object above its nose); but many real maps are ambiguous without intention. Ways of overcoming the difficulty are obvious – once it is realised that ambiguity is possible, and what the 'wrong' interpretation is likely to be. If the pupils are accustomed to maps in which water is indicated by the colour blue, the water-area could be so coloured; place names could be inserted so as to minimise misinterpretation; and so on.

The geometrical figure in Fig. 4 provides another typical example. It may appear as a parallelogram with two diagonals, or as two overlapping triangles on the same

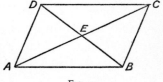

FIG. 4

base – and there are four such pairs – or as four triangles with a common vertex, or even as a solid figure. Here again it is not difficult to suggest how the requisite feature might be made dominant. Often the mere naming of the required figures ('. . . . triangles ABC . . . and ABD . . .') is enough; or the teacher might trace them with a finger; and the use of coloured chalk frequently focuses attention on the relevant items.

Restructuring as Shift of Emphasis

The phenomena referred to in this section are not very different from the events referred to under the head of Fluctuation of

Figure and Ground, but for verbal material, and auditory material generally, the concept of Emphasis is more appropriate. The following sentence,

'So this is your husband!'

will change its meaning as the emphasis changes from one word to another, particularly the words 'this', 'is', and 'your'.

This is, of course, a very simple illustration. Often the emphasis has to be given, not merely to one word rather than to another, but to a sentence, a paragraph, a chapter, a generalisation, a principle, a particular historical event, a method of solution, an arrangement, a proviso, and so forth. The underlining of printed words, or the loud-voiced statements of certain facts, are but simple means of emphasising the relevant aspects of the material to be understood. Sometimes the relevant emphasis may be obtained by sheer repetition, or by requiring pupils to write about the aspect to be stressed, or by the arousal of emotion, or even by the simple expedient of telling the pupils that this is important, and why.

On the negative side, inadequate consideration of the role of emphasis in understanding can result in the unwitting emphasis of irrelevant aspects of the lesson-situation, leading to misunderstanding or puzzlement. Anecdotes and visual aids can be useful, but on occasion they may steal the show, put the crucial aspects of the lesson into the shade. The teacher who is unfamiliar with the slang vocabulary of his or her pupils may do more than reveal ignorance; his unintentional use of emotionally-toned words may take over the emphasis intended for something quite different.

Restructuring as Regrouping

A third mode of restructuring is illustrated by Fig. 2. It illustrates also the phenomena of Figure and Ground and Emphasis, but it exemplifies clearly the way in which parts of a pattern can 'regroup' themselves without physical movement. This concept of Regrouping is particularly relevant, but by no means peculiar, to mathematics. The Gauss series provides a useful example.[1] The terms of this series: 3 7 11 15 19 23 27 31 35 39 43 47 51 55 59 63 can be summed by adding from left to right, or right to left, but as young Gauss observed, a more elegant procedure is to take the numbers in pairs, beginning with the extremes ($3+63=$ 66), and working inwards ($7+59=66$, $11+55=66$, and so on). Each of the pairs totals 66, and so the sum of the series is 66 multiplied by the number of pairs. In other words, add the first and last terms and multiply by half the number of terms in the series. Since the procedure can be shown to apply to any arithmetical series (in which there is a constant difference between successive terms) the solution can be expressed tidily as

$$\text{Sum} = \frac{N}{2}(A+L) \quad \text{where } A \text{ and } L \text{ are the first and last terms,}$$
$$\text{and } N \text{ is the number of terms.}$$

One could, of course, rewrite the terms in these pairs, or below the original series write the reversed series – as in the customary formal proof – but if understanding is required, these latter procedures themselves depend upon the observer's first having regrouped the terms without physical rearrangement.

Another example: to find the square of a number consisting of an integer and one half (such as $8\frac{1}{2}$ or $3\frac{1}{2}$), proceed as follows. Multiply the integer (8) by the number one larger (9), and to the product add $\frac{1}{4}$ (making $72\frac{1}{4}$). Similarly, to find the square of $3\frac{1}{2}$ one would proceed thus:

$3 \times 4 = 12$. Add $\frac{1}{4}$. Answer $= 12\frac{1}{4}$. The square of $3\frac{1}{2}$ is $12\frac{1}{4}$.

Assume that the reader is unfamiliar with this dodge, and is puzzled by the success of its operation. Will regrouping lead to his understanding? Can regrouping constitute an explanation? The general form of an 'integer and one half' is $a+\frac{1}{2}$. If we now find the square of $a+\frac{1}{2}$, either by using the familiar formula for $(a+b)^2$ or by multiplying, we get

$(a+\frac{1}{2})^2 = a^2 + a + \frac{1}{4}$, which can be regrouped as $a(a+1)+\frac{1}{4}$.

[1] For a more detailed account of this example see Wertheimer (55).

But the last expression instructs us to do exactly what the dodge did, namely to multiply the integer (a) by the number one larger $(a+1)$, and add $\frac{1}{4}$. The dodge is but a regrouping of the same basic data.

Whether the above will be accepted as an explanation will, of course, depend upon the reader's familiarity with elementary algebra. If he is familiar with it, the steps shown above will be familiar, and the whole thing will make sense: the dodge will be seen as no more than an alternative grouping of terms. But if he cannot follow the argument, it will not be an explanation – a point which illustrates the earlier statement that understanding involves seeing the thing to be understood as a particular instance of something one already knows.

Although mathematics provides a wealth of examples of this mode of restructuring, one further illustration must suffice. Many pupils, asked how to find the area of a triangle, will reply, 'Half the base times the altitude', which is not, of course, wrong, but if asked to prove it some pupils will begin by putting a mark halfway along the base, and then drawing the altitude – and get no further. The difficulty is, usually, that these pupils did not ever find the area of a triangle in this way. What they found was the area of a parallelogram (base times altitude) which they halved for the area of the triangle. But instead of grouping the formula as $\frac{1}{2}$(base times altitude) they now group it as half-base multiplied by altitude. The new grouping is not in accord with anything they already know.

That meaning can alter by a regrouping of spoken words is too familiar to need illustration. And 'phrasing' applies, of course, not only to words but also to music. Here, however, regrouping shades almost imperceptibly into physical rearrangement – as effected by pauses, punctuation marks, italics, and so forth.

Restructuring as Rearrangement

While there are many instances in which understanding can be effected by causing a fluctuation of Figure and Ground, or by shifting the Emphasis, or by Regrouping, there are also many instances in which it is necessary, or at least much more convenient, to make a physical rearrangement. In written English, for example, there is a limit to the use of italics, parentheses, dashes, and so on. Often the only way to avoid ambiguity is to rewrite. Extreme examples are given by classic instances like:

FOR SALE. Bulldog. Will eat anything. Fond of children.

WOMAN wants washing Tuesday afternoons.

TO LET. Furnished rooms. Suit married couple or naval officer and wife.

In cases like these, rewriting the advertisement is the only solution.

More complex examples are to be found in the teaching of a variety of subjects. In history, for instance, which arrangement leads to the better understanding: beginning with ancient times and following the chronological order, or beginning with the present day and working back? Again, the formal order of items required for a geometrical proof is not always the order most appropriate for the initial understanding. Is it always desirable to begin by defining our terms? Or is precise definition better postponed until basic ideas have been developed? In a science course is it always desirable to begin with experiments? Is the teacher who first understands himself more likely to understand how his pupils think and act and feel? Or is he more likely to understand himself if first he gains some understanding of people in whom his interest is more objective? Should one try to learn a foreign language by first listening and speaking only? Or should one begin by looking at printed words and sentences? Obviously a discussion of such issues is far beyond the scope of this book. I mention them in order to indicate the relevance and extent of the issue of Rearrangement.

Restructuring as Change of Context

One of the roads near Jordanhill College has several churches which display texts to the passing public. One morning, having observed and read these notices, I was somewhat taken aback to read the following:

HALF HOUR SERVICE FOR HEELS

It was, of course, an advertisement in a shoe-repair shop, but its significance for me was affected by my recent past experience, by the context in which it was read.

On several occasions I have asked half my student-audience *not* to look at the projection-screen while I read from it the words

'Pas d'elles yeux Rhone que nous.'

The majority of those students who watch the words on the screen take longer to hear the familiar phrase 'Paddle your own canoe'. The (pseudo) French context apparently affects the meaning of what is heard.

That meaning can and often does change with a change of context is well known, but the point is worth emphasising because its relation to teaching is not always appreciated. It is generally accepted that one's pupils may lack the background necessary for the full understanding of what one is trying to teach. What is less generally recognised is that one's pupils will in fact have backgrounds of one kind or another, and that what one is trying to teach will not remain entirely meaningless but will often take on a meaning which is quite wrong. Often it is only when the teacher can take time to question the pupil at some length (or build up the questions over several years and over a variety of pupils) that he realises how completely he has been misunderstood; and often that misunderstanding can be traced to an inappropriate background. (Much of that background, admittedly, the teacher can do little to alter.)

Examples of how understanding may be gained, or altered, by change of context are not difficult to provide. The significance of an historical event (the outbreak of a war, a treaty, a trade pact, a loan) may alter as one learns more about the circumstances in which it occurred; the significance of a scientific discovery is enhanced when one knows something of the thinking current at the time, or of the social climate in which the discovery was made; a problem of discipline may change in character when the teacher learns more about the family background and personality traits of the offender; and many problems of teaching become understandable and susceptible of solution as one's knowledge of learning increases.

The Technique of Explaining

I have mentioned five ways in which restructuring may be effected: by causing a fluctuation of Figure and Ground, by shifting the Emphasis, by bringing about a Regrouping, by actual Rearrangement of the material, and by altering the Context. All these nevertheless have the same basic function, namely to ensure that it is the cue which is seen, that is, becomes the forceful aspect of the lesson-material. These are, in effect, ways of explaining; but perhaps the most remarkable thing that can be said about them is that in contrast with the mystery that often surrounds words like 'explain', 'see', and 'understand', there is nothing very remarkable about them. Each one of them is essentially something that is already well known to almost everyone. Yet explaining is often very difficult. Why? If the technique of explaining can be described as simply as the fore-going sections were intended to suggest, why is it often so difficult to give an explanation?

One answer, deducible from what has been said already, is that pupils may fail to understand because they lack the knowledge of which the thing to be understood is a particular instance. My neighbour would not understand the queer noise in his house if he knew nothing about air currents and pipes, and the reader lacking all knowledge of algebra would not understand the dodge for squaring $8\frac{1}{2}$ – at any rate not as I tried to explain it. But while this may be true, it raises no insuperable difficulty, because the teacher can take steps to provide the necessary information, and provide it in such a way that it is likely to be retained. Sometimes the provision of that information is itself called 'explaining', but it seems more appropriate to treat it merely as the imparting of information which has to be retained (discussed in the next chapter), and to use the term 'explaining' as I have already defined it.

A second possible answer is that attempts at explaining may fail because the pupil is too stupid to understand. This could, of course, be correct, because the extent of a pupil's understanding of various scholastic material depends upon the extent of his intelligence (though, of course, upon other things also). But this is not the whole answer, because teachers know only too well that morons do not become mathematicians; the experienced teacher has learned, fairly accurately, just how much each of his pupils is capable of understanding. The chronic and nagging problem is that attempts at explanation often fail even when it is almost certain that the pupils concerned *are* capable of understanding. At any rate, this is the problem which besets the teacher who is conscientious enough to see it and honest enough to admit it. What is the solution?

There are, I think, two principal answers. One, obviously, is that the pupil does not *want* to understand. Doubtless this is often true but, without denying the essence of such an answer, our previous discussions of motivation (pp. 88 and 119) indicate that as it stands it is not of much help. In practice what we have to deal with are *behaviours*, in particular the behaviours from which the want, or lack of want, is usually inferred. For understanding, the crucial behaviour is that of persisting. The learner has to stay with the material long enough for restructuring to take place. If he gives up after only a few seconds the cue may not have the opportunity to leap out at him, to become the forceful feature, and understanding may fail to occur. If the reader has had to stare at the frontispiece for some time before the other face appeared, he will be in a position to appreciate that point. The fundamental issue here is that the learner must be induced to keep attending to the material he has to understand. For those pupils who pride themselves on being smart, or on being good at this sort of thing, or who are interested in the subject to which the material pertains, there is little if any difficulty, because what they have to do here already fits into an established mode of behaviour. For the others, the same principle (fitting into an established mode of behaviour) applies, but in their case the fitting will have to be engineered by the teacher – a point discussed earlier. It may have to be demonstrated, for example, that by understanding this material, and only by doing so, can the learner achieve one of his own goals. Also, since satisfaction may be a necessary condition of repeat-performance, it should be ensured that, when the learner does understand, satisfaction ensues. Since in many cases satisfaction derives from the mere solving of difficulties, especially when they are presented in the form of puzzles or challenges, the teacher may on occasion make use of that fact also.

The other answer relates not so much to a failure on the part of the pupil as to a specific failure on the part of the teacher. Its essence lies, not in difficulties inherent in the methods of making the cue the dominant feature of the material, nor in the pupil's motivation, but in the teacher's failure to make perfectly clear to himself, at the outset, precisely what the cue *is* in the case in point. How can he hope to make the cue clear, dominant and outstanding for his pupils if he is not himself perfectly clear as to what it is? How can he help his pupils to see it if he has not seen it clearly for himself? Precisely *what* has to be the figure (rather than the ground)? Exactly *what* is to be emphasised? *What* grouping or arrangement or context is required, and in aid of *what*?

These questions serve to emphasise the point that one cannot just 'understand' the material; one has to understand *something by it*. The pupil does not merely have to 'see'; he has to see this rather than that. To explain is not simply to clarify; it is to make clear some specific aspect of the material. Accordingly, the first task of the explainer must be to decide precisely what it is that has to be given clarity and be the object of the pupil's seeing. Because of the purpose they had at the time they were used, many of my illustrative examples in this chapter were very simple in that respect. Many scholastic examples, however, are less straight-forward. To revert to some earlier examples: if we wish a pupil to see that this is a problem in Profit and Loss, what is it that he has to see? If he is to understand a problem as a case of subtraction, to what aspect of the problem must we draw his attention? What is the crucial feature which has to become dominant? In any given instance, what is the cue?

The answer to that question is not, of course, a matter for psychology, but must derive from the teacher's own intentions and knowledge of the subject-matter in hand. What our analysis here has done is formulate the *question* the teacher must ask himself in every instance – 'What is the cue, here, that the pupil must see?' Indeed, in some complex instances the question must be asked of several different aspects. The following examples illustrate this point.

To solve a problem it is usually necessary to see what sort of *problem* it is, that is to understand the problem itself. But it is possible to see what sort of problem it is and yet be unable to solve it. Moreover, even when the solution is demonstrated, the pupil may not be able to see what matters. In other words, he may fail to understand the *solution* even when he has understood the problem. Furthermore, a pupil may understand both prob-lem and solution, separately, and yet fail to see *how the solution is a solution* of the problem. Many adults understand the problem of a fault in their television picture, that is, see exactly what is wrong with it – for example, it keeps turning over, top to bottom. They may also understand the relevant instruction in the booklet provided – 'Twist knob A, etc.' – and can remedy the fault by following it. Fewer will understand how their following of the instruction solves the initial problem. It could, of course, be objected that if we fully understood a problem we should at once know how to solve it and how the solution was indeed a solution; but this, I think, is a quibble, an unjustifiable extension of the meaning of 'understand'. There are many occasions on which, it would be generally agreed, we understand a problem perfectly well, such as the problem of getting more money, but are stuck for a solution. Nor does our understanding of that problem necessarily let us understand an offered solution – such as a complicated piece of business on the stock-exchange. In general, understanding a problem is one thing; understanding its solution is another; and understanding the relevance of the solution to the problem is another thing again. In many instances, therefore, the teacher will have to go out of his way to make clear not just one point but several.

Explaining, Understanding, and Insight

Since the purpose of explaining is the promotion of understanding, it follows that on those occasions on which we do give explanations we are preventing the pupil from 'doing his own understanding'. For this reason it is sometimes said that the teacher can do too much explaining – the implication being that an advantage is to be gained by our leaving the pupil to understand without help. The desirability of a pupil's understanding without help we may take for granted; but it is a matter for experiment whether the pupil who is subjected to a great deal of explanation will lose or fail to develop the capacity for understanding without assistance. One might indeed propose the contrary hypothesis, that the pupil who is consistently given explanations and derives satisfaction therefrom will get into the habit of expecting to find things understandable, and will himself look for explanations when none is given. Experimental evidence is required; the issue is still open.

Also, if we consistently explain things to our pupils, are we at the same time teaching them to understand, in a general way? Can we help them to *learn* to understand, so that they will show insight – that is, understand without the assistance of someone else's explanation? Here again adequate experimental evidence is lacking, but from what is known of understanding and explaining it is reasonable to infer that such learning is possible. Within certain limits the learner can be his own explainer. He cannot, of

course, restructure the to-be-understood material in direct accord
with the cue which has to be seen, for the reason that while he is
still trying to understand he does not know what the cue is. But
he can bear in mind that restructuring is necessary, and in consequence can resort to various procedures which will have the effect
of loosening the structure the material already has and making it
assume other structures – thus increasing the likelihood of the
relevant structure's appearance. For example, using previously
successful instances as analogues he can try to *regroup* the material
of his present problem, or even physically *rearrange* it. (If he cannot
follow an argument from beginning to end, but the end makes
sense, he may be able to follow it by starting with the conclusion
and working backwards. That sort of procedure is sometimes
effective in geometry.) Or he may focus his attention on items
which, so far as he can see at present, are mere *background*. (In
some crossword puzzle clues, for instance, a quite small word
may be much more significant than its ingenious camouflaging
would suggest.) He may deliberately give *emphasis* to aspects of
the problem which seem to be of no importance. (Sometimes the
student discovers that the key to a complex passage in a textbook
is to be found in an almost parenthetical sentence to which he had
previously paid little heed. The same point is illustrated by many
modern cartoons: the sting lies in some tiny detail half-hidden in
the corner of the picture.) And he may try moving the problem
into some other *context*. (For example, 'How would So-and-so
deal with this?') A special form of change of context is exaggeration: the problem is 'blown up', so that its inherent principles
are more likely to become apparent. This procedure is easier for
the teacher than for the learner, because the former knows just
what aspects call for exaggeration; but the learner nevertheless
can try different exaggerations in succession.

   As I have said, however, experiment on these issues is required;
the above suggestions are based on only a restricted number of
observations. As we shall see later, however, some of them relate
fairly closely to what is known as Transfer of Training, examined
in Chapter 10.

Summary

Explaining is a complex topic, and in a book aiming to deal with a variety of teaching-techniques I have been able to do little more than select and exemplify what seem to me to be its most significant practical aspects. This chapter is already a mere summary but I shall nevertheless venture to summarise its main points, expressing them as instructions.

1. Before even attempting to explain anything to your pupils, state to yourself as clearly and succinctly as possible what it is that calls for explanation. A problem? A solution? An event? A procedure? A technique? A cause? A rule or regulation?

2. State to yourself as clearly and succinctly as possible exactly what it is that the pupil has to see within the material decided upon in 1. What has he to see? This particular word or phrase? That line? This particular principle? That colour? This shape? It is useless to assert that he has to see 'the meaning' of the material. *What* meaning? Precisely *what* is it that the material has to mean? Exactly *what* thing is to be the centre-piece of the pupil's comprehension?

3. Ask yourself whether the pupil has ever seen that thing before. If he has not, there can be no *recognition* and therefore no understanding. It is necessary to ensure that he is familiar with what he has to see before he can be led to recognise it within the instance in question.

4. Assuming that *recognition* of the cue, as decided upon in 2, is possible, devise the learning-situation in such a way that the cue is likely to become the most dominant feature of it. Sometimes the mere naming of, or pointing to, the cue will be enough, but on many occasions it will be necessary to resort to more complex procedures, such as effecting a fluctuation of Figure and Ground, a Shift of Emphasis, a Regrouping or even physical Rearrangement of the material, or a change of Context.

5. These procedures can be effective, however, only in so far as the learner keeps with the material long enough to allow

restructuring to take place. This raises the problem of motivation, which in turn demands that the pupil's present task should be fitted into some established pattern of behaviour, and that, when he does understand, the understanding should result in satisfaction of some sort.

6. To older learners the teacher may be able to pass on, for their private use, some of the restructuring procedures used in explaining. Though experimental evidence is as yet inadequate, it seems probable that by doing this the teacher may be helping some of his pupils to learn how to understand.

8 · Teaching for Recall

Recalling – A Special Case of Remembering

The subject-matter of this chapter is often discussed under the general heading of 'Remembering', but that term is too wide for our purpose here. This chapter is concerned with verbal-numerical material, like poems, stories, formulae, number-facts, proofs of theorems – knowledge or information; whereas it is not uncommon to speak of someone's remembering actions, like how to drive a car or to play billiards – remembering how to do things. This latter group of items can be classed under the heading of 'Skills', and will be discussed later. Also, even when we do restrict our discussion to verbal-numerical material, remembering can take three different forms. I shall concentrate on only one of these, but it can be made clear if we first consider briefly all three.[1]

First, I may remember something by *recalling* it: that is to say, either aloud or 'in my head' I actually state the proverb, tell the story, answer the question, and so on. But second, there are occasions on which I cannot recall what is required yet am able to *recognise* it once it is shown to me; although I may be unable to recall a name, my ability to pick it out from a list indicates that I must nevertheless have remembered it after all. Third, although unable either to recall or to recognise the material, I may show that I must have remembered something of it by *relearning it more economically* than I learned it before.

This chapter concentrates on recall, because recalling is the form of remembering most often required in school. (The conditions governing the other two forms of remembering are however very similar to those governing recall.)

---

[1] That there are three forms of remembering is, of course, a verbal argument – as will be apparent from what follows.

'The Memory'

Before examining the conditions governing recall we may first look at what is often referred to as 'the Memory', because some popular usages of that term get in the way of understanding.

When someone remembers very little of what he has seen or heard we often say he has a 'bad memory'; when he remembers a great deal we say he has a 'good memory'. In themselves these ways of speaking are harmless, and often convenient. The danger arises when, in using them, we assume we have *explained* why the person has remembered so little, or so much. In accepting a spurious explanation we may fail to seek a legitimate one which could give guidance to our practice.

The only evidence that someone has a good memory is the observation that he actually does remember a great deal; and so, when we say that he has a good memory we are merely stating the same fact in different words. It would therefore be improper to say that he remembers a great deal *because* he has a good memory. That statement merely says the same thing twice, with the word 'because' between.

For scientific purposes the explanatory statement must relate the to-be-explained event to some other event which can be observed independently of the event to be explained. The statement that John remembers so much because he has such a big head would meet this requirement, because size of head can be ascertained without reference to how much is remembered. But, of course, there is a second requirement: the relationship expressed by the statement must be one that is known to hold good generally. On that count our example would be unacceptable, because in fact size of head and extent of remembering have no regular relationship. We shall, of course, look at more valid explanations later in this chapter. The immediate point is that the first of these two requirements excludes 'good memory' as an explanation of why someone remembers so much: 'good memory' cannot be ascertained independently of our ascertaining how much the

F

person remembers. (Essentially the same point applies, of course, to 'bad memory'.) And if we cannot observe, by itself, 'good memory', we can never show whether there is a relation between it and the amount remembered. On this ground reference to 'memory' would be scientifically useless, not because the alleged relationship is invalid, but because it cannot be shown to be either valid or invalid; it is not testable at all.[1]

Perhaps I should remark, however, that there is a type of occasion on which reference to someone's good or bad memory does explain something. If, to my surprise, a pupil recalls a very long poem, his teacher might explain that the boy had a very good memory. This would not, of course, explain why the boy remembered so much, but it could explain the teacher's lack of surprise at the boy's performance. She is saying, in effect, that this particular performance is characteristic of the boy, is an instance of the kind of thing he usually does, and so is to be expected. If, however, a pupil performed badly, and similar reference were made to his 'bad memory', there would be a danger of supposing that nothing we as teachers could do would make the boy any better. His 'bad memory' (that is, strictly, poor performance *so far*) might perhaps be the consequence of some constitutional weakness, but it might be the consequence of inattention, lack of interest, or something of that kind. The linguistic convenience of 'good memory' and 'bad memory' is probably outweighed by the dangers inherent in such phrases, and it is perhaps wiser to avoid them.

The kind of criticism I have been making is in effect a criticism of what is known as Faculty Theory. A mental faculty (such as the Memory) may be regarded as an agency by virtue of

[1] What I have just said about scientific explanation relates to the subject-matter of the previous chapter in the following way. There I said that to explain something is to show it to be a particular instance of some specified kind. Here I have said that the relationship expressed by the explanation of some particular event (John remembers a great deal) must be known to hold generally. Any event is scientifically explained, then, if its *relation* to some other event is a particular instance of a relation known to hold generally.

Moreover, what I have been trying to do in this footnote is to explain scientific explanation – by showing that it is a particular instance of the general principle that something is explained when it can be seen as a particular instance of some specified kind.

which some performance is enabled. Thus in saying that the boy's good (or bad) performance was due to his good (or bad) memory, we should be presupposing a faculty of memory. Likewise in saying that his clever (or stupid) behaviour was due to his high (or low) intelligence, we should be presupposing a faculty of intelligence. As already noted, the crucial objection to this is that in citing the Memory we are referring to something which cannot be ascertained independently of the performance to be explained.[1] In seeking an explanation of recall we must go beyond mere talk of good memories and bad memories. If our explanations of good and bad recall are to be useful, they must refer to other circumstances altogether.

Recall as a Threefold Problem

The problem of recall is customarily envisaged as threefold. I cannot now recall someone's name if I never knew it in the first place. First, then, there is the problem of *acquiring* the material at the outset. Nor can I recall it now if in the meantime it has been completely forgotten. Second, then, there is the problem of *retaining* (not forgetting) what I once acquired. And even if (as later recall would prove) the name has not gone completely from my mind, yet for some reason I may not be able to bring it to mind now. This is often referred to as the problem of *recall* (as such). About this third aspect, however, we can be a little more precise. If I did once acquire the material, and it is still available for recall (not forgotten), my present failure to recall can be attributed to the absence of something which would serve to bring the material to mind. I am not likely to recall the name,

[1] From the psychologist's standpoint many other criticisms of Faculty Theory are, I believe, irrelevant. The denial of the 'existence' of a faculty of memory belongs to metaphysics, not science, just as much as does the assertion that it does exist. Also, the demonstration that various recall-performances (rote, substance, visual, auditory, etc.) do not correlate very well invalidates a 'unitary' view of memory, but (as some writings exemplify) permits the view that there are several faculties of memory. Nor is it proper to reject Faculty Theory on the ground that a faculty is the product of reification, because an account of the conditions governing an item's occurrence in thought is not at once an invalidation of its scientific usefulness; indeed that sort of argument can be shown to be circular.

for example, if someone asks me the time, or whether it is raining, or even what was the name of 'that student' who was here at College two years ago. If the name is still available for recall, what is needed is an appropriate *reminder*.

Even with that amendment, however, the threefold problem of Acquiring, Retaining, and Reminder is by no means so clearcut as it first may look. If a pupil does recall what is required, it is plain that he must have previously acquired it, in the meantime has retained it, and that there has been a suitable reminder. The practical difficulty arises when he does not recall. His failure to recall might be the result of failure to acquire, or failure to retain, or the absence of a suitable reminder. Let us check these in order. The only way to test that he has acquired the material is to test him immediately after the lesson; but such a test requires him to recall, and if he fails to recall there is the possibility that our test questions are not appropriate as a reminder. (I am assuming that in so short a time he will not have forgotten – if he did acquire). As for the second aspect, Retaining, a test of retention also requires recall, and in this case failure to recall might be the result either of forgetting or of the absence of an appropriate reminder – it being assumed that he did initially acquire. (There are many occasions on which we suppose we must have forgotten something – only to recollect it later in what, presumably, were more appropriate circumstances.) As for the third aspect, Reminder, we can know that something is in fact an appropriate reminder only in so far as the pupil does recall; but if he fails to recall there is the possibility that the material never was acquired, or in the meantime has been completely forgotten. The three aspects are inextricably bound together: we cannot separate them to test them.

The solution proposed here is to abandon this threefold view and restructure the whole problem from a practical standpoint.

Recall as a Special Case of Learning

The problem can be made to change its character and become manageable if we look first at the issue of the Appropriate

Reminder. If I fail to recall the required name when I am told what the person in question does for a living, or that he is married to the fishmonger's sister, or has a red and white sports car, but do recall when I am told that he has a grey streak in his hair and a slight stammer, the reason must be that at some time in the past this last item of information became connected to or associated with the person's name, whereas the other bits of information did not. In other words, that last piece of information, about the hair and the stammer, is the cue of a past instance of learning, the cue to which my recalling of the name is the response, whereas the other pieces of information are not cues to that response.

Once I do recall the person's name I may, of course, recall also that he is a cost accountant, has a two-tone sports car, and that his brother-in-law has a fish-shop, but although I may have known these things, and they are recalled once I recall his name, they do not necessarily serve as cues to the recall of his name. A certain cue may serve to elicit a certain response, but the content of that response may not serve to elicit the recall of the cue. Recalling, in this connection, is often a one-way street. If my wife asks me if I can remember what dress she wore at the last staff social, I may be unable to do so; but had I been shown the dress I might have recalled, gratuitously, that the staff social was the last occasion on which she wore it. This point is often obscured when we speak in terms of 'associations', for if A is associated with B, it seems sensible to suppose that B will be associated with A. If, in contrast, we think in terms of cues and responses, the one-way traffic is easier to comprehend.

A more significant advantage of envisaging recall as a case of learning, however, is that it results in a profitable shift of emphasis. The view described in the previous section almost suggests that if we wish a pupil to recall something, we may have to hunt around until we are lucky enough to discover a suitable reminder. But once any case of recall is seen in terms of learning, for which the teacher is responsible, it becomes obvious that he can and indeed should specify not only what is to be recalled but also what is to be the cue to its recall. There would be little educational value in helping the pupil to establish a complex response without also ensuring that that response was made in the appropriate circumstances.

On this view, then, the problem of the Appropriate Reminder changes its complexion: it is no longer a problem of discovery but of decision. The teacher must decide to what cue the recall-response is to be made. The problem of Acquiring becomes the problem of promoting an instance of learning. That the instance had been effected could be tested by presenting the cue, without a prompt, as soon as it seemed that the pupil had learned. And the problem of Retention becomes the task of ensuring that the same response can still be given a considerable time after the prompt has been withdrawn.

To recapitulate, to recall something is to show that an instance of learning has been effected, the recalling being the response to some specified cue. Recall is nevertheless a special case of learning in so far as the term 'recall' is used to refer to verbal-numerical material, and in so far as it implies that the response can still be given a considerable time after the instance first was effected.

Rote-recall and Substance-recall

In an educational context it is customary to distinguish two forms of recall-response. When the pupil recalls the material in almost exactly the same form as it was presented by teacher or textbook (word for word, for instance), we speak of 'rote-recall' or 'rote-memory'; but when what is recalled is the essence or gist of the matter, we speak of 'substance-recall' or 'substance-memory'. Plainly, a child may be able to recite something by rote, yet be unable to recall the essence of it in his own words; and on occasion he might be able to tell us the theme of a story but be unable to repeat it word for word. Sometimes, of course, a child will be able to do both; ability in the one does not preclude ability in the other.

For some purposes this distinction between rote and substance can be a useful one, but like many other distinctions it is neither so useful nor so simple as it may first seem. A given piece of material may have several 'substances', such as its plot, its literary style, its verse-form, its attitude to social or other issues, its author's purpose, its historical significance. To speak simply of 'the' substance would be somewhat naïve. As for rote-recall, what is it to include? The same words – in their correct order, the same phrasing and emphases, and so on? Again, if the gist of some matter is itself verbally expressed by the teacher, and the pupil understands it, is his subsequent recall of the teacher's very words rote-recall or substance-recall? Can there be rote-recall of the substance?

These are largely verbal problems, concerned in effect with what the words 'rote' and 'substance' are to mean; but I think we can best deal with them, not by argument, but by ignoring them, for there is a more efficient way of solving the practical issue.

The teacher is always concerned with particular instances, and in every case he will have to decide, not whether he wishes rote-recall or substance-recall, but on the particular response he wants.

In recalling the proof of a theorem, for example, will it be enough that the pupil should repeat what is printed in his book, word for word, with exactly the same figure; or should he be able to prove the same theorem with a figure slightly different from the textbook illustration, and differently lettered? Should the order of steps in the proof be the same? If a different figure, different in what ways? In any instance, I suggest, the particular response required should be clear in the teacher's own mind. Whether or not he chooses to call it 'rote' or 'substance', or some subdivision of either of these, is beside the practical point.

In many cases, of course, the required response cannot be specified by our stating the words which are to be used; it will have to be specified in respect of what the words or other symbols are to mean.

The Conditions Governing Recall

Since recall is a case of learning, the conditions governing recall will be basically the same as those governing any other cases of learning, namely the conditions in which the four requirements of Cue, Force, Prompt, and Reinforcement are met. When the required recall-response and the cue to it are relatively simple, teaching for recall is essentially habit-training. Also, when the situation which has to elicit the recall-response is a complex one, the learner will not be able to respond in the required way unless he understands it – so that explanation may be needed. Since habit-training and explaining have already been discussed we may concentrate, in this chapter, on instances of recall in which the cue is relatively simple but the response is relatively complex. This kind of case would be exemplified by the request to prove Pythagoras' Theorem or to recite Walter de la Mare's 'The Listeners'. It is exemplified also by essay-type examination questions, like 'Give an account of some methods of habit-breaking'.

Because of this restriction, little need be said here about the Requirements of Cue and Force. The forcefulness of the cue was discussed in connection with habit-training, and ways in which a cue could become forceful were considered in the chapter on Explaining. As for the cue itself, it was noted earlier that what the cue has to be in any instance must be decided, not by psychological investigation, but by the teacher himself in the light of his educational purpose. The cue for the recall of some learned material, however, may not always be a question, demand, or reminder interposed *ad hoc* by a teacher, examiner, or indeed anyone. When the pupil meets some practical problem or social situation, often he will have to recall, without the aid of well-directed questions, whatever information is appropriate to deal with it. The teacher may therefore deem it advisable to make the cues for some instances not questions, not verbal demands, but situations as similar as possible to the kinds of situation the pupil will meet beyond school.[1]

[1] See also the chapter on Transfer.

We may concentrate here, then, on the conditions relating to the Requirements of Prompt and Reinforcement. In the following sections I have summarised the findings of some of the experiments relevant to these requirements.[1]

The Curve of Forgetting

One of the most general findings about recall is given in what is usually known as the 'curve of forgetting' (Fig. 5). It is based upon

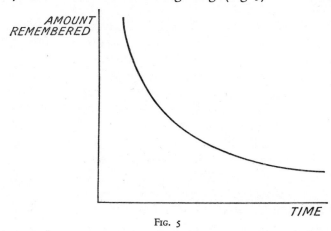

Fig. 5

a variety of experiments involving different types of material and different types of learner. Indeed, probably we should not speak of 'the' curve of forgetting at all, because different materials and different learners produce somewhat different results. For 'meaningful' material for example, the curve falls less steeply, and does

[1] In what follows I have departed from the custom followed by most textbooks of educational psychology and quoted experimental findings without describing the techniques and details of the experiments themselves. I have done this because my purpose here is to help the student-teacher relate experimental findings to his work in the classroom, and because (I believe) an account of these experiments (as contrasted with their findings) would merely be a distraction from the main issue. Experiments relating to habit-training were quoted, but in that case the experiments themselves were illustrative of the techniques the teacher has to use, whereas in the present case they are not. I do believe, however, that the teacher should become familiar with the experimental bases of his practice – though in a different context. The requisite information can be obtained from many different textbooks of educational psychology.

not fall so far, as compared with the curve for 'nonsense' material. For this reason I have omitted figures from the diagram. For all verbal-numerical material, however, the curve has the same basic shape, a shape which indicates the general form of forgetting.

First, it falls with the passage of time – which supports the popular view that as the days pass we forget more and more of what we once knew. In this respect the curve provides a warning against over-optimism: almost everything our pupils commit to memory is subject to forgetting, and the greater the time since they memorised it, the more they will have forgotten.

But second, the curve does not fall as a straight line; it is negatively accelerated. The amount forgotten is not directly proportional to the time. Nor does forgetting speed up as time passes. On the contrary, as time passes, forgetting slows down. The steepest drop appears very soon after memorising – for most scholastic material within the first two or three days. Thereafter there is a gradual levelling out.

A third indication is given if we look at the curve in a different way, namely by relating, not the total amount forgotten to the time that has passed since memorising – as we did above – but the amount forgotten in a given interval of time to the amount that was retained at the beginning of that interval. Just after memorising, a lot is known, but a lot is soon forgotten; in a later interval, less is there to start with, but less is forgotten in that interval; and very much later there is very little left, but very little is forgotten. As Osgood (36) has suggested, it appears that whatever may be the factors determining forgetting, their effect is proportional to the amount retained at any given moment. While there appears to be a 'slowing down' of the forgetting of the *total* amount of material initially memorised, yet this third indication suggests that that appearance may be misleading. Forgetting may work at the same rate, so to speak, on what is available for forgetting at the time.[1]

---

[1] The justification of this statement is that in many cases the graph is approximately a straight line when the amount remembered is plotted not against the time but against the logarithm of the time.

As was said, the curve provides a warning against over-optimism; the teacher should know that so much is forgotten so soon after the pupil has finished memorising. In this connection it is sometimes inferred from the curve that revision should begin very early, within two or three days of the lesson in question. As will be noted shortly, the substance of that inference is valid, but it is not deducible from the curve of forgetting. If we revise adequately very soon after memorising, then (by definition of 'revise adequately') the curve will rise to the top again. But without other evidence we cannot assume that that revision will have any effect on the curve's subsequent shape. For all we know we may see only a repetition of the curve we should have had without that revision, as if I had hitched up my trousers immediately after putting them on but without tightening my belt. Certainly if we revise two days after memorising, we shall have less to relearn than we should after two weeks, but *if* there is no effect on the shape of our subsequent retention there is little advantage in revising so early. For one thing, in another two days we should be back where we started, and so on for ever. For another, since the curve is negatively accelerated it could be argued that it would be more economical to postpone revision until the curve had begun to flatten out. (The amount to be relearned after fourteen days, for example, would be less than seven times the amount to be relearned after two days.) In fact, early revision does have a beneficial effect, but we know this, not from the evidence provided by the curve of forgetting, as is sometimes assumed, but from evidence derived from experiments of a different kind, noted in the next section.

Overlearning

To 'overlearn' something means, not that one is overdoing the learning, but that one is continuing to practise the material beyond the stage at which perfect reproduction can just be achieved.

In general, overlearning does result in better retention: in a given time, less of the material will be forgotten. This finding answers, in part, the question raised in the previous section, because overlearning is in effect very early revision, revision immediately after perfect recall is achieved.

Experiment nevertheless indicates that there are limits beyond which it is unprofitable to overlearn. Although overlearning does pay dividends in retention, yet these dividends appear to be subject to a law of diminishing returns.

Osgood (36), and Hunter (23), quote an experiment in which the subjects were given twice as many trials (learning periods) as were found to be necessary for perfect reproduction. This was called '100 per cent Overlearning'. On another occasion the subjects were given only half that number of extra trials. This was called '50 per cent Overlearning'. The two curves of forgetting were of the same basic form, though the former dropped less than the latter, and the latter less than when there is no overlearning; but the rate constants became less as the amount of overlearning increased. 100 per cent overlearning did not improve retention very much more than did 50 per cent overlearning. The improvement is not directly proportional to the degree of overlearning; the effects of overlearning are also negatively accelerated.

The main point nevertheless remains: very early revision does pay dividends in retention. It will be apparent, however, that these experiments in overlearning still do not answer the question of when is the *best* time for revision. They do show that early revision pays dividends, but they do not prove that we would not get at least as good, or even better, dividends if we invested the extra learning at a later time.

On this point the experimental evidence is very thin, but from the findings noted in this and the previous section we may deduce that if the material is to be recalled both within a week or so after learning and also a long time after learning, immediate revision (overlearning) will be preferable, especially if there is subsequent revision also, though it can be done at ever-increasing intervals.

Consolidation

Recall can be tested immediately after the pupil has been memorising, or it can be delayed until some time later. When the results of these two testing-procedures are compared, it is sometimes found that recall after a delay is better than immediately after memorising. The effect is most marked when the material is 'meaningful' to the learner, and in such instances delayed recall may be superior even after several days.

The graph here will, of course, be different from the classic curve of forgetting. At the beginning the curve will rise, instead of falling – though thereafter it will fall. It will be obvious, however, that the curve cannot rise if the initial recall was perfect. The two curves are not contradictory: curves of forgetting are based on perfect initial recall, whereas the kind of curve we are discussing here is not.

The phenomenon indicated by the initial rise is customarily referred to in terms of 'reminiscence' or of 'consolidation', but since the former term has several rather different meanings in psychology I have used the latter. The general answer to the question of why delayed recall should be superior is that it takes some time for complex material to sort itself out, to become organised, or to 'consolidate', even without conscious thought on the learner's part. This is by no means the whole, or even the only answer to that question,[1] but I doubt if the various answers, as yet, have a direct bearing on the teacher's work. Of much more direct significance is the fact itself. If we test immediately after a period of memorising, we may gain a quite misleading account of what the pupil has learned. The results may be poor, not because the pupil has not been working, but because of the immediacy of the testing. Were the material given time to consolidate (or whatever else it does), then the results might be better.

It does not follow, however, that immediate testing does the learner any harm. On the contrary, immediate testing may serve

[1] For a discussion of the point see Osgood (36).

to show which parts of the material should receive emphasis in subsequent revision. The only danger seems to be that by forcing the pupil to make a response he has not learned, he may make a wrong response – which may stick. Nor does the consolidation-phenomenon run counter to what has already been said about overlearning. Apparently overlearning aids consolidation.

'Whole' and 'Part' Learning

If I have to memorise a passage of prose, or a short speech, or a poem, how should I tackle it – in pieces or *en bloc*? This kind of problem is often discussed under the head, 'Whole and Part Learning', although there are in fact several different 'Part' Methods of memorising, and what is usually called the 'Whole' Method is not essentially different from these others.

In the Pure Part Method,[1] as applied to the learning of a poem, the learner memorises the first line, then the second line, then the third, and so on, until he knows each single line. Thereafter the lines must, of course, be joined. In the Progressive Part Method he memorises the first line, then the second, then these two together; thereafter he memorises the third line, and then the first three together; and so forth until all are memorised. In the Repetitive Part Method he memorises the first line, but instead of proceeding to deal with the second line by itself, he practises the first two lines together. When that pair is known as a pair, he then deals with the first three lines together, and so on; with the exception of the very first line, no line is ever dealt with by itself.

In the Whole Method, the learner reads the whole passage right through – usually on many successive occasions. At first sight this method seems to obviate the need to join the parts, but that appearance is almost certain to be misleading. All but the very shortest and simplest of passages will break, spontaneously, into parts as the learner reads or hears it. Our calling it a Whole Method does not prevent the material's having parts

---

[1] The nomenclature used here is taken from McGeoch and Irion (31).

for the learner himself. On examination, then, the Whole Method turns out to be another form of Part Method, in which each of the parts is read (or recited) only once, in turn, until the whole passage has been read, when the operation is repeated. In making this point I am not, of course, suggesting that the so-called Whole Method is useless but only that its name may be misleading, and that since it is in effect another sort of Part Method, we should not be surprised to discover that its results are similar to the results obtained by the other three.

It will be apparent, I think, that the basic problem here is not whether we ought to learn by wholes or by parts (which is a very nearly meaningless question anyway), but is the problem of discovering which is the most efficient way of joining together whatever parts there are. I say 'whatever parts there are', because the parts experienced by the learner will not necessarily be the same as those intended by the teacher or experimenter. In an illustration used a moment ago I assumed that the parts to be joined were lines, but some older learners might be able to grasp a pair of lines, or more, in 'one gulp'; in which case the two or more lines in question would not require joining. On the other hand, if a pupil cannot repeat a whole line after hearing or reading it, although he could repeat any one of its words on request, apparently in that case joining is required *within* the line.

Whatever the parts to be joined may be, however, joining can be envisaged as having the same basic form. Eventually the various prompts have to be abandoned, and the tail-end of one part must become the cue to the next. For example, if the parts were lines, and each line was known by itself, the teacher would have to drop the prompt consisting of the giving of the first word or two of each line, and the tail-end of one line would have to become the cue to the recital of the next. The memorisation of a complex response can be envisaged as the establishment of a series of little instances of learning, a series of habits, the end of one response being the cue to the next response, and so on. The relative efficiencies of the various methods of memorising may therefore be interpreted in respect of the degree to which they fulfil the conditions governing the formation of habits – Contiguity, Sequence, Repetition, Satisfaction, and so on.

As I hinted a moment ago, however, experiment indicates that no one of the four methods we have been discussing is absolutely better than any of the others. There is some evidence that the Progressive and Repetitive Part Methods are a little superior to the Pure Part Method; that for older learners the Whole Method is often preferable but also that the best method for any learner is likely to be the method to which he has become accustomed.[1] A method which is superior to another in one respect is likely to be inferior in some other respect. That this is so can be seen by our looking at these methods, albeit briefly, in the light of the conditions known to govern the forming of habits.

In the Pure Part Method, for instance, the learner may have to repeat one and the same line before he knows it; and if he does this he is likely to establish an irrelevant connection, namely between the end of that line and the beginning of that same line – instead of the beginning of the following line. The conditions of Contiguity, Sequence, and Repetition get to work, so to speak, on the wrong things. That particular difficulty is dealt with more effectively by the Repetitive Part Method and the Whole Method. But the Repetitive Part Method (and the Progressive Part Method also) entails a great deal of repetition of the earlier lines, probably far beyond optimum overlearning (see p. 167). And the Whole Method, though apparently fulfilling to a large extent the conditions of Contiguity, Sequence, and Repetition, may fall down on the conditions of Satisfaction. In each of the two more complex Part Methods, it is not long before the learner has something to show for his work; at some stage he can claim that he now knows half the poem, and so is less likely to give up. In the Whole Method there may be no demonstrable result until the whole poem is known. There will, of course, be a stage at which half the total time will have been reached, but the learner scarcely can claim then that he now 'half knows' the whole of

[1] See, for example, McGeoch and Irion (31) and Osgood (36).

the material. Indeed on this ground we might predict one of the experimental findings noted above – that the Whole Method is rather less appropriate for younger learners, because the younger the learner the sooner satisfaction is likely to be needed.

What has just been said may seem to run counter to what appears to be a popular belief at the present time, namely that psychology has shown that Whole Methods are the best. That belief may stem from the finding that Whole Methods are the most appropriate for *understanding*. For example, to get the gist of a book it is usually advisable to read it at first fairly quickly, right through, rather than to try to memorise each of the chapters in turn. So far as memorising is concerned, however, there seems to be little to choose between the different methods.

The implication of the findings on 'Whole and Part' methods is that the teacher should try different methods with his own class, and observe which are the most suitable, for that class and for different types of material. A Whole Method is likely to be preferable for older learners or for relatively short materials; a Part Method for younger learners or for relatively long material.[1]

Distribution of Practice

'Distribution of Practice' refers to the problem of the most efficient use of a given total time for memorising. Is it better to use up all the time in one continuous period ('massed practice'), or to spread the total time over a number of shorter periods at different times ('distributed practice')?

The answer provided by a variety of experiments is that, in general, distributed practice is the more effective. If, for example, a student has a total of three hours available for the study of a chapter in a textbook, three separated periods of one hour each

[1] My apparent pre-occupation with poetry as the subject-matter of memorisation is not intended to suggest that poetry is the only material worth memorising, or even that poetry should be committed to memory at all. I use it here merely because it is easier to refer unambiguously to specific 'parts' (lines, stanzas, etc.) of poems than to refer to parts of prose, speeches, and so on, without quoting specific examples.

(say one hour per evening for three evenings) will generally be better than three hours' continuous study.

Just what length the periods (adding up to the given total) should be, or how many of them there should be, depends, of course, upon the kind of material to be studied, its length, its complexity, its form (prose, poetry, mathematics, etc.), as well as upon the learner's intelligence and familiarity with the subject to which the topic belongs, and so on. A useful point to keep in mind, however, is that the learning-period should not be so short as to finish while the learner is still 'warming up', or so long as to continue after the learner has become bored. (The learner himself is not always the best judge in this connection, for as he becomes tired his criticism of his own performance may become indulgent.) The crucial point is that he must remain fresh – or keep the topic fresh. One way of doing this is to switch from one topic to another – so long as the successive topics are not very similar, for then the one may interfere with the other. (See next section.) For example, if he has three different subjects to be studied over three evenings of three hours each, instead of dealing with the subjects one per evening he could spend one hour on each subject each evening.

It will be apparent that unless one knows the details of the work to be done, and knows also about the age and intelligence of the learner, one cannot give detailed advice about distribution of practice. I can therefore but repeat the general finding, namely that some form of distributed practice is usually preferable to massed practice. The teacher will have to experiment with his own class to discover the best sort of distribution for his particular circumstances, though keeping in mind the general maxim that a little often is usually better than a lot at once.

Proactive and Retroactive Inhibition – Interference

If a learning period devoted to topic A is followed by a learning-period devoted to topic B, the recall of the one topic may be adversely affected by the other topic. When the earlier topic inhibits the recall of the later, the phenomenon is known as 'proactive' ('acting forward') inhibition; when the later topic inhibits the recall of the earlier, the phenomenon is called 'retroactive' ('acting back') inhibition. For convenience, however, and other reasons also,[1] the two may be embraced by the more general term 'interference'.

Experiment on this issue reveals that the degree of interference increases with degree of similarity of subject-matter and also with degree of proximity in time. A period on the geometry of the circle is unlikely to interfere very much with a lesson on French verbs, even when the two periods are contiguous; but a lesson on French verbs is likely to interfere with a lesson on Latin verbs, especially if the two periods are close together in time.

That interference of this sort takes place cannot, of course, be inferred merely from the observation that the pupil's recall is faulty, because poor recall could be attributed to other circumstances, such as inadequate memorising in the first place, or the giving of an irrelevant cue. Its extent has to be demonstrated by comparing the recall-performances, in the same topic, of matched groups of learners, groups differing only in respect of succession of topics. That interference occurs can be inferred, of course, from the observation of little pieces of one topic in the recall of another. For example, it is not until pupils have learned the basic multiplication facts that they answer questions like 'Six and Seven?' with the product rather than the sum.[2] And pupils who are learning these two different languages frequently use Latin words in French proses.

As these two simple examples illustrate, interference may be explained in part in terms of poor discrimination. The pupil may give the same response to two items which look the same to him. He fails to distinguish the two cues. This suggests that although during the days or weeks in which he is acquiring the different topics these topics should be kept separate, yet at some stage his

---

[1] So-called retroactive inhibition is an interference, not with something that happened earlier, namely the memorising, but with the *recall* of the earlier topic *after* the later topic has been studied. But we may suppose that the interference-factors are operative at the *same* time as the recall is attempted. (Similarly for 'proactive'.)

[2] See Thyne (52).

attention may have to be drawn to the crucial differences. I put the issues in that order because there is evidence to suggest that cues are the more readily distinguishable when the learner has acquired different responses which may be attached to them.[1]

Active Recitation

While it is possible to remember what one has read more or less passively, yet experiment indicates that retention is usually enhanced if the learner tries to recite what he has been reading, while he is still engaged in memorising it. He should, of course, have the text at hand, so that he can avoid learning the wrong things.

It is not difficult to see why this condition should be an effective one. To recite, during learning, is to practise the very thing one will have to do when the text is removed. The learner should, of course, ensure that he recites what will in fact be required. If he will have to recall the main points of a chapter, for instance, he should recite these points, and not the text line by line. In general, the textbook should be used as prompt: it should be studied in such a way as to ensure the form of response which will be ultimately required. (See also p. 254.)

Wanting to Remember

It is sometimes said that we forget things because we did not intend, or want, to remember them. We sometimes tell pupils to 'try' to remember what we have been teaching them. Is the view implied by comments of that sort in accord with the facts? Is it true that an intention or want to remember is a condition of subsequent recall?

Most of us, I think, could quote instances in which we should not have remembered so well unless we had made a point of remembering. Although I have never tried to remember the names of hundreds of students I meet, yet when I have a special

---

[1] See the chapter on Transfer, particularly p. 218 ff.

reason for knowing a student by name, and want to use his name later, I usually do recall it. On the other hand, everyday experience indicates that there are many occasions when we want to remember something but are unable to do so; the title of a book or the name of a hotel someone has recommended, a joke, a job to be done. At the time, we really do want to remember it ('I must remember that!'), but it slips our memory. Also, there are many occasions when we do recall things we never intended to. A scene from last night's television play, a catchy tune, a casual remark, may 'impress itself on the memory' without my having wanted it to do so. If I receive a telephone call telling me I have won ten thousand pounds, or that my wife has been injured in an accident, I do not have to think, 'You must keep that in mind!'

In general, although a want to remember may sometimes help, yet there are occasions when it does not, and other occasions when it is not even necessary.

Typical of the experimental evidence relevant to the solution of this problem is an experiment [1] in which the same lists of material were given to two groups of subjects. One ('intentional') group was told that the lists would have to be recalled later; the other ('incidental') was told that they were to evaluate the material listed – but not told they would have to recall it. The experiment was nevertheless designed in such a way that it could be ensured that both groups learned the lists to the same criterion; in fact, the scores obtained for immediate recall were the same for the two groups. As popular opinion might have predicted, however, the 'incidental' group required more readings of the lists than did the 'intentional' group to reach the same standard of immediate recall. But when both groups were tested nineteen days later, both for recognition and recall, the difference in scores was negligible. (Should there be any doubt about the negligibility of the difference, the insignificant difference was in fact in favour of the 'incidental' group.) To apply these results to our present problem we must assume that the former group would have formed a 'want' or 'intention' to recall, and that the other group,

---

[1] Quoted by Osgood (36), Chapter 13, referring to Biel and Force.

or most of its members, would not; but that assumption is at least as reasonable as those we make in everyday discussions of this problem. The conclusion of the experiment is that when degree of initial learning is held constant, intention to remember adds nothing to the degree of retention.

Since it is known that degree of subsequent recall depends upon the degree of initial learning – for example, if something is to be completely recalled later, it must be completely learned in the first place – the practical implication of the experiment seems to be that a want to recall after some time will be of use only in so far as it is expressed in initial *learning*. This serves very well to explain the three contingencies noted in the second paragraph of this section. In those instances in which a want to remember is effective, the want has expressed itself in learning the material at the outset. In those instances in which a want is not effective, the subject has not done the necessary learning. He may say, sincerely, 'I must remember that!', but for one reason or another does not go out of his way to learn it, to *commit* it to memory. (In many cases, I believe, the reason is that he does not know how; for example, to use the method of Replication exemplified by the illustration of the car heater on p. 107). And in those instances in which a want to remember is not necessary, the initial learning has occurred without intention on the subject's part. The material is attractive, has force for him; a prompt is at hand; his immediate success is satisfying; and so he does not need to form a 'want' to remember.[1]

To the main point already made two others may be added. When we want to recall something on a future occasion, we sometimes do more than learn it thoroughly in the first place; we also refer to the material between-times, and so derive the advantages of additional practice. In such cases we should expect an 'intentional' group to score over an 'incidental' group lacking the additional learning-periods. Even so, the advantage would be attributed, not directly to the 'want to remember', but to the additional practice in which it was expressed. Second, students

---

[1] *Cf.* the traditional distinction between 'intrinsic' and 'extrinsic' motivation.

generally will bear witness to the view that once the occasion for recall is past, the material tends to be forgotten. A practical implication is that if the teacher wishes the material to be retained for a long time he should ensure that the kind of subsequent occasion relevant to the learning in question is not merely the answering of questions in an examination or the writing of an essay. Although the occasion for recall must arise in school, it should be the *kind* of occasion the learner will meet, and knows he will meet, in a wider context. The recalling must be made a part of a set of activities in which the learner already engages and which will continue to engage him.

To summarise: a 'want to remember' must also be a 'want to learn', because it is upon the thoroughness of the initial learning that the efficiency of subsequent recall depends. If I want to remember a student's name, in the sense that I want to be able to address him by name next time I see him, I must *learn* to address him in this way. I must ensure that I have heard his name aright, and address him by it *now*. In general, in the presence of the cue (sight of student), and while I have a prompt (student's having just told me his name), I must perform the very response (saying his name) I want to be able to make to that cue (sight of the student) on any occasion. As for the teacher's inducing the learner to 'want' to remember, that task becomes the task of inducing him to want to learn; and that issue has already been examined in previous chapters (pp. 88 and 119), where it was argued that a want to learn is in effect the manifestation of *behaviours* which permit of the fulfilment of the basic requirements of learning. That view is illustrated very clearly by the present case. Everyday observation and experiment alike indicate that what is commonly referred to as a 'want to remember' is useless unless it is expressed in the very behaviours which fulfil the conditions governing recall. Not only so, they indicate that when these conditions are fulfilled a 'want to remember' is unnecessary. (Indeed, when these conditions are satisfied we may discover that we remember things we 'want' to forget.) Apparently the various 'thoughts' customarily taken as evidence of a want to remember ('I mustn't forget that!', 'I'll tell that story at the party next week!', 'I'll need to keep that in mind!', and so forth) will be useful only in so far as they are *cues to the behaviours of learning*, such as practising the required response in the presence of the cue, or in a replica-situation, overlearning, and so on.

Since remembering is a case of learning, the teacher should apply here the same motivational principles as were suggested earlier. If the material does not have a direct appeal, it must be introduced in accordance with activities in which the pupil already engages, and must be a part of them. In this account I have said nothing of the Freudian view of forgetting, but it is of interest to observe that material which is 'repressed' is usually 'out of accord' with the subject's established ways of thinking, acting, or feeling. It does not 'fit into' a dominant mode of behaviour. The Freudian view, and the view I have been advocating here, are probably not so very different. The same view may explain also why 'meaningful' material tends to be retained better than material which is nonsensical or not understandable by the learner: as was argued in the previous chapter, material becomes meaning-ful, or understood, when it appears as a particular instance of something the subject already knows. Meaningful material, then, already has the context necessary for prolonged retention.

Summary

1. Decide as precisely as possible just what recall-response is required. If, for instance, some piece of knowledge is to be recalled, decide just what kind of response would be acceptable as evidence of the retention of that knowledge.

2. Decide just what kind of situation is to elicit that response. In what sorts of circumstances should the knowledge be recalled? In other words, specify the cue of the instance to be effected.

3. Choose a prompt appropriate to the recall-response required. This might be a textbook, notes, or the teacher's own oral recital.

4. If the material is relatively long, or the pupil relatively young, divide the material into parts, and encourage the pupil to tackle the parts. For older pupils or shorter material a Whole Method may be more appropriate.

5. Whichever of the above methods is used, try to distribute the total time available so that the pupil has several periods of study of the topic rather than one long and intensive period.

6. Encourage the pupil to try to 'say' what he is memorising, rather than merely read passively. He should also be advised as to *what* he is to try to recite, for instance main points rather than consecutive lines – depending upon the educational purpose in question.

7. Encourage the learner to continue to memorise beyond the point at which he can just reproduce the material perfectly.

8. Test for recall very soon after the pupil has been memorising, though bear in mind that immediate testing may give too low an estimate of the results of the pupil's work. It will nevertheless indicate where emphasis is needed in subsequent revision.

9. Revise the material, in the first instance, within two or three days of first memorising. Thereafter the revision periods may be spaced out at increasing intervals.

10. So far as possible, avoid teaching two very similar topics close together in time, especially when the topics are new to the learners. Later it may be necessary to make explicit the points likely to be confused.

11. Since material which is meaningful and interesting to the learner is usually acquired faster and retained longer than is other material, it is profitable to try to ensure that the pupil understands what he is to memorise, and is interested in it, before he attempts to memorise it. By doing so, the teacher is in effect fulfilling the motivational requirement that the activity to be learned should be part of some wider activity in which the learner already engages.

12. Since knowledge which the pupil finds rewarding to possess is likely to be retained longer, try to ensure that what he memorises can be put to successful use.

9 · Teaching as Training in Skills

What is a Skill?

'What is a skill?' poses a verbal problem, and as in previous cases our answer will be based on common usage. Typical of performances commonly accepted as skills are dancing, typing, tying one's shoelaces, driving a car, dressmaking, planing a piece of wood. Of course, not everyone who does these things is skilful at them; these are skills only if they exhibit certain characteristics. What are they? When they are skills, what do these performances have in common?

One obvious feature is their complexity: analysis of any skilful performance shows it to consist of several movements. In some instances these movements are, in the main, successive. The typist strikes one key, then another, moves the line-spacing lever, depresses the space bar, and so on, in succession. In other instances the constituent movements are, in the main, simultaneous. In starting a car uphill, the driver has to release the handbrake, let in the clutch, depress the accelerator pedal, steer, and watch the traffic conditons all at one and the same time. Sometimes a skill consists of both simultaneous and successive movements – as in driving a car. In every case, however, there is complexity of movement.

But second, although the analysis of a skill shows it to be complex, yet in skills generally the constituent movements are so highly organised that they appear as a unity, a coherent whole. Successive movements are so smoothly dovetailed that the joins are almost imperceptible; simultaneous movements are harmoniously blended in concert. The fingers of the skilled typist do not poke here and jab there; they seem to dance over the

182

machine. The skilled motorist, far from dividing himself into bits in order to perform in different ways at the same time, exhibits a high degree of coordination.

Even complex organisation, however, is not enough. The performance would not usually be called skilful if some of its constituent movements (even if smoothly blended with the others) were unnecessary. The skilled typist does not withdraw her hand from the keyboard after each key has been struck, and the skilled carpenter does not lift the plane a foot from the plank after each sweep. A skill achieves its effect with economy of behaviour.

Once this third feature, of economy, is made explicit, it becomes apparent that we cannot ascertain whether a performance is a skill by merely looking at the performance itself. To decide that this or that movement is unnecessary, we must have asked, 'Unnecessary for what effect?' The behaviour of the golfer at the tee may exhibit a smooth organisation of movement and economy of effort – he has a beautiful swing – but it is not skilful if he misses the ball or drives it into the rough. The performance must not only be intrinsically harmonious but also achieve its intended effect.

A skill might be defined, then, as an economical organisation of behaviour achieving an intended effect.[1] But while that definition expresses in a succinct way what is implied by common usage, yet as it stands its usefulness to the teacher is small. In particular, the behaviour required in any skill is indicated only by reference to the effect it has to achieve; no indication is given about what the behaviour itself has to be. Instead of offering a description of the golfer's swing, it says in effect merely that the golfer must do whatever has to be done if the ball is to go where it is intended to go. Such an account is plainly of little practical

---

[1] This will not suffice as a *psychological* definition, because it presupposes a value-judgment instead of referring directly to the performance itself. The point is in accord with Guthrie's assertion that psychology is concerned with behaviours, not actions (17). For a more general discussion see Lewin (28). On that ground the term 'skill', as commonly understood, is not a psychological term at all. A way out of the difficulty is implied by what follows in the text.

use. Very often the learner himself will see perfectly well what the effect of his performance has to be; he wants his trainer to tell, show, or otherwise instruct him in what he has to *do* in order to achieve it. For practical purposes, in any instance, we need not merely a description of the intended effect but primarily a description of the behaviour in which the learner must engage.

There is, of course, a solution. True, in the first place we must compare the effect of the subject's performance with the effect intended, for otherwise we should not know that the performance was indeed skilful. But when we see an intended effect achieved, we can examine the performance which in fact achieves it, specify the essence of that performance, and subsequently instruct other learners in it.

But even this is scarcely enough. A skill does not consist of movements in a vacuum. The ball will rise from the tee and travel to its intended landing point only in so far as the swing is addressed to the ball at the outset – as it lies still on the tee. The finger movements of the typist, no matter how well organised, will produce the required business letter at the end only in so far as they are directed to the appropriate keys, levers, and so forth, at the beginning. In general, it is not enough to specify the performance – even when it has had the intended effect; we must also specify the way in which the movements relate to the situation in which they occur. In other words, the complex organisation of movement must be envisaged as a *response* to some specified kind of situation. Finally, in so far as the specified kind of situation did not get the specified response but got some other response when the learner previously met it, the acquiring of a skill will be the effecting of an instance of learning.

Four Basic Problems

As the examples at the beginning of this chapter illustrate, the term 'skill' covers a variety of performances; and yet the fact that it is possible to establish a definition which embraces them all, and that skills are instances of learning, suggests that for every skill the same basic conditions must be fulfilled. It is with these basic, general conditions, common to all skills, that this chapter is concerned. The teacher will, of course, have to fill out these general conditions with details peculiar to the particular skill he has to teach – typing, dancing, handwriting, swimming, and so on.

A useful approach to these conditions consists in making explicit the particular problems which are to be solved by these conditions. These problems may be seen as being four in number.

In some relatively simple skills, the learner can already make the movement required, but is now required to make that movement in response to a different sort of situation. For example, the trainee letter-sorter may be already able to flick a letter into the appropriate box or bag – so long as he looks at the box or bag; but now he may be expected to flick the letter into the appropriate receptacle with scarcely a glance at it. The cue to that particular throwing-movement has to be, not the seen receptacle, but the address on the envelope. Similarly, even the tyro typist can strike the right key if she first looks at it, but the expert will make the same striking movement in response only to the sight of the letter on the document to be copied. Since the mere sight of the address on the envelope, or of the letter on the document to be copied, will not intially get the required response, these are instances of learning, and are of essentially the same sort as the cases discussed in the chapter on Habit-training. The dividing line between skills and habits is an arbitrary one – as is illustrated by the fact that what may be a skill for the young learner may be a habit for him a year or two later. Since habits have already been discussed, we need not consider this problem here.

In many skills, however, the learner has to make a movement he has never made before. These 'new' movements may be seen as falling into two classes. Some movements are obviously complexes of simpler movements. As noted already, the skill of driving a car can be seen as a series of smaller skills, like changing gear, releasing the handbrake, steering, and so on. In such instances it is often convenient to deal first with the component skills and then have them joined together. The problem of joining, or 'organisation', is considered in the next paragraph. But some movements, though new, cannot be conveniently broken down into component movements. Typical of this class is the skill of using a saw, or a plane, or a scythe. In these and similar cases the new movement has to be acquired *en bloc*. Here then is a second problem, namely of how the trainer can help the learner to acquire such skills.

But third, as noted above, some skills can be envisaged as consisting of various component movements, and it is often convenient to help the learner acquire each of these, and then help him to organise them into a coherent whole skill. This problem of organisation of movements into one smooth total movement will arise, of course, whether the component movements were 'new', or whether they were 'old'. For example, the movements of changing gear, letting in the clutch, and so on, could be 'new', but they have to be organised. Similarly, the typist will have to organise the various 'old' key-striking movements into a coherently economical complex skill of typing.

The fourth problem is an extension of the third. If the typist is to become skilled, she will have to do more than strike each letter-key in response to the sight of the appropriate letter on the document to be copied. That method would entail her looking at one letter, striking a key, looking at the next letter and striking another key, and so on; and although some speed might be acquired in this way, greater speed will be achieved if she can respond, not to single letters one after the other, but to patterns of letters, words, or even phrases, on the sheet she is copying. In general, the most economical organisation of movements requires an organisation of what were initially distinct cues. The pianist 'takes in' a whole musical phrase from the sheet of music, and plays it as a whole; and the expert pianist will take in very much more. A fourth problem, then, is how *cues* can be organised into whole patterns.

The last three problems are now discussed in turn.[1]

---

[1] The classification of problems just offered is based on a classification of skills suggested by Freeman (15).

Training in New Movements

In this section 'new movements' refers to movements which can be conveniently acquired all in one piece, without initial breaking down and subsequent organisation. By 'conveniently' I mean that the movement does not appear to *have* pieces into which it could be broken, or that the trainer knows from his past experience that it is usually possible for the learner to make the new movement without its first being broken down into parts. A simple dance-step could be a case in point.

In terms of the four basic requirements of learning, the crucial issue here is that of Prompt: the trainer has to introduce something which will ensure that the learner behaves in the new, required, way. Kinds of things that may serve as prompts have already been discussed in connection with habit-training – verbal instructions, models, or combinations of these. With skills, of course, the prompts will usually be more complex.

Models

Some of the difficulties associated with the use of models as prompts were pointed out earlier: the learner may copy 'the wrong way round'; his seeing what has to be reproduced is not the same as his going through the movements necessary to effect the reproduction; he may copy irrelevant aspects of what is demonstrated; the model itself may distract attention from the cue. In connection with skills, however, the last point is less relevant, because the learner may have to *learn* to copy the model, and so will have to give all his attention to it. In such cases the response will have to be made to the cue later.[1] Models used in training in skills may nevertheless introduce a new difficulty.

Very often the learner will be able to 'follow' the demonstration only when the expert slows down his performance: the normal quickness of the expert hand deceives the learner's eye.

[1] A similar point could be made in connection with habits. Strictly, however, the model will not be serving as prompt until it shapes the response made to the cue itself. A reason for defining 'prompt' in this way was given earlier. See p. 56.

But in slowing down his usual performance the expert will often change it also in other ways. It will lose not only speed but also coherence. What was smooth becomes jerky, and so on, so that what the learner sees is not, strictly, a skilled performance at all. It is not difficult to see why this should happen. In slowing down his performance the expert has to pay attention to details of execution to which he usually pays no attention at all; quite often the expert's skill is all in his hands, or feet; he himself has forgotten how he does it – if ever he knew. And since he has to focus his attention on certain details he may fall down on others. For many skills it is advisable that the demonstrator should show both a version at normal speed and also a slowed-down version, or even show one segment after another, but with each segment in the normal time. Sometimes a slow-motion film is helpful, and yet what is seen on such a film may look very different from the skill at normal speed.

It was noted a moment ago that the learner may have to give all his attention to the model. This raises another problem. Should the learner look also at his *own* movements? If he is watching a demonstrated dance-step, should he look also at his own feet, to see what they are doing, and compare their movements with the movements of the demonstrator's feet? In some instances he may have to observe his own movements, because otherwise he would be unable to judge whether they were in fact a good copy of the model, but if he cannot look at both at once the comparison may be unreliable. And the learner may not be a good judge. Probably the most effective procedure is for the *trainer* to indicate where modification is needed, while the learner continues to watch the trainer's demonstration. Thus the trainer, while demonstrating, might comment, 'Left arm higher!' or 'Spring higher on the count of One!', or something of the kind.

Verbal Instructions

As was noted, models may often be supplemented by verbal instructions. The verbal instructions may be used either to effect a modification of an imperfect copy, or to draw attention to the crucial aspects of the model itself.

There are occasions, however, when a verbal instruction by itself may serve as a prompt for a new movement. Typical of such instructions are the directions on some tools or gadgets. ('Take handle *A* in the right hand, so that lever *B* points downwards; then turn knob *C* in a clockwise direction. . . .') Instructions of this sort, of course, are often accompanied by a diagram, which is almost the same as a model. What is customarily known as a 'recipe' could come into the same category. In many such cases a demonstration would be simpler, but there are learners who have considerable difficulty in following a visual model, and pick up the new movement more easily if it is indicated by words. If words are used, however, without a demonstration, it will be necessary to ensure that the learner knows the precise meanings of the words the trainer is using. In a great many cases the trainee will first have to learn what the words mean – by watching the movements as the trainer names them.

Also, as will be noted again later, verbal instructions to oneself, once they have been memorised, can be a useful aid to organisation: the learner tells himself what he has to do next.

Positive rather than Negative Guidance

Both in demonstrating and in instructing verbally it is usually better to indicate to the pupil what he has *to* do than to indicate what he should *not* do. This point was illustrated at the end of the second-last section. 'Left arm higher!' is usually better advice than 'Don't keep your left arm so low!' 'Both hands behind the chisel!' is usually more profitable than 'Don't put your other hand in front of the chisel!' Likewise, one would demonstrate the actions the learner has to imitate, rather than actions he might make but should not.

One reason for the preference is that while a negative instruction ('Don't . . .') may on occasion prevent the learner from doing what he should not do, yet it may give him no advice at all about what he should do, and so leave open the possibility of other

G

undesirable performances. Similarly for the demonstration of unwanted performances. Another reason is that the very mention of an action, even when accompanied by a ban on it, may lead even the most co-operative learner to perform that action. For example, if a class of students who have been sitting almost completely still for ten minutes are asked to try not to move their feet within the next thirty seconds, some of them will find the task almost unbearable; and many of them will move their feet when the thirty seconds is up. Another reason, particularly relevant to demonstrations, is that when the learner tries later to recall what he had to do, the 'picture' he gets may be the picture of the demonstration he was *not* to copy – but that negative qualification may be forgotten; all he may remember is what he saw his teacher doing.

There are nevertheless instances in which it will be well-nigh impossible to avoid giving negative advice; but in such cases, it is generally agreed, only the very grossest errors should be pointed out in the early stages of training.

Putting through the Motions

When the learner fails to follow a verbal instruction, or when his attempt to copy the model is far from satisfactory, it is tempting to get hold of him physically and 'put him through the motions' which are required. It is not difficult to understand why there is general agreement that this procedure is usually ineffective. If the learner follows a verbal instruction, or imitates a model, he is himself making a response, actually doing what he is ultimately required to do; but if he is to be 'put through it', he must relax, and allow his fingers, arms, legs, and so forth, to be moved, not by his own muscles but the by trainer. He is not then *making* the movements at all, and so is not practising what he is required to do.[1] Indeed, unless he relaxes completely, he may be making small movements which are the very opposite of the movements he is required to make, for he will tend to resist, even if only very slightly, the pressure exerted by the trainer.

[1] *Cf.* the distinction between passive reading and active recitation discussed on p. 176.

There does seem to be some value, however, in the trainer's physically *preventing* movements which should not be made. For example, he might prevent the learner's hand rising from the typewriter, or stop an extreme arm-swing, and so on. This procedure links up with a further point, discussed in the next section.

Inhibiting Unnecessary Movements

There are many instances in which the learner contrives to make the required new movement, but makes at the same time several other movements which are unnecessary. The child who is learning to write may make the movements necessary for the production of the required letters, but he may also protrude his tongue, hold his whole body in an almost rigid position, and so forth. The learner-driver may operate the controls properly enough, and avoid accidents, but sit crouched over the steering-wheel. In many such instances these extra movements or muscle-contractions are not only unnecessary but also have a deleterious effect on his performance.

These examples illustrate what is often referred to as 'diffusion'. The beginner appears to be unable to make the required movement 'clean': he cannot separate it from other movements. He may be able to raise both eyebrows at once, but cannot raise one at a time; or in playing the piano his left hand tends to do the same as his right – as in a mirror. If we try to stop the unnecessary movements, we are likely to discover that we have stopped the required movements also. On the other hand, if we allow the extra movements to continue, we may find in time that they have become part and parcel of the performance, to the extent that any attempt to remove them results in the performance's falling to pieces.

In connection with this problem a *laissez faire* attitude on the part of the teacher may be as safe as any other. For one thing, the observation of subjects who are acquiring skills indicates that in time the extra movements tend to drop out; very few adults or older children protrude their tongues when writing, although

their teachers may have done nothing to eliminate such movements. The experienced driver is more relaxed than the learner,
though no one ever trained him to be so. For another thing,
emphasis on the irrelevant movements, gestures, and so on, at
the beginning of training may have the effect of making the
learner even more tense, and so increase rather than decrease the
diffusion. There is nevertheless the danger that some of these
unwanted movements may persist and become built into the
final performance, and there are ways in which they may be
removed before they have become permanent aspects of the
response.

One way, noted in the last section, is the physical prevention of
the movement. If the typist wastes time by looking at the keyboard as well as the copy-material, a screen can be inserted
between the keyboard and the learner's eyes. Another procedure
is to induce the learner to make some *other* movement which is
incompatible with the movement which looks like becoming a
fixture. (*Cf.* the Method of the Incompatible Response, p. 108).
This other movement too may be unnecessary, but if it is changed
from time to time, there is less chance of any of these movements
becoming a permanent part of the total performance. Even mild
punishment (such as saying 'Tongue!' to the child whose
tongue writes letters in the air), can be effective. As a general rule,
success is more likely if one deals with these irrelevant movements
one at a time. As I have suggested, however, it may be preferable
to let the irrelevant movements disappear with time.

Knowledge of Results

There is ample evidence that improvement in skills depends
to a large extent upon the learner's having knowledge of the
results of his performance. He needs to know how he is getting
on – if he is to get on still better. Knowledge of results apparently
serves the same function as does comment from the trainer, though
less directly, and only in so far as the learner is able to deduce
what modifications in performance are necessary. For example,
if the shots on the target are too far to the left, obviously he must

aim farther to the right. If he hears that the note is sharp, the learner-violinist must stop the string a little farther from the bridge. As this last example illustrates, however, knowledge of results will be of no value if the learner is unable to effect a comparison of his results with the results intended; if, for instance, he cannot hear that the note is sharp.

Also, even if the learner can detect a difference between his actual result and the result required, improvement is most likely when the comparison indicates how improvement can be effected; that is, as noted above, when the learner can deduce the necessary modification – to shoot farther to the right, or to stop the string farther from the bridge, even when perfection is reached only in consequence of a series of approximations. Improvement is still possible, however, when the learner cannot deduce what he must do. So long as he is able to detect that his result is unsatisfactory, he can resort to 'trial and error' behaviour until the required effect is achieved. It will be apparent that if he cannot detect when his result *is* satisfactory, trial and error will be of no value, for he will not know when to stop modifying his performance.

The degree of skill achieved in this connection will depend, of course, upon the standards the learner has set himself. If, in his own opinion, the result he has achieved is good enough, knowledge of the result is unlikely to lead to further improvement, and he will at best continue to give the performance which is 'good enough'. This latter point serves to illustrate the view that there will be persistence of the performance which does produce the required result, not merely because it does produce that result, but because the learner is satisfied by the comparison he has made. In effect, it is the satisfaction produced by the performance which serves as reinforcer. The educational moral, then, would be that 'good enough' is *not* good enough; if it is satisfaction which reinforces, the learner's level of aspiration will have to be kept high, or else he will be satisfied too easily.

On the other hand, if the learner keeps trying, yet never has any sense of satisfaction, he is likely to give up. An appreciable lack of satisfaction or success is a sort of punishment, and is likely to lead to an avoidance-response to the whole project. (A very similar argument could be couched in terms of Expectancy-fulfilment instead of Satisfaction. See p. 85). And the educational moral from that point could be that the learner must have *some* satisfaction even when his performance has not yet reached the required standard. This may be effected by the teacher's pointing out to the pupil that some aspect of his performance is better than it was. Without being dishonest, the trainer may profitably express approval of even slight improvement.[1] Also, if the learner continues for some time without any improvement, or even slips back a little, he may be told, quite honestly, that this sort of thing is characteristic of the acquisition of all skills. Graphs of learning, particularly for motor skills, are characterised by ups and downs, and plateaux. And, of course, it is no help to the learner if his teacher becomes discouraged before the learner himself does so. The points made in this paragraph relate to the issue of Knowledge of Results in this way: the teacher may go out of his way to point out results which *are* good – so that the learner will continue in his attempts to improve.

A final point: if the learner is to have knowledge of results, he must be able to see what the results are. In some instances it may be sufficient if the trainer gives him the necessary information, but in others he will have to see them for himself. If, however, the results follow immediately upon the performance, the learner may not be able to observe both. In some forms of tracking apparatus, for example, the performer cannot watch his own movements and at the same time watch the white spot on the screen. Which should he watch? I think this example obviously provides its own answer: he must watch the effects of his performance, not the performance itself. In general, where the learner may watch *either* performance *or* results, he must watch the results, and modify his performance accordingly.

---

[1] *Cf.* Skinner's method of 'shaping' behaviour by reinforcing even the smallest moves in the right direction. See p. 250 ff.

Eye on the Ball

The issue raised in this paragraph is similar in some ways to the issue just noted. The golfer must certainly watch where the ball goes, that is, the result, and so cannot watch his own movements. But, of course, the movements will be skilful only if he first hits the ball, and it is almost an axiom of golf that one must keep one's eye on the ball and not on one's stance, or swing. Likewise, in preparing to hit the oncoming tennis ball, one must watch it, and not one's racket, or arm movements. In shooting at a target, attention has to be given, not to the trigger-finger, but to the bull; and in drawing a line on the blackboard, from point *A* to point *B*, the teacher will have to keep his eye, not on his moving hand, but on point *B* – his 'target' in this case.

In general, attention has usually to be given, first of all, to the 'target' – that is, the situation to which the skilled movement has to be a response; and then has to be given to the result of the movement. Only rarely has attention to be given to the actual movement itself. But if attention is not given to the movement, how do we contrive to retain it? How do I know what to do, next time, if I have never noticed what I do? The answer is that here I am dependent not upon my visual but upon my kinaesthetic sense, the sense of 'feel' in my muscles, joints, and tendons. It is in this sense-modality that the skilled performer, when he makes a mistake, can 'feel' something is wrong; or, when he is on form, can feel that he is so.

Strictly, then, although we may not be looking at our own movements, yet they are nevertheless being perceived – kinaesthetically. In terms of kinaesthetic perception we might add another explanation of why it is often desirable that the learner should not concentrate on the skill he is practising, but should relax, and 'let the skill look after itself'. Not only (as noted already) may concentration on his movements increase diffusion; if the concentration is visual, it may interfere with the learner's kinaesthetic perception. Just as someone may be so busy listening that he cannot see something, so the learner may possibly be interfering with his own 'feel' of what he is doing.

It will be apparent that if the remembered 'feel' of a performance can be an aid to its recurrence, the learner should not be allowed to become familiar with performances which are undesirable.

Distribution of Practice, and Consolidation

With motor skills, as with verbal-numerical material, distributed practice is generally more effective than massed practice. Another interesting parallel with Recall is that in the intervals between the practices consolidation appears to take place. To repeat the quotation from William James, we learn to skate in summer and to swim in winter. Although the 'material' here is movement, yet some sort of organisation occurs during intervals of rest.

Consistency in Coaching

Some writers have suggested that although trainers *A* and *B* may be equally good trainers, yet many learners benefit by having the same trainer throughout the learning-period. The reason is probably that while the differences between the trainers have no direct bearing on their efficiency, yet these differences may loom large for the learner, put him off and distract him from the demonstration or comment to which he should be giving his full attention. The condition of Habituation is probably as relevant here as it is in Habit-formation.

The Learner's Motivation

Since learning a skill usually calls for greater persistence, more prolonged attention to the demonstrator, and a greater capacity for tolerating set-backs than does habit-forming, there is considerable point in the view that the learner must be well motivated if the skill is to be acquired. In other words, he must 'want' to acquire the skill in question.

The principle here is nevertheless exactly the same as before. A 'want' to learn is useless unless it is expressed in the very behaviours which permit the fulfilment of the basic requirements of learning;

and for practical purposes the trainer's task consists of discovering and employing means of making these behaviours occur. In particular, he has to exploit a mode of behaviour in which the learner already engages, and which produces satisfaction or at least will continue under its own inertia.

Skills very often satisfy that latter requirement, because by acquiring a skill the pupil is enabled to do something which brings him satisfaction – a sense of achievement, a raising of prestige, and so forth. If one of his modes of behaviour takes the form of doing (or trying to do) what his older acquaintances do, and these acquaintances have acquired the skill in question, little if any persuasion will be needed. In this connection teachers sometimes try to link up a skill with sport, or engineering, or scouting; but while this may work very well for those pupils who are interested in these topics, it is unlikely to work for the pupil who is not interested in (say) sport and has no ambitions in that direction. Ideally, the teacher should exploit the pupil's own forte, something to which he is already committed, something entailing what is currently labelled 'ego-involvement', something at which he really 'fancies himself'. In practice, unfortunately, some pupils seem to fancy themselves at nothing susceptible of exploitation; they have no hobbies, little or no ambition, no enthusiasms; but it nevertheless appears that some such mode of behaviour must be found – even if at the outset it is no more than doing what his teacher demands and taking pleasure in the extrinsic rewards that (should) accrue.

Since this issue has been discussed already, I need not repeat it further. So far as complex skills are concerned, however, one point merits emphasis. Some skills take a long time to acquire, so that the satisfaction to be derived from accomplishment is a long way from the early attempts. Accordingly, in one way or another the teacher should try to arrange intermediate satisfactions. Wherever possible the skill should be taught in such a way that although it is not perfect it will nevertheless yield dividends in part-accomplishment. Illustrative of this approach is the present-day practice of teaching the piano-pupil to play real tunes very early in his tuition, and of showing handwork pupils how to make simple, but nevertheless genuine, objects long before they have learned all the techniques necessary for the skilled tradesman.

The Organisation of Movements

Successive Movements

A typical example of the organisation of successive movements is the operation of starting a car engine. The learner will have to check that his handbrake is on and that the gear-lever is in neutral, then switch on the ignition and press the starter-button. Each of these movements, let us suppose, can now be made in response to a verbal cue – even if at first the learner-driver has to be shown how. Suppose also that he has learned these verbal cues by heart, and in the right order: 'Check brake, check gear, switch, starter'. (This jingle will itself be a learned response to the situation in which he has to start the engine.) When ready to start, he will mutter, 'Check brake' (and check it), 'Check gear' (and check it), and so on.

At this stage there is a little series of habits, a series of responses (checking brake, checking gear, switching ignition, pressing starter), each of which is made to a verbal cue. At the final stage, however, the verbal instructions will have dropped out, and the movements will follow one another in succession, and without apparent pause. How this final stage is achieved can be explained in terms of the concepts used in connection with habit-training. As the one movement (say checking brake) comes to an end, the learner gives himself the verbal cue ('Check gear!') to the next movement, and proceeds to carry out that movement. If he does this many times, the state of affairs reached at the end of one movement will regularly precede the verbal cue to, and the actual making of, the next movement. But this is the pattern required for the establishment of a habit. In the present case the verbal cue will now act as *prompt* (or unconditional stimulus) for the required movement, and by regularly and immediately preceding that prompt, the state of affairs at the end of the preceding movement will become the cue (or conditional stimulus) to the following movement. Eventually the verbal instruction, like the food powder in Pavlov's experiment, can drop out. Moreover, the smoothing of the pattern can be explained by reference to the tendency of the response to be made closer and closer in time to the conditional stimulus. (In the Pavlov experiment, it will be recalled, the dog eventually salivated *before* the food powder was given; with time, the interval between CS and Response becomes shorter.) The dropping out of the verbal cue ('Check gear!') does not leave a gap; the response of checking gear closes up against the conditional stimulus, the state of affairs produced by the preceding movement – the 'movement-produced cue' as it is sometimes called.

This explanation indicates that in attempting to join together distinct movements the teacher will have to bear in mind and put into operation the conditions found necessary in connection with habit-training. In particular, the verbal cue, whether given by teacher to pupil, or by the pupil to himself, will have to be in contiguity with the tail-end of the preceding movement.

Simultaneous Movements

The child who is learning to play a piece of music on the piano may learn to play, first of all, with one hand, and then with the other; but eventually has to play with both hands at the same time. Patterns of movements, initially distinct, have to occur simultaneously.

One basic difficulty in the kind of case just illustrated is that when attention is given to the one hand, and what it is doing, the performance of the other hand suffers; but the more skilled the performances with the hands one at a time, the less the interference is likely to be. Another difficulty is that of keeping the movements of the two hands in the required relationship. In the example just cited a way out of that difficulty is implicit in what is required. Both hands must conform to the same time, the same rhythm – this third factor, of rhythm, serves to effect the necessary relationship between the two patterns of movement.

There appears to be widespread agreement that rhythm is a valuable aid to organisation generally, and learners sometimes are required to perform to music. This in turn nevertheless raises another difficulty: the slower learners in the group may be hurried to such an extent that they get lost and make more mistakes than they are capable of coping with, whereas the faster learners are held back. A similar point, which may be referred to as Speed and Accuracy, is discussed in a later section.

The Organisation of Cues

A high degree of skill, it was noted earlier, requires not only an organisation of movements but also an organisation of what were previously distinct cues. So long as the pianist reads the music note by note, he will not become skilled; the morse telegraphist who hears only single letters as he receives, and can send only by breaking down the spoken or written word into letters, will never be a skilled operator; the pupil who can write only word by word will never write fluently. If improvement is to be effected, the cue-units must increase in size or complexity. For the pianist, for example, finger-movement patterns must eventually be responses not to successive single printed notes but to printed phrases or more. How can this be achieved?

First, a negative point which is sometimes forgotten: even if the learner can take in, visually, a printed musical phrase, that complex cue will not evoke the corresponding complex response unless he has already learned to perform the complex behaviour in which it consists. The mere sight of the complex visual pattern does not serve to organise the distinct, 'small', responses previously made to that cue's parts. Many youthful guitarists, for example, learn to play not by reading staff notation but by following chord-patterns consisting of dots on a symbolic representation of the fret-board; the dots show where the finger-tips have to be placed. Such a learner may be able to place *one* finger on the required string and behind the required fret, and even be able to distinguish a variety of chord-patterns in print; but he will not be able to respond directly to these until he has first learned how to organise his finger movements. When he gets even two fingers right, the others may slip or lose pressure; or he may find that he cannot stretch his fingers wide enough; and so on. The organisation of cues remains useless until the movements (simultaneous in this case) themselves become organised. It is only when the previously distinct movements have become organised that the complex visual pattern can become a cue to the complex response.

Second, it appears that the organisation of cues is itself facilitated when the learner can already behave in the complex way the complex cue will require. Why this should be so is not difficult to suggest. Take the same example again. For the guitarist the printed material is, in effect, a set of *instructions for action*. Accordingly, what he notices on the sheet are likely to be the signs relating to what is already familiar to him, namely the actions he can already perform. Similarly, a printed melodic phrase is more likely to be recognised *en bloc*, once the pianist has, so to speak, 'the feel of it in his fingers'.

In making this latter point I do not mean, of course, that the learner will be able to ignore the constituent parts of the complex cue, as if in seeing a whole word or phrase he could ignore the letters constituting it. What I am referring to is a shift of emphasis. Instead of seeing each letter of a word, or each word of a phrase, or each note of a chord, more or less in isolation from the others, the skilled performer will see them in relation; and the 'them' are as necessary as is the 'relation'. What he will see is a pattern, but he must be able to distinguish patterns differing in even one element. My point was that this pattern-aspect of the material will become apparent more easily if the learner can already perform in the way which is to be a response to that aspect.

Third, recognition of the cue-pattern and ability to perform the complex behaviour are not enough. The latter has to become a *response* to the former. The complex fretting-movement has to become a response to the complex printed chord-pattern; the complex speech-performance has to become a response to the whole word or phrase; and so on. But this problem we have already considered, for once the complex cue is instantly recognisable and the complex behaviour is smooth, the problem is essentially the same as that of habit-training.

Breaking Down a Complex Skill

In the preceding sections we have been considering how movements, simultaneous and successive, can be organised or joined together; and how simple cues can be built into one complex cue. From what has been stated, however, it might be inferred that the requisite parts are already 'there', so to speak, waiting to be joined, whereas this is obviously not so: from the total skill which the trainer has in mind he has already selected, wittingly or not, a particular set of component pieces. The parts which the pupil has to learn at the outset, and subsequently join together, are the results of a previous break-down.

When the same method of teaching a skill has been used for many years that point may not be appreciated. The traditional 'parts' are treated as if they were the natural, inevitable, and only possible parts. Traditionally, the pupil learns to read by concentrating on single letters, to write by concentrating on the various 'strokes' handwriting requires, and so on. The fact that a mode of analysis is traditional does not, of course, indicate that it is necessarily inefficient. My point here is that a skill may be broken down in many different ways, some more useful than others, and that unless we realise this is so we may fail to select the system of parts most appropriate for learning and teaching.

For each skill (swimming, reading, handwriting, piano-playing, etc.) the teacher will have to consult the recent literature on the relevant topic, for it would be impossible to make even a summary of it here. All I shall venture to do is cite three general principles which should guide the teacher's practices.

First, the teacher should always be alive to the possibility of analysing the skill in a new way. If he tries to keep an open mind he is likely to find that a skill may become 'restructured' in the same way as did the diagrams in Chapter 7.

Second, from what he knows of the means, and difficulties, of joining movements or organising cues, he may be able to select a system of parts which can be joined more easily than can the parts he is already using. (Letter *names*, for example, as used in the alphabetic method of teaching reading, do not easily join to form spoken words). Also, if each part is as large as the learner can cope with, the number of joins will be minimised.

Third, and perhaps most important, he should try to select parts which are such that even the learning of the parts themselves produces satisfaction in the learner. I still recall the disappointment and boredom I experienced when, having been told I was going to learn to write, I did no more than cover pages with up-strokes, down-strokes, loops, and other meaningless squiggles; and the pleasure I had had in copying real words from books and newspapers at home, before I started school. 'Jam yesterday, jam tomorrow, but never jam today!'

The next three sections relate to the same basic problem.

Speed and Accuracy

A problem common to the acquisition of new movements, the organisation of movements, and the devising of suitable 'units' in the first place, is that of speed versus accuracy. If the learner is allowed to proceed very slowly (as when the model itself is demonstrated slowly), he is likely to make fewer mistakes, but his performance may fall short of the speed required.

Where accuracy is all-important, as in some crafts, and time is negligible, the solution is simple: there must be from the outset an all-out concentration on accuracy. A great many skills, however, call for both accuracy and speed, and there are few if any tasks where accuracy is of no importance at all. In such cases, where should the emphasis be placed? Does it matter which aspect is dealt with first?

Two experiments throw some light on that issue. Solley (48), in an experiment involving striking at a target, used three groups of subjects. One group was instructed to go all out for speed, another was to stress accuracy, and the third was to give equal emphasis to both. After the initial training period, in which the results indicated that these three different sets of instructions were being observed by the respective groups, all three groups were instructed to place equal emphasis on speed and accuracy. The results of this second part of the experiment showed that what happened there was influenced to a significant extent by the earlier period of training. Although now attending equally well to accuracy, the group which had been trained to emphasise speed still maintained speed, whereas the subjects who had first concentrated on accuracy now lost accuracy when required to work faster. In an experiment by Sharp (43) involving three groups of subjects who were required to work at different speeds, it was found that the greater the speed demanded, the greater was the number of errors per trial, and the greater also was the number of trials needed. That part of the findings is in accord with common expectation: but although the fast-working group needed more trials, yet less total time was required for complete learning. (A trial for the fast workers was, of course, shorter in time than was a trial for the slow workers.) Apparently the subjects who were obliged to begin at a fair speed could improve their accuracy in a shorter total time than those who began by concentrating on accuracy could improve their speed. All the subjects were, of course, trying to be both accurate and fast.

The extent to which the results of these laboratory experiments can be applied to skills generally is, of course, debatable; but they do suggest that, when speed is to be of considerable importance, the learner should be made to work fairly fast from the outset. It seems that accuracy gained at low speeds does not readily transfer to high speeds, although the leaner who begins at a fairly high speed can improve in accuracy. Where both speed and accuracy are important, however, the evidence suggests that the learner should stress both from the beginning.

Whole and Part Learning

In the discussion of Recall it was suggested that some form of Part Learning is usually preferable to Whole Learning – unless the material is relatively simple or the learner is experienced in the kind of task to be undertaken. Very much the same point can be made in connection with skills. Indeed, it has been presupposed in some of the foregoing sections. Organisation presupposes that part-skills will be learned, and then joined; and the section on Training in New Movements implied that these movements would be relatively simple.

Some writers [1] have nevertheless suggested that while part learning may be appropriate for the organisation of successive movements, yet it may be inappropriate for simultaneous movements. The examples often cited seem to imply, however, that what is meant is that in some skills the learner should be advised against dividing up the skill in a *longitudinal* way – such as practising with one hand at a time when learning to juggle two or more balls. (Indeed, it is difficult to see just how he *could* practise with one hand at a time.) But it is possible that he might divide up the skill into time-intervals – that is, practise with both hands a small segment of the skill.

Distribution of Practice

Some distribution of practice, as opposed to massed practice, appears to be as desirable in the organisation of movements as it is elsewhere.

Interference and Transfer

In the chapter on Recall it was noted that when two tasks are similar, and come close together in time, one may interfere with the other. The same observation can be made of skills. When we have just been using one sort of hand-tool, a chisel

[1] Maier (30) for example.

for example, it is often difficult, at first, to switch to the use of another, such as a tea-knife. Again, it may be more difficult to teach a boy to swim if he has already been learning without guidance than if he is starting from scratch; some of the movements he has acquired may interfere with the new movements the trainer wishes him to make. In some ways this is the same sort of problem as arose in Habit-breaking.

On the other hand, it is observable also that in learning one skill we may be thereby helped to acquire another. From the one we may 'pick up tips' which can be transferred to the other.

Just how and in what circumstances one skill will help, or will hinder, the learning of another is obviously a question of considerable practical importance; and because of its complexity it has been allocated a whole chapter. All that need be said here is that interference, and likewise helpful transfer, is usually at its height in the early stages of training. Accordingly, it is in the early stages that very careful supervision is required.

Summary

This chapter has been concerned only with general conditions, conditions common to a great variety of skills. A summary of these will therefore be general indeed. It may nevertheless be useful to indicate in one section some of the most important points.

At the outset the teacher must specify the nature of the performance required, and specify it as a response to some specific kind of situation.

Once this is done, the performance or skill required may be seen as falling into one of four rather different categories. The learner may already be able to behave in the required way, but has to behave in that way in response to a different kind of situation. This is essentially the problem of habit-training. But the required movement may be new for the learner. If so, it may be taught *en bloc*, or divided into parts which have to be organised eventually. Further, if a high degree of skill is to be achieved, what were once distinct cues must themselves become organised.

A new movement, to be obtained *en bloc*, may be induced by means of a model, or a verbal instruction, or some combination of these. A special difficulty here is that the model may have to be slowed down; it may therefore cease to be a good model. Nor is the task complete even when the model is well imitated or the instruction is closely followed; the new behaviour-form has still to be tied to the cue of the instance to be effected. 'Putting the learner through the motions' is seldom effective, almost certainly because he is not practising what he will be required to do, and may indeed be making contrary movements. In some cases, however, physical inhibition of gross movements may be useful. Where it is necessary to criticise the learner, criticism should be restricted at first to the grossest errors.

Knowledge of results is usually necessary for improvement, though that depends upon the learner's levels of aspiration, and upon his ability to deduce the modifications that are required. If he is to continue in his task, however, he will need intermediate satisfactions, and the teacher should strive to find *something* to praise from time to time. The trainer should try to analyse the skill into parts which not only can be joined without too much difficulty, but also are such that their accomplishment is itself a source of satisfaction. Also, when the older learner becomes discouraged he may be told, truthfully, that the acquisition of skills has ups and downs, and plateaux. Where the learner has to choose between observing his own movements and observing the results of his movements, he must generally choose the latter – though help may be given by the trainer in indicating what modifications of movement are needed.

The same bias towards observation of the environment, rather than the movements themselves, is desirable in connection with the cue, or target. The learner must 'keep his eye on the ball', and not upon his swing.

Distribution of Practice is as relevant here as it is in Habit-training; and consolidation between practice periods seems to occur here too.

In organising successive movements, the verbal or other cue to one movement must be kept contiguous with the tail-end of the previous movement, so that that cue can be dropped and the tail-end of the previous movement will become the cue to the beginning of the next movement. Organisation of simultaneous movements is likely to be most effective when the part-movements themselves are very well known; and in some instances rhythm is an aid to such organisation.

A high degree of skill requires that cues, as well as movements, should be organised. But these complexes of cues will be useful only if the complexes of movements have already been established. And once they have been established, the learner will have to practise making them as responses to the complex cues.

Where speed is of considerable importance, the learner should begin with a fairly high speed of performance, and be allowed to gain in accuracy at that high speed; but where accuracy is at least as important as speed, he should begin by paying attention to both. Negatively expressed, initial concern with accuracy only is rarely effective.

The whole skill and also its parts should be fitted into and made a constituent part of the pupil's established activities.

10 · Teaching for Transfer

What is Transfer?

Many school subjects are justified not only on the ground that they are of direct value to the pupil, now or later, but also on the ground that in learning them he thereby learns other things. Mathematics, for example, is sometimes said to train the pupil to think clearly; nature study to develop his powers of observation; team games to foster a social sense; and so forth.

This issue – whether by learning to do one thing we are thereby making it easier for us to do something else – is customarily discussed under the head of Transfer of Training, or simply Transfer. But our learning to do one thing might, of course, make it *less* easy to do something else. The term 'transfer' covers that possibility too. If the learning of something, T_1 – which might be a habit, a skill, a topic or indeed anything at all, facilitates the subsequent performance of something else, T_2, there is said to by 'positive transfer' from T_1 to T_2. If, on the other hand, the learning of T_1 makes T_2 less easy to perform, there is said to be 'negative transfer' from T_1 to T_2. And if the learning of T_1 makes no difference at all to the subsequent performance of T_2, there is said to be 'zero transfer' or 'indeterminate transfer' from T_1 to T_2.

There is a further refinement. The terms 'positive' and 'negative' refer only to the direction of the transfer, but its amount is also important. If the amount is large, in either direction, the transfer is 'high'; if small, in either direction, it is 'low'. 'High negative transfer from playing the banjo to playing the guitar' would mean that playing the banjo had a very bad effect on one's subsequent playing of the guitar. 'Low positive transfer from Latin to French' would mean that by learning Latin one was helping oneself, just a little, in French.

These, however, are no more than illustrations of what the terms mean: their content might well be false. In general, all that has been said in the last two paragraphs comes to no more than a definition of terms. Such definition is necessary in answer to the question of what transfer is, but we have still to find out the facts. Does transfer occur at all? If it sometimes does, under what conditions? What direction does it take, and to what extent, in particular instances?

Facts of this sort are patently worth knowing. We cannot hope to train pupils to deal with each and every specific situation they will meet when they leave school, and much of our teaching rests on the assumption that by learning certain topics now they will transfer something of what they have learned to the world outside. Even within school the issue is important. If there is reasonably high positive transfer from T_1 to T_2 (that is, when T_1 is learned before T_2), but not from T_2 to T_1 (when T_2 is learned first), it will be advantageous to teach T_1 before T_2 rather than conversely. If there is negative transfer from one topic to another, it will be helpful to know the conditions in which the effect can be minimised. If we hope for positive transfer, what can we do to make it positive, and as high as possible?

Unfortunately, facts that are worth knowing are not always available; and although there have been very many experiments on Transfer, yet at present few of the cautiously established findings have a clear and unambiguous reference to the complex tasks of the teacher in school. (One reason for this is that in order to obtain clearcut results it is often necessary to deal, at first, with very restricted aspects of a problem.) A few pieces of information are nevertheless better than none, and while we await the results of further research we can make the most of what we already know. Indeed, as I shall try to show in this chapter, Transfer is not a unique phenomenon, distinct from learning, but can be envisaged in terms of it, so that we can bring to bear on this problem a considerable amount of information we already have about learning generally.

'Types' of Transfer

Although all cases of transfer can be fitted into the general picture given in the last section, yet it is customary to distinguish various 'types' of it; and before we begin to look at explanations of transfer it will be convenient to consider what types of transfer there are.

Learning-to-Learning Transfer

In an educational context 'transfer' means often, not simply the effect of our learning T_1 on our performance of T_2, but the effect of our learning T_1 on our *learning* T_2. For example, will learning Latin make it easier for us to *learn* French? Of course, we cannot possibly experiment to find out what our learning of French would have been like if we had *not* learned Latin first. In no case can we make the learner start again from scratch. The most we can do is compare the performances of two different groups of learners, groups matched for previous attainment, intelligence, and so forth, so that we can discover whether the group which first learned Latin shows any superiority over the other group in the subsequent learning of French. In the interval between learning Latin and learning French, of course, both groups will be doing *something*; and the group which did not learn Latin will of necessity have been doing something else. All we can do in this connection is note carefully what both groups were doing, and if possible control what they do.

Stimulus Generalisation

The dog in the Pavlov experiment quoted earlier (p. 65) was trained with a buzzer of a particular pitch, but subsequently it was found that the animal would salivate in response to buzzers of different pitch. A rat, trained to make an approach-response to a card marked with a square of a particular dimension, and to make an avoidance-response to a card marked with a circle of a particular diameter, will subsequently make these responses to squares and circles of different sizes.[1] This sort of phenomenon is usually called 'stimulus generalisation', the term suggesting that a response made to some particular, specific, stimulus will 'generalise' to other similar stimuli.

Transposition

Typical of this type of transfer is the phenomenon examined in an early experiment by Bingham (3). Chicks were trained to peck at grain on a 6-inch circle, and to avoid a 4-inch circle – where the grain was glued to the pattern. Subsequently it was found that the chicks, confronted by a pair consisting of a 4-inch circle and a 3-inch circle, would choose the 4-inch circle. They now chose the very circle they had previously learned to avoid; but in a sense they were doing the same thing – choosing the *larger* circle of the pair. Other experiments of a similar kind have shown that the subject will continue to choose (for example) the *darker* shade of grey, although in doing so he is rejecting the very shade he previously learned to choose. The reader familiar with the phrase, 'transposing a tune', will see why the term 'transposition' is used here: instead of reacting to the characters of the elements of the situation, the learner reacts to some sort of relationship between them. (Or at least so it seems.)

Mediation

The term 'mediation' is sometimes applied to instances of transfer when it appears that the learning of T_1 is of help in the performance of T_2, if T_1 and T_2 are each related to some concept. This concept 'mediates' between T_1 and T_2. For example, if I have learned to stop a window rattling by pushing a little piece of folded paper between window and window-frame, and now I am bothered by a door which blows open, the concept 'Wedge' may mediate, and I now apply to the blowing-door situation some of the responses I previously made to the rattling window.

[1] More detailed accounts of the experiments quoted in this chapter will be found in (6), (25), (27), (36).

Learning How to Learn

Several experiments have shown that subjects who are set to learn lists of nonsense-syllables (like 'rop', siz', 'bir' . . .) become quicker, with practice, in their memorising, even when no two lists have syllables in common.

Rats which are set to run mazes become quicker in finding their way through mazes, even when no two mazes are the same. And in Harlow's (18) famous experiment with monkeys it was found that although at first his subjects took many trials to choose the correct (rewarded) member of a pair of objects (the monkey having to be rewarded several times, or punished several times, for taking the right, or wrong, object of that pair), yet as the number of such pairs was increased the subjects became quicker and quicker in learning. Finally, after considerable practice in being rewarded or punished, one trial was enough. One punishment for choosing the wrong object of a pair was sufficient for consistent subsequent choice of the other object; and one reward for choosing the right object was enough for consistent subsequent choice of that object. Harlow found similar effects for children.

Since results of this kind seemed to indicate that what the subjects were doing was improving their methods of learning, phenomena of this sort are often subsumed under the head of Learning How to Learn.

Perhaps we should not read too much into the names used to categorise these types. Most cases can nevertheless be fitted into one or other of them, and with this general picture in mind we may now consider various ways in which transfer has been explained. Patently we must find some explanation of it, for how else are we to gain insight into what we must do if transfer is to be promoted?

The following sections deal with this latter issue in a more or less historical way, because although some of the earlier views are not based on facts, many people still hold and often express them. It may therefore be salutary to see what they are.

Formal Discipline

Usually the Theory of Formal Discipline is expressed, when it is made explicit at all, in terms of Faculty Theory (see p. 158). Thus it might be asserted, or implied, that mathematics trains the Reason, the memorising of poems or lists of dates develops the Memory, and so on. As I remarked before, however,[1] statements expressed in terms of Faculty Theory are not susceptible of test at all. To be verified they must be translated out of faculty-language. To say that mathematics trains the Reason seems to be equivalent to saying that learning mathematics will improve reasoning generally; that is, one will improve in dealing with *any* task calling for reasoning. That hypothesis can be tested. All we need do to invalidate it is show that there are tasks, calling for reasoning, which are done no better despite one's training in mathematics. Similarly for the Memory, the Judgment, and so on.

Once the hypothesis is expressed in this way it becomes almost self-evidently false. Common observation indicates that while the student of mathematics sometimes thinks more clearly about mathematics, yet he may improve not at all in his thinking about other issues such as religion or politics. Obviously false or not, the hypothesis has been subjected to experimental tests, and all of these have made it abundantly clear that transfer of this 'wholesale' variety does not take place. One of the earliest of these was the memorising-marathon undertaken by William James – who found that after committing to memory many lines of *Paradise Lost* his subsequent attempts to memorise still more lines were no better. Indeed James found that his later performance was rather worse – a result he attributed to fatigue. Admittedly some of these early experiments lacked the necessary controls; and later investigations, like those exemplified in the previous section, have shown that transfer certainly occurs. To return, however, to our historical account: although small positive and negative transfers were observed even in some of the early inquiries, many of these

[1] See footnote to p. 159.

tended to be overlooked – probably because the results were so very different from what the Theory of Formal Discipline implied. One of the results of this experimental debunking of the 'wholesale' nature of transfer, as implied by that theory, is described in the next section.

Specificity of Learning

As one might have expected (with wisdom after the event), one of the consequences of the invalidation of the wholesale view expressed in the Theory of Formal Discipline was the emergence of an equally extreme theory in the opposite direction. To risk an oversimplification, it said that learning is always specific; you learn precisely what you learn, that and nothing more.

Since, as the examples already cited prove, transfer does in fact occur, it might seem that this 'Specificity Theory' must be invalid; but the matter is not quite so simple, and I shall try to show later in this chapter that that theory is not so mistaken as at first it seems.

To return to our historical review: whether the Specificity Theory (as we may call it) did effect changes in educational practice, or whether it merely gave support to changes that were taking place anyway, is difficult to say, but at any rate, some of the changes that were in accord with it would almost certainly be regarded, nowadays, as being in the right direction. Drudgery could no longer be justified (by those holding the new theory) by reference to training in Perseverance, Memory, Patience, and so forth, and many tasks of no obvious intrinsic merit disappeared from the curriculum. The emphasis now tended to be on the child's interest, the topic's utility or aesthetic quality, and the like. Moreover, if T_2 cannot be learned merely by one's previously learning T_1, but T_2 is worth acquiring, patently T_2 itself must be taught. (This conclusion, if not the argument supporting it, is in line with more recent findings; even when there is positive transfer from T_1 to T_2, the transfer is rarely if ever perfect, and T_2 can be acquired more efficiently by our learning T_2 directly than by our awaiting some transfer from T_1).

Desirable educational effects of a theory nevertheless do not prove that theory's validity; and as was remarked a moment ago, transfer certainly does take place. There may be no wholesale transfer, as implied by the Theory of Formal Discipline, but neither is there no transfer at all, as the Specificity Theory seems to say.[1] The truth is either somewhere between, or on a different level.

Common Components

Everyday observation of children in school suggests that the learning of one topic is unlikely to have much if any effect upon another if the two topics are quite unlike. One would scarcely expect the study of classics to have an effect upon the pupil's performance on the football field. We should expect an effect only if the two topics were similar in some way. The learning of formal English grammar might be expected to have a positive effect on the learning of a foreign language; basic arithmetical procedures might be expected to affect the learning of algebra. Also, if the two topics were similar we might on occasion expect a negative effect; the learning of the one topic might confuse him in his learning of a similar but not identical topic.

To say that two topics are similar is, of course, to imply that they have something in common; and a view of Transfer, based on this notion of common components, was advanced explicitly by Thorndike and Woodworth towards the beginning of the century. It said, in effect, that transfer would occur if the two topics had components in common, the amount of transfer being a function of the number of common components. To take a simple, if obvious, example: if a pupil has learned certain addition facts (such as $9 + 7 = 16$), and these particular addition facts are involved in multiplying by a two-figure number, to that extent his having learned to add will facilitate his multiplying. Also, the greater the number of addition-facts he has learned, the greater will be the help he gets in this type of multiplication-problem.

---

[1] '*Seems* to say' – because, as I hinted at the beginning of this section and shall show later, the theory is not so mistaken as some extreme statements of it suggest.

The example just cited manifests transfer – in the sense in which 'transfer' is customarily defined, and was defined at the beginning of this chapter. It is nevertheless in accord also with Specificity Theory, for the example does not presuppose that the child's having learned certain addition facts will help him to find the two products which have to be added; it implies only that he will be helped when he is adding them. The transfer depends upon his doing in the second case something which is exactly the same as what he did in the earlier case. Indeed, the name sometimes given to the Thorndike-Woodworth hypothesis – the Theory of Identical Elements – makes that point explicit. Whether such instances should be referred to as cases of transfer at all is, of course, a verbal problem, but as I have just said, they are in accord with customary usage of the term. The student who has not given much thought to the matter may nevertheless feel somewhat disappointed. It is transpicuous that T_1 will facilitate T_2 if T_1 is itself part of T_2. It is almost like saying that our learning to strike red-headed matches will 'transfer' to our striking blue-headed matches. This may be plain, but it is so plain as to seem banal, a come-down from what we might have expected transfer to be.

The Theory of Common Components, however, is not quite so simple as it might seem. To continue our last example: in learning to add, the pupil will have learned not only certain specific number-facts but also certain procedures, such as 'carrying'; and one would expect such a procedure also to facilitate his adding within the complex multiplication. This suggests that the common components may not necessarily be bits and pieces of the given material but also procedures used to deal with it. In fact, the Thorndike-Woodworth Theory did refer not only to the material but also to procedures or methods, principles, and even attitudes. Even with this extension, however, the fundamental point remains: transfer is dependent upon common components of one sort or another. And that point is basic to subsequent theories also. They are more precise, but all of them presuppose that transfer is dependent upon something common to T_1 and T_2.

The Bruce-Wylie Laws

At the end of the last section I implied that the theories so far considered were insufficiently precise – a view which can be justified by our looking at the types of transfer already described. Although the Theory of Common Components may well be valid, it is not obvious in a given case just what it is that has to be common. Nor does the mere reference to common components indicate what direction the transfer will take. If 'common components' applies to transfer generally, how does it come about that transfer is sometimes positive, sometimes negative?

That question is answered by what are sometimes called the Bruce-Wylie Laws – after the two investigators whose findings they embrace (5), (56). The first law says that the *amount* of transfer depends upon the degree of similarity of the stimuli involved in the two situations (the situations of T_1 and T_2). The second says that the *direction* of the transfer depends upon the compatibility of the responses to these situations.

These laws, which will be illustrated in a moment, make explicit several things left unsaid by earlier theories. First, they distinguish clearly between the two basic aspects of learning, namely situation and response. Second, in doing so they imply that transfer consists essentially in *doing* something in T_2 which was first learned in T_1; in other words, transfer consists essentially in the carrying over of some *response* from T_1 to T_2. Third, the laws distinguish between, by referring separately to, amount and direction of transfer: the amount of transfer is related to the situations, the direction to the responses. But the laws also raise new problems. Often it is well nigh impossible to make precise measurements of 'degree of similarity of stimuli'; and 'compatibility of responses' is not always easily specificable in particular instances. As I shall try to show later, however, these difficulties are not crucial from the teacher's point of view. We may therefore concentrate on the more basic issues. In particular, we may interpret the first law as meaning that if there is *some* similarity between the two situations, there is likely to *be* transfer of one kind or another; its amount we may ignore meantime.

Here is a simple example which incorporates that point. Suppose that a child has learned to write to dictation words like 'cuff', 'muff', and 'puff', but so far has not tried to spell words with a similar sound but a different spelling – like 'rough' and 'enough'. In such cases the situation is the word-as-heard; the response is his writing the word. If, now, he tries to write the word 'enough' in response to his own dictation, and what he has already learned about 'cuff' and 'muff' affect what he now writes, he will write ' – uff'; and in that case we should speak of negative transfer. On the other hand, if the word he decides to write (for the first time) is 'stuff', and the same past experience affects him, he will write ' – uff', and we should speak of positive transfer.

That example is in accord with, and illustrates, the two Bruce-Wylie Laws. 'Similarity of stimuli involved in the situations' implies that the two situations have a common component.[1] In the instance in which there was transfer (positive) from 'cuff' to 'stuff', the common situation-component is the sound common to these two words-as-heard, namely the sound of 'uff'. And the corresponding writing-responses to that component may be said to be compatible, for they are exactly the same, namely writing 'uff'. On the other hand, in the instance in which there was transfer (negative) from 'cuff' to 'enough' (written 'enuff') there is again a common situation-component, namely the sound common to these two words-as-heard, but now we may say that the writing-responses are incompatible, in the sense that they ought to be different, namely writing 'uff' and writing 'ough'. Whether there will be any transfer at all (irrespective of sign) seems to depend upon whether the situations have a common

---

[1] The common component may be a compound of several identical stimuli: that is, stimuli each of which has an identical opposite number in the other situation. Or on two stimuli may be identical, but they may be similar: that is, one stimulus in the one situation may have something in common with one stimulus in the other situation, and another stimulus in the one situation may have something in common with a stimulus in the other situation. The term 'common component' covers a variety of possibilities.

component, are similar. The direction of the transfer seems to depend upon whether the responses to that component, in the two situations, *ought* to be the same or *ought* to be different. If they are, and ought to be, the same (as in 'cuff' – 'stuff'), the transfer will be called positive; and if they are the same but ought not to be (as in 'cuff' – 'enough'), the transfer will be called negative.

That the sharing of a component, the similarity between the two *situations*, cannot determine the direction of the transfer, and relates only to the issue of whether there will be any transfer at all, may be illustrated by our focusing attention on one aspect of our example. Not only was there similarity inside each case; over the two cases there was a common component, an element which was exactly the same in both. The sound common to 'cuff' and 'stuff' is the same sound as is common to 'cuff' and 'enough'; but there was positive transfer in the one case and negative transfer in the other, and so it cannot be the common situation-component, the 'similarity of situations', which determines the direction the transfer will take. The direction, as already noted, is a function of the responses, not of the situations.

Our example, as I said in introducing it, says nothing of 'degree of similarity' of stimuli nor of 'degree of compatibility' of responses, and so does not illustrate all that the Bruce-Wylie Laws assert. But it adds two points they do not make. Having argued that 'similarity' of stimuli presupposes a *common* situation-component, I was able to speak in terms not merely of 'similarity' but of 'identity'. The sounds of the whole words, 'cuff', 'stuff', and 'enough' are only similar, but they have an aspect in common, something which is the *same* in all. This way of viewing the matter, I suggest, solves by restructuring them the problems of 'degree of similarity' and 'degree of compatibility'. A fundamental aspect of the first problem is that any two situations may be 'similar' in several different ways. 'Van' is like 'ran' in having three letters, in having two letters in common, and in having a common sound; but in some ways 'van' is like 'truck', for both are nouns and have similar meanings. Clearly we cannot say which word, 'ran' or 'truck' is *more* like 'van' until we have specified the criterion of similarity. The solution suggested by our example is that instead of speaking merely of 'similarity' we *specify what is identical* in or common to the situations. (A pedagogical advantage of that solution is noted in a later section.) Further, by reference to the specified common situation-component we can speak not merely of the 'compatibility' of the responses to the situations as wholes, but, where appropriate, of the *identity* of the responses to the components the situations have in common.

The view just expressed cannot, of course, claim to be a novel one, for it can be inferred from our considering at once the Bruce-Wylie Laws and the Thorndike-Woodworth Theory of Common Components. This abstraction from the two theories nevertheless seems to have greater precision than is achieved by either theory alone. Indeed, as I shall argue in the following section, still greater precision, and so greater utility, can be achieved if we make use of the Specificity Theory also.

A Theory of Transfer in Terms of Learning

In this section I shall try to show that transfer can be envisaged in terms of the concepts already elaborated to deal with learning.

As was illustrated in the discussion of Understanding, any situation may appear as one of several possible kinds, the kind it appears to be being a function of the particular feature (probably complex) which is forceful. (See again, in illustration, the diagrams of Chapter 7.) Suppose now that the learner is faced with a situation which in many respects is new to him. Although he has met many problems involving addition, subtraction, multiplication, and division, yet never before has he encountered a problem quite like this:

'What number exceeds 12 by 4?'

Now although this problem is new for him, yet if he perceives it at all it will be of *some* kind for him; *some* feature will be for him its forceful feature, the feature to which he gives his attention. For the moment let us not say what that feature is. Instead, let us

H

call it simply, F_f. That is to say, F_f is the feature which in fact has force for the learner in question. Suppose also that F_f is already the cue of some established instance of learning; whenever F_f, in any situation, get his attention (has force), he will respond in the way peculiar to that established instance. Then in the present situation he will respond in that way.[1] But, irrespective of the nature of that established instance of learning, this will be a case of transfer, because what he now does in the present situation is being affected by what he has already learned. T_1 is affecting T_2. Moreover, it is in accord with the Thorndike-Woodworth Theory and the first Bruce-Wylie Law. There is a common component, namely F_f; and it is a component of the situations, their basis of similarity.

But what direction will the transfer take? Suppose that the feature which is forceful (F_f) for our young learner is the phrase, '12 by 4', and that (as sometimes does happen) a phrase of that form has become for him a cue to multiplication. Then his response will be his saying, 'Forty-eight!' If, again, such a phrase, by being part of the longer expression, 'Divide 12 by 4', has become a cue to division, he will answer, 'Three!' If, however, he attends not only to the two numbers but also to the partly obscured phrase, 'exceeds by', and if, in accord with his previous learning of the meaning of the words, that phrase is already a cue to addition, he will respond by saying 'Sixteen!'

The first two answers are wrong (negative transfer) and only the third answer is right (positive transfer); but if the direction of the transfer has to be not only observed, but also explained, we must look at more than the mere results.

Transfer occurred, of course, in all three cases; and it occurred in so far as the forceful feature, F_f, of the present situation was for the learner the cue of some established instance of learning – the instance differing from one case to another. But the direction of the transfer depended upon something else, now made explicit.

---

[1] This is a matter of logical necessity, for if he does not respond to the present situation in that way, either F_f is not its forceful feature (he has misunderstood the situation), or else F_f is not the cue of some established instance of learning – both of which contingencies are out of accord with what we supposed.

It was positive when the feature F_f, which was in fact forceful, *should* have been the forceful feature; that is, when it could be said that the learner had *understood* the present situation; that is, when F_f was the *cue* (intended) of the present situation. To include the point made in the previous paragraph: we get positive transfer when the forceful feature of the present situation *is* its cue and when it is also the cue of some established instance of learning.

It was negative when F_f, which was in fact the forceful feature, should *not* have been the forceful feature; that is, when it could be said that the learner had *misunderstood* the present situation; that is, when F_f was *not* the cue (intended) of the present situation. We get negative transfer, then, when the forceful feature of the present situation is not *its* cue, and when that feature is the cue of some established instance of learning.

In elaborating this view of transfer I have, of course, referred to only one example; but that point is irrelevant to the main argument because the example was no more than an illustration of a purely logical deduction. The argument nevertheless is not yet complete, because all I have shown so far is that when the conditions stated in the last two paragraphs hold good, there will occur events which are cases of transfer. I have not shown that these conditions will suffice to cover *all* types of transfer. Such a demonstration would be very lengthy, if possible at all, and so I shall rest content to show that the view described above can cover the types already noted earlier in this chapter.[1] Further, even if it could be demonstrated that these conditions do cover all types, I should still have to show that the conditions not only were sufficient but also were necessary. That demonstration would also be somewhat lengthy, and I shall not attempt it here, but some of the parts of the necessary argument will be mentioned here and there in the following sections.

The essence of the view I have been proposing in this section

---

[1] I say, 'if possible at all', because 'What is Transfer?' is a verbal problem, and I doubt if at present there is sufficient agreement to warrant my abstracting a definition acceptable by everyone. I shall not attempt to prove the point here, but I believe that if we accept what the majority of psychologists *imply* when they speak of 'transfer', the condition referred to above can be shown to be all-embracing, on purely logical grounds alone.

is that any case of transfer is in effect no more than one would expect within any specified instance of learning. If the forceful feature of the present situation is indeed the cue of some established instance of learning, of necessity the learner will respond to the present situation as he responds in that established instance, for the reason that the present case *is* a case of that very instance.[1] In general, the present situation, which is said to exhibit transfer, may be seen as no more than a late situation in the series of situations any instance of learning involves.

Such a view is in effect a restatement of Specificity Theory, because what I have suggested is that there is no such thing as transfer *in addition to* learning. What we customarily choose to call transfer is no more than is implied by the logic of learning itself. Why the present view is not quite the same as the usual expression of Specificity Theory can be answered more simply if we turn aside for a moment and ask another question. If transfer is simply what we should expect of any instance of learning, why did transfer ever become a special issue? Why do many textbooks still devote a special chapter to it (as indeed I have done here)? Why not simply include it in the discussion of learning, without even using the word 'transfer'? One answer is that despite vast improvements in psychological experiment and theory since the days of Faculty Psychology, many of the concepts then employed are still with us. Several psychologists have made this point in other connections, and it may well be true of this issue also. But, I suggest, another reason is that many a so-called case of transfer does not *obviously* come within an instance of learning; such cases *look* different, and so are given a special name. And one reason of their not being obviously in accord with some instance of learning seems to be that, in the case in question, we have failed to realise that that instance was indeed established. The pupil has learned more than we imagined we had taught him, more than we gave him credit for. Some examples supporting these suggestions will

---

[1] Strictly, I need not include reference to the forcefulness, in the present situation, of the cue of the established instance, because if that instance is in fact established, its cue will be forceful in every case of that instance. I retain the reference merely for emphasis.

appear in the following sections; for the moment we may return to the point that the present view is not quite the same as the usual statement of Specificity Theory. If certain cases of learning are not obviously cases of learning, there is no logical objection to our *calling* them cases of transfer, for they may well *look* different; and if we do apply the term to such cases, it would then be illogical to say there is no such thing as transfer. That is why, instead of denying the occurrence of transfer, I said there is no transfer 'in addition to' learning. It belongs within learning, and is strictly not even a special case of it; we learn what we learn, though it often *seems* that we learn more.

Finally, why call this view a 'theory'? In accord with the definition of that term earlier in this book (p. 51) I have given it that name because it does not derive from experiment, nor does it propose hypotheses which might be tested; it is only a way of looking at the events customarily called transfer-phenomena. It is nevertheless an explanation of these events, in envisaging them as particular cases of something more general, namely learning. Also, it implies that we need not look for special hypotheses in connection with these phenomena: if transfer is after all within the area of learning, we can apply to it what we already know about learning generally – the conditions governing understanding and misunderstanding, remembering, and so on.

Application to 'Types' of Transfer

Stimulus Generalisation

In the case cited earlier (p. 211), it will be recalled, the dog was trained to salivate with a buzzer of a certain kind, but subsequently salivated in response to buzzers of rather different pitch. If the term 'stimulus generalisation' is no more than the name given to that sort of phenomenon, as just described, exception can scarcely be taken to it. It nevertheless suggests not just that the dog was *trained* on a buzzer of pitch P_1, and subsequently responded to buzzers of pitches P_2, P_3, and so on, but also that initially the dog *learned* to respond only to buzzers of pitch P_1, and subsequently (so to speak) 'did some generalising'. It would be naïve to assume, however, that subjects always learn precisely what we intend or what we suppose they have learned; they may well have learned rather less or rather more. How then should we find out precisely what the subject had learned in the first place? So far as our ascertaining the nature of the cue is concerned (our present problem), we should have to alter the situation in various ways and observe the variations which still elicited the specified response (such as salivation), and those which did not. From such observations we could then infer what the cue in fact was – namely whatever is common to the variations (of situation) which elicited the response in question.[1] If we now apply this point to the Pavlov experiment, and observe that salivation is elicited when the pitch of the buzzer is varied, we must infer that the cue to salivation was *not* a buzzer of specific pitch but was something common to all these sounds – a sort of 'buzz-quality'. Likewise, in the square-and-circle experiment also noted earlier (p. 211), we should have to infer that the cue to the approach-response was *not* a square of specific dimension but was something common to all the squares but lacking in all the circles – squareness, perhaps, or even mere rectilineality. In general, the *actual* cue to the specified response may be more general and less detailed than the experimenter has taken for granted; the subject of the experiment may have been less discriminating than was supposed.

Here is the essence of the argument. The 'generalisation' thesis presupposes that, in the initial instance of learning, the cue was 'ungeneralised', or less general than what is common to the situations to which the subject now makes the response in question. The thesis is therefore suspect unless that presupposition is tested. But the situations which could indicate that the cue was indeed more general than the 'generalisation' thesis presupposes are themselves the very situations cited to support that thesis. Patently

---

[1] This relates to the logical point (Part One) that full confidence in a specified instance's having occurred can be achieved only when there is an infinite series of situations sharing, and sharing only, the cue.

we cannot have it both ways. In so far as variation of the response-eliciting situation is necessary to the ascertainment of the cue to that response, the 'generalisation' thesis becomes untenable.[1]

If, then, we accept that the cue, initially, was more general than the subject was given credit for, cases of stimulus generalisation can be fitted into the theory outlined in the last section. Even in the so-called transfer situations the subject is still doing what he learned to do in the first place. It only looks different because the observation of the initial instance was faulty – largely because of the set-up of the initial training-situations, particularly their relative invariability.

Transposition

The argument here is very similar to that sustained in the previous section. Here also we cannot know what the cue to the response was until we vary the situation. If the subject still chooses the larger circle, or the darker grey, this suggests that this is what he learned in the first place. Moreover, there is nothing very surprising about such a phenomenon. Choice of the specific shade (as contrasted with the darker shade) is the more sophisticated performance. And if the subject is indeed doing now what he did in the initial training-sessions, the very notion of Transposition becomes redundant.

Mediation

This type is more complex. In some cases the so-called mediating concept may have occurred to the subject before he met the transfer-situation, but we may not appreciate the point until we observe his tackling of some new situation. The mere fact that a concept is common to, or mediates between, two ostensibly different situations does not itself prove that the concept did not

---

[1] There is, admittedly, a complication. In those cases in which it is relevant and possible to measure the *intensity* of the response (as by observing the rate of flow of saliva), it appears that the intensity of the response tends to decrease in accord with the extent of the variation of the (ostensible) stimulus. As the pitch becomes less and less near to the original pitch, the intensity of the salivation decreases. That finding could be interpreted in terms of a highly complex cue, but does not, I believe, affect the main argument.

occur until the second situation was met. For example, the subject may conceive of Quadrilaterality (though probably without his having that name for it) without having to experience all possible types of quadrilateral; parellelograms might well be enough. Likewise, a fairly adequate concept of Dog might be achieved although the subject had met only a few dogs. If 'dogginess' is shared by all dogs, and is a character of any dog, it is at least conceivable that the subject will spot that feature after only one encounter with one dog. And if Quadrilaterality, or Dogginess, was the feature to which the subject responded in the earlier situations, it is for him the cue of that situation. And if in fact he has learned to respond in the required way to that cue, he will respond in the same way to the second situation, because it also contains that same cue.

On the other hand, there may well be cases in which the concept, or common feature, is not apparent to the subject until he meets the later situation. The necessary abstraction may not occur until this later situation arises. If, however, that abstraction is achieved, the subject will thereby re-envisage, re-understand, the previous situations. Indeed, it is only in so far as he does so, and so can see the present situation as being of the same kind as these previous situations, that he will make to the present situation the same response as he made to these previous situations. Even in this case, then, it is appropriate to say that transfer occurs in so far as the cue of the present situation is at once the cue of an established instance. True, it may be only when the subject meets the new situation that he 'realises' what he learned before, but it is nevertheless this 'what-he-learned-before' which accounts for the so-called transfer – 'so-called' transfer because here also the phenomenon can be fitted into the concepts of learning.

Learning-to-Learning Transfer

As was noted in the corresponding section earlier in this chapter, transfer may occur not only from one instance of learning to the *doing* of something else, but from one instance of learning to another instance of *learning*. But if the latter instance is *not* the same as the first instance, as the above sentence implies, how can such a type of transfer be fitted into the present theory? How can the new situation-response complex be a case of some established instance if it is a different instance?

There seem to be two answers to that question. First, and obviously (in the light of what has been argued already), the allegedly new instance may not be a new instance at all *for the learner*. It may only *look* different, because the trainer has underestimated what the subject has in fact learned. The essence of this suggestion has already been discussed in the foregoing sections.

A second answer is that although the two instances may indeed be different, yet *part* of the latter instance (to which transfer is said to have been effected) may be an established instance. (Or, in more complex cases, several parts of the new instance are established instances.) For example, the learning of one foreign language might facilitate the learning of another if (for instance) both languages entailed gender agreement between adjective and qualified noun. Latin would help one learn Spanish in so far as some of the Spanish words had Latin stems, and had the same meaning. Playing the guitar would facilitate one's learning to play the banjo in respect of fretting the strings firmly, plucking the strings in the required way, and obtaining harmonics. But the transfer would not be complete, partly because the established instance (plucking the strings in a certain way in response to the printed music, for instance) would be only a part of the total new instance, and partly because some aspects of the established instance (or some established instances) would be in opposition to the responses required in the new instance. For example, the same printed chord requires one finger-pattern of fretting on the guitar, a different pattern on the G banjo.

On this view, then, the total amount and direction of transfer would be the *resultant* of the effects of the various established instances. There would be a certain number of 'minuses' – on account of the different finger-patterns, and so on; and a certain number of 'pluses' – on account of firm fretting, plucking, and so forth. In general, learning-to-learning transfer may be envisaged as involving a complex of several established instances, the net result being the resultant of the various positive and negative transfers.[1]

Learning How to Learn

Though useful enough for some purposes, the expression, 'Learning How to Learn' seems to be rather too sweeping – in the light of the evidence so far produced. From some finite group of instances one could scarcely learn *all* that might conceivably be learned about how to learn. The evidence suggests that what does happen is that the subject learns to make a specific (if complex) response to some specific (if complex) kind of situation. Consider again Harlow's experiment quoted on p. 213. In each of the successive trial-sessions the monkey was presented with two objects. The choice of one object resulted in reward, the choice of the other did not. At first, however, the re-presentation of the same pair of objects did not always result in the monkey's making the previously rewarded object his first choice. After many trials with different pairs of objects, however, consistency was achieved. In this case it is possible to state precisely what was learned. The monkey learned to make an approach only to the object which resulted in reward last time he saw it. The object-rewarded (so to speak) on the previous occasion is now the cue to the approach-response. Earlier, that cue (object-rewarded-last-time) did not consistently get the approach-response; sometimes it was ignored in favour of the other object. There was therefore a change of response to the same cue. Previously, over several trial-sessions, the response to the class 'objects-rewarded-last-time' was a mixture of approach and avoidance; now it is consistently approach. The monkey has learned to choose a 'once-rewarded' object, and to reject a 'once-punished' object.

Whether this kind of case qualifies for the appellation of Transfer is, I think, doubtful, but the main point remains. It can be embraced by the theory just as the other cases can. What the

---

[1] It seems unlikely, however, that the resultant could be determined by a straight-forward algebraic addition.

subject does in the very late situations is to make the same response
as he learned to make earlier.

Whether we can *teach* pupils how to learn is a complex and
lengthy question, and cannot be dealt with adequately here.

Left-Right Transfer

A type of transfer not mentioned so far is sometimes known as
Left-Right transfer. After we have learned to write, or use
almost any tool, with the right hand, we find that we can write,
or use the tool, with the left hand also – though seldom quite so
efficiently. Just *how* this comes about is an almost purely physiological issue and cannot be discussed here. I mention it merely
to illustrate further the earlier point that *what* the subject learns,
in the first place, may be more than we give him credit for.

Transfer in School

For details of transfer-experiments on school subjects the reader
is referred to texts on educational psychology.[1] All I need mention
here is that there is considerable evidence that transfer is likely to
be increased if the learner makes explicit the principle or aspect
on which transfer depends. The expression 'makes explicit'
is nevertheless rather vague, and liable to misinterpretation. What
it seems to mean, for practical purposes, is that the learner's
attention be directed to the cue, the feature intended to be common
to the various situations. In other words, he should be helped
to *understand* them (see Chapter 7). And this, it will be recalled,
is precisely what our theory implies (p. 223). A brief summary of
implications for teaching is given in the next section.

Teaching for Transfer

In view of the long discussion of transfer we have had so far,
this last section may seem unduly short, but if our arguments have
been valid the matter could scarcely be otherwise. The chief

---

[1] A short summary is provided by Kingsley and Garry (25).

implication of the theory we have been advancing is that transfer is not something additional to learning but is embraced by it. Accordingly, the requirements and conditions of transfer have already been considered in earlier chapters. To put the point more strongly, we do not need to discover special conditions governing transfer, because transfer itself is not special. Strictly, indeed, we need not use the term 'transfer' at all. Its continued use seems to be a matter of historical precedent rather than of psychological necessity, but since the phenomena discussed in this chapter are usually classed under the head of Transfer, it has been convenient to maintain that usage. All I need do now, however, is restate some of the points already made in earlier chapters.

The main practical implication for teaching is that when the teacher wishes to promote transfer (which must, of course, be transfer from some specific issue to some other specific issue), he should first make explicit, to himself, precisely what sort of response is required, and precisely what *kind* of situation is to elicit it. As was noted before, he cannot give the pupil practice in every specific situation that will be met later, but he can try to ensure that the required response is made to the *kind* of situation, that is to the *cue*, he has in mind. In other words, the teacher will not rest content with the required response to the several situations he has been able to provide; he will try to ensure that that response is being made to the *cue* shared by these situations, which will be also the cue of the situations the pupil will meet later. This, it will be appreciated, is a demand that the pupil should *understand* the situations, for to understand something is to respond to its characterising feature, its cue.

How such understanding may be promoted was discussed in Chapter 7, but it may be pertinent to repeat that a basic requirement here is that the teacher himself must be perfectly clear as to what the cue is in the case in question. In transfer-language, the teacher must make explicit to himself what the common component is to be. If, for example, he is to teach one language in such a way that there will be positive transfer to another, he must discover what the relevant common component is. If the study of geometry is to help the pupil to reason more effectively elsewhere, the teacher will have to make explicit to himself, and make forceful for the pupil, the component common to the two topics. (There can, of course, be transfer without teaching. My point is only that it is more likely to occur if the teacher acts in such a way as to promote it.)

Mere understanding is nevertheless not enough, because it requires only that *some*, any, response be made to the cue. (See Chapter 7.) If the pupil is to respond to the 'transfer-situation' as he learned to respond to the 'training-situations', it will not suffice that he makes *any* response to the cue; he must make the response specified, because the transfer-situation is but one of the situations of the instance of learning in question. Accordingly, as was noted a moment ago, the teacher must make explicit not only what the cue is to be but also the sort of response it has to get. In many cases that response will be complex, but the more complex it is the more desirable it is that the teacher should make explicit its essential nature.[1]

Finally, since understanding appears to correlate with intelligence, we should expect transfer (which is largely a matter of understanding) to be greater the more intelligent the pupil is. Both everyday observation and some experimental evidence support that, and so serve to support the view taken here.[2] With individual differences in ability this book has not been concerned. Its aim has been to show that certain general principles and procedures can be applied to all topics and to all learners. The moral of the point may nevertheless be suggested. It is not that transfer is unlikely when pupils are of low intelligence, but that such pupils will require longer and more detailed explanations if what they learn in school is to be put to use outside it.

---

[1] I have spoken here of a 'sort of response', and the reader will appreciate that this point has been presupposed throughout the book, for no two behaviours are identical, in the sense of involving exactly the same physical movements.

[2] See, for example, the evidence produced by Kuenne, quoted by Bugelski (6).

11 · Teaching by Programming

Teaching-machines, Programmes and Programmers

Some of the more complicated teaching-machines look like television sets. There is a window in which the pupil can see a piece of information, and a row of button-controls which he can operate. When he has read a piece of information he can press one of the buttons, and new material will appear in the window. Sometimes the machine (by means of the words in the window) will ask him a question, and offer him several possible answers. If he chooses Answer C, he will press Button C, and a new set of words in the window will tell him whether he was right or wrong. If he is right, the machine will then take him further on. If he is wrong, the machine will explain his error and probably tell him to press the button which will recall the previous material in which he went wrong. (See p. 248 ff.).

Sometimes the material in the window will be pictures, or maps, or diagrams. These will appear just when they are needed. The machine is made in such a way that it will show the pupil the right things at the right juncture in the lesson.

Since each pupil has his own machine, and the answers he gives indicate to the machine what *it* must do next, each pupil receives tuition appropriate to his needs. For the same reason, he can proceed as quickly or as slowly as his ability allows.

This certainly *looks* like teaching; and teaching-machines have been with us long enough to demonstrate that pupils do learn when they use them, even when the machines are much simpler than those just described. Yet, ingenious as the machine may be, it is reasonable to argue that the pupil learns, not from the machine, but from the material (information, questions, etc.) stored inside the machine and allowed to appear, a little piece at a time, in its window. This organised body of material, usually printed on a long roll of paper or film, is called a 'programme'; and one might suggest that if anything here can be said to teach, the teaching is done not by the machine but by the programme it presents. A good machine will make the most of a good programme, but from a programme consisting of misleading or irrelevant information, ill-conceived questions, faulty explanations, and the like, the pupil will learn little or nothing. His learning depends far more upon the programme than upon the mechanism which is no more than a device for presenting it.

Programmes have nevertheless to be written by someone. Someone has to decide what information the programme is to contain, how it should be arranged, what questions should be asked, when they should be asked, what sorts of explanations are needed, and so on. Ultimately the quality of the pupil's learning depends upon the knowledge and skill of the person who wrote the programme in the first place. In this sense, a teaching-machine has a teacher inside it. Perhaps we should say, then, that the teaching is done, not by the machine, nor even by the programme, but by the programmer – the person who wrote the programme for the machine to present.

Since the purpose of a programme is to promote learning, the programmer must be a good teacher. But while programmes written by a poor teacher will almost certainly be poor too, a programme written by a good class-teacher will not necessarily be a good one. Programme-writing, or 'programming', is a special skill, acquired only at the expense of much time, practice, guidance, experiment, thought, and patience. There is at present a demand for good programmes, but that demand cannot be met merely by the existence of large numbers of experienced teachers. There is urgent need of people who have acquired the special skill programming requires.

Since programming is a skill, and not just knowledge of it, obviously one chapter of one book cannot turn even the most willing reader into an expert programmer. If he decides to try to write a programme, he should study thoroughly some of the texts devoted to that end. (See bibliography at the end of this chapter.) He would benefit also from a practical course in which he actually writes under the guidance of a skilled practitioner. The teacher who has already a knowledge of the basic principles of learning will nevertheless start at an advantage because programmed learning not only conforms to these same conditions but manifests them in a very precise way.

For the reasons just mentioned, this chapter aims, not to train the reader in the skill of programming, but rather to describe the essential nature of programmed learning and how it fits into the pattern of learning described in earlier chapters. Its goal is the reader's understanding, with which he should be the more able to acquire the practical skill of programming, and also to assess critically and intelligently programmes written by others, so that he can decide whether he would be wise to use them for his own pupils. He may discover too, as many other teachers have done, that although he never publishes or even completes the programme he has tried to write yet he acquires greater skill in planning his own techniques of teaching.

What is a Programme?

A teaching-machine is basically an apparatus for presenting the learner with a programme. At first, students of programmed learning sometimes find their attention focussed upon the machines and how they work, but the essence of programmed learning is the programme itself. Teaching-machines are constructed to suit the needs of programmes, and not conversely. Indeed, as we shall see later, programmed learning need not make use of machines at all.

As has been implied, the material of a lesson and of a programme are similar; each contains information, illustrations, questions, the remedying of error, and so on. But there are also some important differences.

Neither a lesson nor a programme is presented *en bloc*. Each necessarily consists of parts, but the parts into which a programme is divided are much smaller than what would usually be regarded as the 'parts' of a lesson. The content of a programme appears only a little piece at a time in the window of the teaching-machine, but the point is not that the parts of the programme are made small enough to get into the window, but rather that the window is made small so that the pupil can concentrate upon only one of the programme's small parts at one time. Each of these small parts of a programme is called a 'frame'; and since each frame may consist of only a few sentences (and sometimes less), even a programme of moderate length may have several hundred frames. One basic characteristic of a programme, then, is that it consists of parts, called 'frames', which are very small. (For an illustration see pp. 240).

A second characteristic, already implied, is that a programme has to be set out, physically, in such a way that only one frame is visible at a time. (Were the frames on p. 240 in a teaching-machine, only one would appear at one time.)

The 'steps' *between* successive frames are small too; one piece of information should lead the learner smoothly to the next. Often this requires some overlapping of successive frames, but the main point is that there must be no gaps which the learner cannot bridge. Much the same principle is incorporated in a well-planned class-lesson, but few lessons apply it to every detail of information the lesson contains. A third characteristic of programmed learning, then, is the smallness of the steps between successive frames.

Small frames with small steps between them could nevertheless be arranged in many different sequences, some of which would be more effective than others. What information should come first? At what point should examples be used? And so forth. The same problems arise in class-lessons too, but in programmed learning they are examined in detail. A fourth characteristic of programmed learning is that the frames are arranged in the sequence which will maximise the pupil's learning. To ensure that this goal is achieved, a good programme will have been adequately tested on a sample of pupils before it is published.

Perhaps the most significant difference between programme and class-lesson is that a programme not only presents material *to* the learner; it also requires *from* him a *response* to every point it makes. He may have to fill in a blank (with a word or phrase), answer a question, give a reason, choose between alternatives. The teacher also will seek responses from his pupils, but he cannot hope to obtain a response from each pupil in connection with every point the lesson has made. A programme is designed to do this (and can do it because each pupil has his own copy of the programme). *Why* programmes are so designed will be considered later. In answer to *what* a programme is we need note only that in programmed learning the pupil does not read passively; he has to do something about everything he reads.

Further, a programme is designed so that every response the learner makes will be checked by the learner himself. (If need be, the teacher can check them too.) This procedure allows of immediate knowledge of results, desirable in learning any skill (see p. 192). Once again, however, *why* this procedure is used will be considered later.

Exactly what happens after he checks his response depends upon the type of programme being used. The two main types, 'linear' and 'branching', are described in the next two sections.

Linear Programmes

In a linear programme there is only one sequence or 'line' of frames, which is read by all learners. It has two, alternating, kinds of frame: an information-frame to which the learner has to make a response; and immediately following it a smaller check-frame with which he can verify the response he has just made to the preceding information-frame. (See p. 240 ff.)

Since all learners read all the frames, and in the same sequence, will not the less able learners make many wrong responses? A programme should state for what age or type of pupil it is intended, but even within one class there may be a spread of ability. In fact, most linear programmes get very few wrong responses because the programme is written in such a way that most of the responses will be right. This is effected by various means.

First, since each pupil works at his own rate, he can take more time for points he finds difficult than is usually possible in a class-lesson. Second, although all types of programmes have quite small frames (the largest being no more than one page), the frames of a linear programme are very small indeed, each dealing with only a very small amount of material. Third, since the steps between successive information-frames are small too, new material never appears without previous preparation. Fourth, linear programmes incorporate prompts. Types of prompts used in linear programmes will be examined later (p. 255). The immediate point is that linear programmes are designed so that most of the learner's responses will be right, and prompts further that purpose. Fifth, since the aim of the programme is to ensure that the pupil finally makes the required responses without prompts, the prompts are eventually withdrawn, albeit in such a way as to minimise the chances of his making wrong responses. This is done, in many cases, by gradual reduction of the prompt-material – 'fading' the prompts, as some programmers put it.

The form (not the content) of the following sample-sequence of frames illustrates these five points. (Note that it assumes, as any programme does, certain previous knowledge: in this case, the ability to converse in terms of Cue, Force, Prompt, and Response. Were this sample actually used for instructional purposes, the reader would see only one frame at a time, either by means of a teaching-machine or by the use of a sliding mask. The numbers labelling the frames are not parts of the programme, and have been included here to facilitate reference to them in our subsequent discussion.)

(78)

When, by means of a prompt, the specified response has been made, it must be connected to the cue. The name 'reinforcer' is given to anything which .... cue and response in this way.

---

(79)

connects

---

(80)

In the instance, 'Learning to take care when crossing the street', a reward would be a reinforcer if it connected the .... of crossing the street and the .... of taking care.

---

(81)

cue response

---

(82)

Rewards are not the only things that can connect cue and response. *Anything* which does this is called a ....

---

(83)

reinforcer

---

(84)

What is the function of a reinforcer?

---

(85)

To connect cue and response.

(86)
     Reinforcers are either positive or negative. If they connect cue and response by being *added* to the learning-situation or by being *increased* in amount, they are .... reinforcers.

(87)
     positive

(88)
     If reinforcement were effected by a prize, then since prizes are awarded (and not taken away!), the prize would be a ....

(89)
     positive reinforcer

(90)
     On the other hand, if reinforcement were brought about by the removal of the reinforcer, or by a decrease in its amount, this would be an example of the use of a ....

(91)
     negative reinforcer

(92)
     Because, by taking aspirin, a student once reduced his anxiety at an examination, he thereafter responded to examinations by taking aspirin. The .... was a negative reinforcer.

(93)

anxiety

---

(94)

It was the student's anxiety which was the . . . . because it connected the examination-cue with the aspirin-taking response; and it was . . . . .ive because it was . . . . in amount.

---

(95)

reinforcer negat(ive) decreased
(reduced, etc.)

---

(96)

Pupils sometimes work harder at a school subject as a consequence of gaining more marks in it. In this case, what is the reinforcer? Is it positive or negative, and why?

---

(97)

marks positive because increased in
amount

The sample, though very short, illustrates the five points made above.

Each reader can work through it at his own rate.

Each information-frame is very small, dealing with only a small amount of information.

The steps between successive information-frames are very small too. Frame 80 is linked to the preceding information-frame by being an example of it; and it is not until the third information-frame (82) that the student is asked to respond with the new term 'reinforcer'. (He is nevertheless prepared for it, by means of Frames 78 and 80.) Frame 86 makes a new point, introducing the notions of positive and negative reinforcers, but that point is based upon the concept of Reinforcer presented in the four preceding frames. By small steps of this kind the student is led to Frame 96 in which, confronted with a specific instance of reinforcement, he has to identify the reinforcer, say whether it is positive or negative, and justify the answer he has given.

The sample utilises prompts. In the first frame (78), which introduces a new term ('reinforcer'), the prompt is very heavy. The required response, 'connects', is prompted not only by the sense of the first sentence but also by its containing a similar form of the same word, and for good measure by the phrase 'in this way'. In contrast, Frame 80 does not contain a prompt for the responses of 'cue' and 'response'. To respond correctly here, the student must draw upon his previously acquired ability to identify cue and response in a stated instance. He has to take his (bare) cue from the substance of the frame. The purpose of this frame is, of course, to remind the student of *what* a reinforcer connects. Frame 86, because it introduces the new concepts of Positive and Negative reinforcers, uses broader prompting. For one thing, the frame drops a broad hint, in its first sentence, that his response will have to be either 'positive' or 'negative' (but even in so doing focusses the student's attention on these very terms.) Also, the words *'added'* and *'increased'* (italicised!) are intended to indicate that the right alternative is 'positive'. The same frame (86) illustrates another point: although the prompts 'added' and 'increased' are very heavy, yet they are not artificial, because a positive reinforcer *is* something which is effective by being added or increased in amount. In this case, with some help from the context ('Reinforcers are either positive or negative') it is possible to make the cue of the material do its own prompting. Compare with the following (intentionally bad) example:

Reinforcers are either positive or negative. If reinforcement were effected by a prize, this would be an example of the use of a p . . . . reinforcer.

For the adult reader, the incomplete word 'p.........' is probably no broader a hint than is the word 'added'; but it is doubtful if the use of the former prompt ('p.........') would teach him anything. The response in the two cases is the same, but in the frame just quoted the response is not linked with anything that matters. The point is that prompts have to be judged not merely by their heaviness or broadness but by their appropriateness to the theme of the programme. (See also p. 256 ff.)

As the programme proceeds, however, the prompts for a particular response are withdrawn, though gradually.[1] As we noted, Frame 86 offered the alternatives 'positive' and 'negative', and further prompted the response by means of the words 'added' and 'increased'. Frame 90, however, does not explicitly offer the alternatives; but its introductory phrase, 'On the other hand', immediately follows the response 'positive reinforcer', and is intended to supplement the prompt-words 'removal' and 'decrease'. (The frame illustrates how a previous response can be used to help prompt the next response.) The succeeding frame (92) contains none of these prompts. It does nevertheless use the word 'reduced', which in this context has the same *meaning* as 'decreased'; and the reader is likely to expect that this frame will provide an example of the general point made in the immediately preceding frame. Even so, it illustrates the 'fading' of prompts for a given response. By the time the student has reached Frame 96 there are no prompts at all. (The word 'more' is not a prompt, but is part of the cue, for unless some indication is given as to

---

[1] In view of the definition of 'prompt' given earlier in this text, phrases like 'gradual withdrawal of the prompt' are, strictly, improper. According to that definition, an item either does ensure that the response given is the right one or it does not. Either it *is* a prompt, or it is *not* a prompt; there are no half-way stages, and so a prompt, per se, cannot be 'gradually' withdrawn. What the exponents of programmed learning intend is nevertheless clear enough. As the programme proceeds, the amount of *material* required to *serve* as prompt can be gradually reduced, until there is no need for such material. Ultimately the function of determining the form of the response is acquired by the cue itself. The same point applies to the use of phrases like 'heavy prompt'.

The point would seem to be worth making, because confusion often arises through the failure to distinguish a specific *item* from the *function* it is intended to serve.

whether there were more marks or fewer marks we cannot identify the type of reinforcer.)

Frames 92 and 94 illustrate a further point. Despite Frame 92's stating explicitly that it was the *anxiety* which was reduced, and its saying nothing about anything else which was decreased or increased, the structure of the frame may lead the not very attentive student to respond, incorrectly, with the word 'aspirin'. An additional cause of error could be the fact that this is the first frame in which he has been asked to identify the reinforcer. If it is realised by the programmer, this difficulty can be dealt with in either of two ways. The substance of Frame 92 can be spread over more frames, each having adequate prompts. Or, with the method used here, the possibility of error can be dealt with in the succeeding frame. The check-frame (93) for Frame 92 tells the student what the right response is; but in case he does not see why that is the right response the following frame (94) explains it – as well as emphasising a point of its own. *Should* every required response be adequately prompted; or from time to time should the student be given more difficult frames, even at the risk of wrong responses? This question will be raised again.

The foregoing illustrations of the use of prompts may have seemed unduly detailed, but it is only from the examination and discussion of specific instances that the role of prompts can be fully appreciated. The reader who intends to write a programme would be well advised to study in detail the use of prompts in a variety of published programmes, as well as in texts which discuss them.

Branching Programmes

In contrast with a linear programme, in which all learners have to take the same 'line' (because there *is* only one line), a branching programme can take different learners along 'branch-lines' when this seems desirable. The branch may take the form of a bypass: the pupil who has been doing very well, as indicated by his consistently making right responses even to a succession of difficult frames, may bypass several frames and join the main line ahead of his slower class-mates. On the other hand, a pupil who makes a wrong response may be taken down a 'remedial' branch and given more intensive or simpler tuition before he rejoins the main line – either at the point he left it or very slightly further on. Such a pupil might have to deal with (say) twenty frames, compared with the average pupil who needs only (say) seven frames to span the same stretch of subject-matter.

One of the simpler forms of branching is illustrated by the 'scrambled text'. This looks like an ordinary book, but anyone who tries to read it in the normal way by proceeding from Page One to Page Two, and thence to Page Three, and so on, will find that the text fails to make sense. Page One provides some information – rather more than in a linear frame; but at the foot of the page there is a question, followed by a short list of answers from which the student has to select the answer he thinks is correct. Opposite each of the suggested answers is a page number; and the student, having decided upon his answer, turns to the page numbered alongside that answer. When he turns to the page he has (in effect) selected, he will find that the question is re-stated, and so is his answer. If his answer is right, he will be told that it is right; and the remainder of the page will continue the tuition – until he meets another list of questions at the foot of that page, when the same kind of procedure is repeated. If, however, his answer is wrong, here also the question will be re-stated, with his answer to it; but the remainder of the page will give an explanation of his mistake, followed by the instruction to return to the page where he erred and try again. Such branches are very short. The learner, when he has erred, is taken up a 'side street', given a little talk, and brought back to the intersection with the main thoroughfare. (See p. 248.)

The more complex teaching-machines can do very much the same job. Instead of turning to the appropriate page of the scrambled text, the student presses the button labelled in accordance with his answer; the machine rolls the programme round to the appropriate frame; and so forth. Machines of this kind are of course very expensive (as compared with linear machines and scrambled texts), but some of the best of them can perform operations that would be impossible in a textbook, no matter how scrambled it was.

It will be apparent that unless the machine is devised to analyse responses which the student himself constructs (writing a sentence or saying the answer aloud), the branching type of programme must be restricted to responses which consist of the learner's choosing answers already provided. In contrast with the obvious advantages of remedial sequences and of loop-lines enabling the clever pupil to get on with the learning, this latter restriction may appear to be a major disadvantage. It should nevertheless be remembered that neither kind of programme is a *test*, and does not aim to 'catch out' the student. A well-written branching programme, used by the kind of learner for whom it was intended, will only rarely get wrong choices; but since every programme will get *some* wrong responses, it seems reasonable that it should be able to provide for that eventuality. Also, it may be desirable to oblige the student, now and again, to face up to a really difficult frame, if for no other reason than that difficult frames may remind him that he must pay attention.[1]

It will be apparent also that the writer of a branching programme must have a wide knowledge, not only of his subject-matter, but of the kinds of mistake students are likely to make. (Why list wrong answers nobody would give?) That knowledge can be obtained, of course, by trying out the programme first in a form calling for *constructed* answers, and noting the types of error most commonly made. In noting this, however, one may decide also to modify the frames which received many wrong responses.

Another major difference between the two types of programme is that the branching type does not, or does not obviously, make use of prompts, as does the linear programme. I have inserted the proviso 'or does not obviously' because *some* sort of prompt is a prerequisite of learning, and the right response is in fact prompted

[1] See Angell and Lumsdaine, quoted in (7) p. 143.

by the total frame, in much the same way as a well-written page of an ordinary textbook will enable its reader to answer questions based upon it.

Like the linear programme, however, the material of a branching programme is broken down into small parts, which are arranged in the best sequence. In both cases, the learner has to make some sort of response: in the one case by constructing an answer, in the other by choosing the answer he thinks is correct. The *reasons* for demanding a response are nevertheless different. Crowder,[1] the originator of branching programmes, requires a response not because he believes there is any particular virtue in responding but because it is only by reference to how the learner responds that the subsequent unit of instruction can be adapted to his needs.

The question of which type of programme is the better is too complex to be analysed here. For further discussion of it the reader is referred to the texts listed in the bibliography at the end of the chapter. Some of the main points will nevertheless be raised in the next, and final, section.

Examples of Frames in a Branching Programme

(xxi)

The question was: What is the function of a prompt?

Your answer was: To ensure that the response made to the cue will be the required response.

Good! You are right. Your choosing that answer shows that you are quite clear about the difference between a cue and a prompt. Now let's move on.

Whenever Tom leaves the room, he shuts the door behind him. But Mother is still prompting him. If he is to learn, his door-shutting response must now be connected

[1] In (8), p. 142.

to the cue of leaving the room, so that Mother's prompt can be dispensed with. Various things that might join up a cue and a response will be mentioned in a moment; but *anything* which serves to attach a response to a cue is called a 'reinforcer'.

What is the job that a reinforcer has to do?

(*a*) To make the cue forceful. (p. xxvi)

(*b*) To make sure that the right response is given in the first place. (p. xxx)

(*c*) To connect a prompted response to the cue. (p. xxiv)

(xxx)

The question was: What is the job that a reinforcer has to do?

Your answer was: To make sure that the right response is given in the first place.

Well now! You are *partly* right, because a reinforcer's job is to make sure that the right response is given. But not *in the first place*. That is the job of the prompt. The right response cannot be attached to the cue until it is available for attaching; and it is the function of the prompt to make it available. Once it *is* available it can be attached to the cue; and it is then, and only then, that a reinforcer can operate. Now turn back to p. xxi, read it again, and choose the right answer.

The Psychology of Programmed Learning

This section has two purposes. As its title implies, it aims to give an account of the psychology which relates specifically to programmed learning. Most of this will refer to linear programming because that type derives directly from a particular psychological system, namely that of B. F. Skinner.[1] Crowder, in contrast, states that his type of programme is not derived from any particular psychological theory. The second purpose is to illustrate further the basic requirements of learning described earlier in this text. Because programmed learning raises in an unusually specific way some of the most crucial problems of human learning, a discussion of the basic requirements of learning in this context will enable us to exploit them further and at the same time show in greater detail how they may be fulfilled.

Responses

One of the basic principles of Skinner's psychological system is the 'shaping' of behaviour by means of carefully devised schedules of reinforcement.[1] One of his experiments on animals illustrates what this means.

A pigeon in a training-box has to learn to walk in a figure-8. As soon as it makes even the smallest move in the right direction, even if only by turning its head, it receives a food-pellet. Once the pigeon has learned this small response to the cue (which might be a signal-light, or just the bird's being in the box), it is not given food until it has moved a little further in the right direction. At some stage it must begin to move in another direction (in order to trace out a figure-8), and at that stage it is not given food until that movement has been added to the behaviour already established. By such a series of approximations the whole figure is built or 'shaped'. (Note the similarity of this procedure to the Repetitive Part Method of Memorising. p. 170).

Skinner, regarding the food-pellet as the reinforcer, stresses two aspects of the reinforcement. *Each* of the part-behaviours, increasing in size as the training proceeds, must be reinforced. And each of these reinforcements must be effected *immediately* after the relevant response is made. (Skinner [2] contrasts these two

---

[1] For a fuller account see (45) and (46).
[2] In (45), p. 149ff.

aspects of training with customary procedures in the class-room.)
We shall return to reinforcement later. In the meantime let us
examine the responses.

Even from this very brief account of Skinner's procedure it
will be apparent that the shaping of behaviour necessitates the
trainer's knowing, from the outset, precisely what the learner has
to do at the end. (How could the pigeon-trainer reinforce only
the right responses unless he knew from the beginning that these
were right responses because they would contribute to the final
figure-8 walk?) If the trainer or programmer is to shape this
'terminal behaviour', he must know initially what it has to be.
In the terms of the present text: to effect any instance of learning,
simple or complex, the teacher must first specify the response
required.

That it is a response, a *behaviour*, which has to be so specified
is underlined in all accounts of programmed learning. The
demand is 'Specify your objectives in behavioural terms'.
Although that demand is patently relevant to training in physical
skills, it is by no means obviously relevant to more academic
subjects. Instead of specifying their objectives in terms of
behaviour, teachers usually express them in terms like, 'to
know . . .', 'to understand . . .'. Indeed, when offered the
alternative, many teachers prefer the terms they already use, and
sometimes counter-attack their critics on the ground that the
behavioural specification of educational objectives restricts or
devalues them.

Reluctance to adopt the alternative way of thinking may be
partly due to an antipathy to behaviourist psychological systems;
but one need not be committed to the neobehaviouristic psychology of Professor Skinner to see the need to specify one's
objectives in behavioural terms. Even if we assume (as Skinner
does not) that there are inner mental processes (as contrasted with
cerebral events) of Knowing, Appreciating, and the like, yet at
the same time we can recognise that the teacher must have
evidence that these hidden mental processes have occurred. He
would be a naively optimistic teacher who took for granted that

because he had done his best to explain something his pupils would of necessity understand it; or that because they had read something they would therefore know it. Effective teaching demands *evidence* of knowing (etc.) the matter in question, and that evidence can be provided only by pupil-behaviour which the teacher can observe.

It is of course true that not *any* response will serve as criterion. The teacher has to decide *what* behaviour will suffice; and it may be that after scrutinising a particular programme he will decide that its terminal behaviour does not provide the evidence which would satisfy him. The teacher may be right, but valid as his objection may be in any particular case, it is an objection only to the particular terminal behaviour of that programme, and is not an objection to the basic demand for terminal behaviour. His objection would have to be met, not by the rejection of that demand, but by the substitution of different content leading to a terminal behaviour which *would* provide satisfactory evidence.[1]

The sample given on p. 240 ff. is too short to exemplify terminal behaviour in the full sense, but its 'sub-terminal' behaviour might be described thus: Given an adequate description of a particular instance of reinforcement, the student will identify (name) the reinforcer, state whether it is positive or negative, and explain why it is of that kind.

Once the terminal behaviour has been specified, the programmer can then work out a sequence of behaviours which will lead to it. (Some of the intermediate behaviours may of course be

[1] The above justification is perhaps unnecessarily concessionary. Modern behaviourism does not deny the occurrence of knowing, appreciating, and so on. On the contrary, it is very much concerned with them, and focusses attention on the very behaviours commonly cited as evidence of the mental processes to which these terms ('knowing', etc.) customarily refer. It nevertheless refrains from positing mental processes (as distinct from cerebral events) additional to the behaviours themselves. For the neobehaviourist, exemplified by Skinner, the behaviours in question are not 'evidence' of knowing; they are, rather, evident *examples* of it. Some of the reasons for this approach were mentioned in our earlier sections on Motivation. See also Skinner (45), p. 156, lines 17–32. Gagne (8) seems to be hinting at the same point when he suggests that knowledge, in any particular instance, is an inferred capability making possible the successful performance of a 'class of tasks'.

worth acquiring in their own right.) Obviously, to do this he must be accomplished in the topic to be programmed. To take a (relatively) simple example: What behaviours must the pupil be able to perform before he can 'Add two proper fractions, denominators not greater than 9'? As the reader can discover, obliging oneself to write down every frame in the shaping of even so simple a terminal behaviour is a profitable, illuminating, and sometimes embarrassing exercise in thoroughness.

Why frames are made small will now be apparent. The small responses they require are the 'part-behaviours' necessary for the shaping of the complex terminal behaviour. Why the programme should demand responses at all has already been implied. It is only by reference to the learner's behaviour that it can be discovered whether he has learned what he should. Although Crowder's views and practices are often very different from Skinner's, that answer would seem to be in accord with both.

Strictly, however, the above argument refers only to those occasions when evidence of learning is required. Plainly the *terminal* behaviour falls into this category. But need all the smaller, contributing responses be observable, 'overt' responses? Might not 'covert' responses of thinking the answer, or saying it 'in one's head' be sufficient? If the terminal behaviour is a physical skill it is almost certain that the part-behaviours must be physical also: one could scarcely expect to build up a physical skill from little bits of thought. In general, the bits must be of the same stuff as the whole. Also, a programme has to be tested before it is put into use, and it is only by means of a *record* of all responses made to the frames that one can discover which frames are misleading, or too difficult, and so on. Further, when a branching programme is presented by a machine, it is only by means of an overt response from the learner that the machine can 'decide' what frame to show next. It is nevertheless debatable whether overt responses are *always* necessary.

Some experiments have allowed students to read the programme with the blanks already filled in and underlined, and have shown that learning takes place.[1] It is very probable that the students did make some sort of response to the underlined words, but not the overt sort of response usually required. In some other experiments where it was known that there were covert, but no overt responses, it was again found that learning occurred. Whether the overt or covert response is preferable, however, was found to be a more complex question than is often supposed, because its answer depends upon the kind of material being used and the experience of the students using it. Cummings and Goldstein [2] suggest that unfamiliar or difficult material is not satisfactorily learned by covert responding, and that the reason may be that a complex covert response cannot be reliably compared with the check-frame. Cook [3] takes the view that a covert response is not possible until one has first learned to make the corresponding overt response, and quotes an early study by Gates (16) in which the value of active recitation during learning was found to decrease with an increase in the meaning or sense of the material. Material the learner finds difficult to comprehend apparently benefits most from overt response.

From these and similar studies we may infer that if the learner has not already learned to perform the behaviour constituting the response, we cannot expect him to learn much if we ask him to make only the equivalent covert response; but if he can already perform that behaviour, even if not in response to the situation in question, there is no great virtue in obliging him to perform it now, because the covert response will do. There is nevertheless a proviso: if the same programme allows *both* modes of response, the student may treat as relatively unimportant those frames calling for 'only' a covert response.

The last paragraph may suggest that while overt responses are not always necessary, yet to insist upon them does no harm. *Some* forms of overt response would nevertheless seem to be suspect. Many linear programmes oblige the student to make the overt response of *writing*; and in many cases it is doubtful if the

[1] See Briggs, Goldbeck, Campbell, and Nichols, in (7).   [2] In (8).
[3] In (7).

behaviour of writing is an essential part of the terminal behaviour. Before he writes, he has to *think what* to write, and usually it is the meaning of what he writes, rather than the act of writing, which is significant. If so, having to write may distract him from the main issue. The more practised he is in putting his thoughts into writing, the less serious the danger, but it may be a considerable danger for younger children. (They have to attend to such things as getting the word or words into the space provided). How else an overt response, which may be checked, can be expressed is no easy question, but the point just made does draw attention to what appears to be the crux of the matter. The *basic* issue is not whether the response should be overt or covert, written or spoken, or one of any other pair of alternatives, but rather whether the response asked for is a necessary preliminary to the terminal behaviour. This is the primary consideration. In order to permit the checking of responses, we may have to infringe that rule; but once the rule is clear we can strive to stick to it as closely as possible. Also, with the proviso noted by Cook (above), we can remind ourselves that except for validation purposes it is the *learner* who checks the responses; and that if he is able to check covert responses we need not oblige him to make overt responses which are not essential to the shaping of the terminal behaviour. In the extreme case we might not require an overt response except for the terminal response itself.

The Role of Prompts

In our earlier chapters we had occasion to consider prompts in only a rather general way, and suggested that they might take the form of verbal instructions or models. A linear programme provides opportunity to examine prompts in more detail, because it uses prompts in nearly all its frames.

Skinner (46) distinguishes two kinds of prompt: the 'formal' and the 'thematic'. A formal prompt has the same 'form' as the required response and provides either a model, which the learner has to copy in its entirety, or part of a model, which he has to copy and complete. Here are two examples, overleaf.

Frame X

When the learning of one topic interferes with the recall of another topic learned earlier, the interference is said to be 'retroactive'. To help you remember this term, write it down.

Frame Y

When a reinforcer is effective by being added to the learning-situation, or by being increased in amount, it is called a pos . . . ve reinforcer.

In contrast, a thematic prompt does not model the required response, but operates by its meaning within the theme of the programme. This can be done by the use of words with connotations similar to those of the response-words, by the implication of the frame-context, by suggested contrast, by analogies, and even by the grammar of the frame. The variety of thematic prompts is limited only by the ingenuity of the programmer. Examples of thematic prompts will be found in the sample on pp. 240 ff.

At first sight formal prompts may seem too easy, too mechanical, and to lead only to rote learning. As noted earlier, however, a prompt has to be judged, not by its appearance nor even by whether it is formal or thematic, but by whether it does the job it is intended to do. In illustration consider Frame X. (Usually one should not judge a single frame, because the frames before or after it may make the point we think the frame in question has missed; but Frame X was designed in order to be criticised.) Its first sentence introduces a new term and tells the student what it means. It is possible that he may remember its meaning, but he need not even note its meaning, at the outset, in order to make the response the frame requires. He need look only at the word in quotes and copy it. Assuming that the purpose of the frame is to teach the student what the term means (that is, what retroactive interference is), and not just to ensure that he can spell it, that formal prompt is scarcely the best means.

A basic objection to Frame X, then, is not that it encourages rote learning. (His learning what the terms mean would be rote learning too.) The essential fault here is that the (formal) prompt used is inappropriate to the purpose of the frame. Frame Y is open to the same kind of criticism.

As these two frames illustrate, we cannot properly criticise a prompt on grounds of inadequacy unless we have already determined *why* it is inadequate. That it does not further the purpose of the frame, though a valid answer, is practically useless unless we know the specific purpose of the particular frame. Obviously an intended prompt would be inadequate if it failed to ensure that the response given was the response required; but let us take that point for granted. In many cases, any one of several prompts could ensure the right response: the crucial question is which of these prompts is the best to use. What criterion are we to apply?

Despite the widespread use of prompts in linear programmes, few texts on the subject give a straight answer to that question, or even make the question itself explicit. Yet there is a fairly simple answer. A prompt, as defined earlier in this book, has a quite specific function: to ensure that the response to the cue has the specified form. If the item intended as prompt exceeds that function and not only determines the *form* of the response but also *evokes* it, learning will not occur. The prompt-item must not distract attention from the cue.

The practical implication of this criterion, for programmed learning, is that before we even begin to consider what sort of prompt we should use we must specify not only the response we want but also the cue we want to evoke it. Having done this, but not before, we can select a prompt which *is* capable of ensuring that the response will be the right one, but at the same time is *not* capable of usurping the function of the cue and de-priving it of force. (This is of course an ideal requirement, but the closer we can get to its fulfilment the more likely learning will be.)

In Frame Y, for example, the part-model ('pos . . . ve') is likely to distract the student's attention from the cue, namely 'reinforcers . . . added, or increased in amount'. The response which should be made to that cue may be *made*, but may be made to the incomplete word instead of to the cue. Compare with Frame 86 in the sample. (p. 241).

The criterion just suggested is derived logically from a parti-cular definition of learning, but very similar points are made by Taber, Glaser, and Schaefer (49) who apparently base them on practical experience. (Their concepts, and so their terms, are not the same as mine.) They suggest that 'strong' formal prompts may withdraw attention from the 'subject matter'.[1] Now the term 'subject matter' is somewhat vague. Even the most formal of prompts is unlikely to draw attention away from *all* the frame's subject matter. (If it did, the student would not even know he had to copy the word.) Nor will it matter if attention is diverted from *some* parts of the subject matter if these parts are not crucial. But what parts *are* crucial? These authors say that the function of a prompt is not merely that of ensuring the occurrence of the right response but also that of establishing new behaviour by modifying 'stimulus control'.[2] The prompted behaviour has to be evoked by a *different* stimulus: not by the 'discriminative stimulus' which already evokes that response and may be used as a prompt, but by the 'potential discriminative stimulus' which, it is intended, *will* get that response. They say also that a programme would teach very little if, when the learner was required to respond to new material, responses could be made only to 'established stimuli'.[3] By 'established stimuli', here, they are referring presumably to discriminative stimuli which can be used as prompts. Their latter two points indicate that *eventually* it is to the potential discriminative stimulus that the learner must respond

---

[1] Op. cit. pp. 94, 95.   [2] Op. cit. p. 109.   [3] Op. cit. p. 92.

in the required way; and if we now add their first point about 'strong stimuli' withdrawing attention from the 'subject matter', we may infer that the crucial part of the subject matter is the potential discirminative stimulus. It would appear, then, that although Taber, Glaser, and Schaefer express their points in a different way, and probably make them for different reasons, yet we are substantially in agreement. Any discriminative stimuli intended as prompts should not be so 'strong' as to interfere with the potential discriminative stimulus' *evoking* the response. To repeat the main point in the terms we have been using throughout: the item chosen as prompt should be such that it *will* ensure that it is the right response which is made, but *will not* prevent that response's being made to the *cue*.[1]

Although the points discussed in the last few paragraphs arose out of the discussion of formal prompts, the same criterion applies to thematic prompts too. If the prompt really is thematic, the danger may be less, but the fact that a prompt is effective by virtue of its meaning rather than of its form does not ensure that it is the *cue* which will be the centre-piece of the frame. Nor is the criterion relevant only to *programmed* learning, even if an analysis of programmes serves very well to illustrate it.

The general conclusion is that, wherever it may be used, and irrespective of its kind, an item selected as prompt must have the function of determining the form of the response but not of evoking it. If that function is to be fulfilled, however, the cue must evoke a response so that its form can *be* determined by the intended prompt. The cue itself must have force. That demand in

[1] The word 'strong' may be useful by way of introduction, but to say that a 'strong' stimulus will distract attention is surely tautologous. Only by observing that it *does* get a response can we know that the stimulus is 'strong'. Surely this is what 'strong' *means* here? It was partly to avoid such tautology and the self-contradiction of 'stimuli *not* getting responses' that I distinguished a kind-characterising feature (cue) from an evoking-function (force). Another reason is illustrated above. Stimuli (including potential discriminative stimuli) tend to be identified (?) by reference to the particular responses they are intended to evoke, whereas precision of statement and the demands of practice necessitate an independent specification of the part of the subject matter which is to evoke the response. (*Cf.* 'A division problem is a problem that has to be solved by division.') Whatever we may choose to call it, the *concept* I have called 'cue' seems to be necessary for an adequate description, that is, a working theory, of learning.

turn takes us back to the initial issue of deciding precisely what the cue has to be in any given instance. As will be noted in the next section, this is an issue about which textbooks on programmed learning say little.

The Significance of the Cue

Many textbooks on programmed learning use the term 'cue' as a synonym of 'prompt'. This seems to me to be unfortunate, not just because it conflicts with my usage, nor because it is a waste of a useful term, but for two more substantial reasons. First, despite their often stated synonymity, the terms are not always used as synonyms. To exemplify by referring to a text I much admire, Taber, Glaser, and Schaefer (49) include 'cues' in their index, but all that is said there is 'see Prompts'. Some of their actual uses of 'cue' nevertheless indicate that they are intending something different. They refer,[1] for example, to the 'cues' which tell a dentist whether a tooth may be saved or must be extracted. Surely such 'cues' are in fact the features *characteristic* of this sort of situation? Unlike prompts, these are the aspects of the to-be-diagnosed situation which have to remain, and to which the expert dentist's response must ultimately be made. These are 'cues' in the sense of this text. The two different concepts need two different terms. The second reason is that the concept of a kind-characterising feature (which I have called 'cue') is scarcely developed at all by exponents of programming. Yet such a concept seems to be necessary.

Some authors refer to 'the stimuli' in a frame, but any human learning situation has a multitude of possible stimuli, and so it is not very significant to say that the response initially determined by a prompt must eventually be made to the 'stimuli' of the situation in which the prompt is used. Which stimuli? Moreover, it is doubtful if what is intended to evoke the response can always be described in 'stimulus' terms at all. It may not even be a number or collection of stimuli. It is often an abstraction from them, such as the 'concept' of Five.

[1] Op. cit. p. 41.

A further ground of criticism is that so long as the cue is not clearly indicated we are in no position to make preparations for understanding. To understand something is to respond to the *cue* of the situation. (See Chapter 7.) How can we strive to make the cue forceful (by emphasis, frame-design, and so on) if we are not specific about what the cue itself is? True, some programmers have a flair for writing good frames, and may contrive to emphasise the relevant feature (cue) almost intuitively; but many programmers are less gifted, and it may be that it is for this reason that programmes are often criticised on the ground that they deal only with rote learning. The same point is relevant to Transfer, because Understanding is its essence.

Klaus [1], emphasising the importance of an initial specification of the required response, suggests that the frame should be written round that specification. To this useful suggestion might be added the advice that the cue also should be specified, and that the frame should then be written round both. It is only after the programmer has decided what response he wants, and what cue he wants to evoke it, that he can decide what sort of prompting will be most appropriate. Also, it is only then that he can arrange for the necessary reinforcement. How can he arrange to connect cue and response unless he first knows what both are?

Reinforcement and Motivation

How is reinforcement provided in programmed learning?

The usual answer is that the reinforcer is the confirmation that the response to the preceding frame was correct. (In a linear programme nearly all the responses *will* be right, and from the check-frames the learner can see that they *are* right. A similar comment applies to branching programmes.) Such confirmation immediately follows the response, is given consistently, and so satisfies Skinner's requirements. (p. 250.) Receiving confirmation of one's right answer to a frame is presumably analogous to the pigeon's receiving a food-pellet on making the response the experimenter wants.

[1] Quoted by Deterline (9). See also (8), p. 35ff.

I*

That is nevertheless not the only possible or actual answer. An alternative view, quoted by Taber, Glaser, and Schaefer (49) in the context of programmed learning, is that the reinforcer may be, not the item (food) usually regarded as the reinforcer, but rather the response the learner makes to that item (eating it). Also, as noted earlier (p. 86), there is a widely held view that reinforcement consists of a reduction of a drive (hunger).

It is very doubtful if the *subject matter* of animal-experiments on this issue has direct relevance to human motivation and reinforcement, mainly because they exploit such primitive drives as hunger and thirst, and responses like eating and drinking, which are scarcely appropriate to school-learning. Also, the conclusions from different animal-experiments of this kind are by no means unanimous.[1] Since linear programming is said to derive from such experiments, however, we may nevertheless examine the *procedures* employed in them to see whether they throw light upon programmed learning in particular and human learning in general.

First, to give direction to our examination of the facts of the training-procedures, let us state three major theories:

(a) the reinforcer is some *stimulus*, such as food;

(b) reinforcement lies in a *response* to the allegedly reinforcing stimulus, such as the eating of food.

(c) reinforcement occurs at the level of *drive*, inside the animal, and consists of a reduction of it; for example the reduction of hunger.

These three views, though apparently contradictory, are nevertheless interdependent. It is generally accepted by exponents of the 'stimulus' view that the stimulus to be used as reinforcer must relate to the motive or drive: if a food-pellet is used, the animal must be hungry. That stimulus, almost by definition, will relate also to the response to it. Since the 'stimulus' theorists agree that the reinforcing stimulus must be a 'strong' stimulus, we may assume that it will in fact evoke a response: with the hunger-drive

[1] See for instance Sheffield and Roby (44), as contrasted with Miller and Kessen (34). Both articles are included in (4).

already established, the food-pellet will evoke the response of eating. Also, the response to the alleged reinforcing stimulus is related directly, if more subtly, to the motive or drive. The experimenter creates a drive by (say) depriving the animal of food; but strictly he knows that the alleged drive-state is adequate to his purpose only in so far as the animal does *behave* in a certain way (does eat when food is offered). (If it did not eat, food-deprivation would not further the experimenter's purpose.) As argued in our earlier sections on Motivation, not only may the observable behaviours be said to be the only 'evidence' of an inner motive or drive; it is only from these behaviours that the very concept of Drive or Motive is inferrable. The three views are thus inextricably linked.

Second, a summary of what seem to be the relevant facts of training. When put into a certain kind of situation, such as a training-box with a food-cup and lever in it, and perhaps also a signal light, the food-deprived animal will eat the pellet in the food-cup. Sometimes, however, the food is not immediately available: the animal may have run over to the cup, or press a lever, or walk in a figure-8 before food will appear. In such instances the animal can eat *only if it first* behaves in some other way. In Skinner's terms, the training-design makes the eating-behaviour 'contingent' upon the performance of a preliminary behaviour. What Skinner's type of experiment seems to have shown is that when the eating-behaviour is made contingent upon some other behaviour, and immediately and consistently succeeds it, that other behaviour *becomes* the precursor of the eating-behaviour in the kind of situation in which these conditions previously held. Subsequently confronted by the same kind of situation, the animal will engage in the behaviour upon which, during training, the eating-behaviour had been made contingent.

Skinner's experiments are usually described in the language of operant conditioning, and so there is no mention of prompts (or unconditional stimuli). Unlike his counterpart in classical conditioning who *prompts* the animal to behave in the required way, the operant-conditioning experimenter waits until the required behaviour, such as lever-pressing, appears. As Bugelski has observed, however, it does not follow that no prompts were operative. The *experimenter* may not have prompted the rat to press the lever, or prompted the pigeon to turn to the right, but *something* in the situation must presumably have done so.[1] Also, although there may be no mention of a conditional stimulus (or cue), presumably *something* in the situation must have served as such. In the training-box situation something will take the role of cue to which the rat will eventually respond by running to the lever, pressing it, and eating the pellet then deposited in the cup.

With these points in mind, the training-procedure may be summarised as follows.

The experimenter creates a 'drive-state' (hunger) which will ensure that, given the opportunity (food) to do so, the animal will behave (eat) in the way predictable from the drive-state. Call this the 'predicted response'. When so 'driven', the animal is confronted by a certain cue (training-box and its appurtenances, or some feature of them), and is allowed to make the predicted response (eat). It is then confronted by the same cue but is *not* allowed to make the predicted response. By means of prompts (ad hoc or accidental), however, the animal now behaves in the required way (presses lever). Call this the 'required response'. Immediately after it makes the required response (presses lever) it is given food, which permits the predicted response. Subsequent to the repetition of this training-procedure the animal, when confronted by the same cue, will respond to it, without prompts, by making the required response. The performance will nevertheless deteriorate, or even disappear, unless the required response (lever-pressing) is followed from time to time by the predicted behaviour (eating).

A detailed analysis of this procedure, from which the following theses are derived, is beyond the scope of this chapter, and so the points now made should perhaps be treated as suggestions rather

[1] Op. cit. p. 56ff.

than as valid inferences. (The reader is nevertheless invited to test them.)

The so-called drive-state is not an inevitable condition of training, but is only a means of ensuring that, given the opportunity, the animal will engage in the predicted behaviour. What matters here is not the drive-state per se but the occurrence of a predicted behaviour when opportunity is provided. If he will respond in the predicted way to the *cue alone* (in accord with past learning) we need not contrive a special 'drive-state'; knowing what the cue is we can predict the response it will evoke.

This response must be not only predictable but also of such a kind that it can be made contingent upon the required response. Eating fulfils this requirement. The learner cannot eat until there is food, and the experimenter can therefore ensure that eating does not occur until the learner has first responded as required, by pressing a lever, walking in a figure-8, or saying grace. Also, the behaviour I have called 'predicted' must *be* predictable for the simple reason that we cannot control its time of occurrence if we do not know what it is.

In this procedure learning is effected by the required behaviour's being *enclosed* between what is to be the cue for it and the predicted behaviour which that cue would evoke but for the contingency-control. This 'enclosing' effect is achieved as follows. While the *predicted* response is inhibited by the trainer, the cue for it is presented along with a prompt (ad hoc or accidental) for the *required* response. Were the predicted response not so prevented, a prompt for the required response might be impossible, because there is a very strong connection between the cue and the *predicted* response.[1]

Then wherein lies the 'motivation'? That the animal 'wants' to eat is inferred from the observation that it usually *does* eat, in the circumstances in question, when given the opportunity to do so.

---

[1] To say that there is a 'strong connection' between cue and response is, of course, but a metaphorical way of saying that the probability, or predictability, of the response's being made to the cue is high.

If we now wish to 'motivate' the *required* behaviour, say lever-pressing, and ensure that *it* also will continue to occur in response to the chosen cue, we can infer from Skinner's procedure that we must *enclose* that required behaviour between the cue and the predicted (already 'motivated') behaviour. This inference is essentially the same as the thesis advanced in earlier discussions of Motivation (see pp. 88, 119), but is a more precise version of it. The relevance of this thesis is perhaps most clear in those cases where we need not create a special 'drive-state', but can effect learning by enclosing the new behaviour between a cue and the response which that cue already evokes.

What serves as reinforcer? We may discount Drive-reduction, not on the ground that it is false or irrelevant, but on the ground that a drive-state has to be inferred from the predicted behaviour. Also, as noted, there are many instances in which an established cue-response connection is sufficient. We may discount also the so-called reinforcing stimulus, for human learning at least, on the ground that human subjects are unlikely to learn if they are never allowed to make the appropriate *response* to it. A sweet is unlikely to serve as reinforcer if the child is never allowed to eat it. The 'reinforcing stimulus' is of course necessary, but its function would seem to be to control the contingency of the predicted behaviour. On this view, then, reinforcement consists of the required behaviour's being immediately succeeded by the predicted response to the same cue.

Support for this view is given by some experiments by Premack (41). He has concluded that a response can be reinforced if immediately succeeded by another response which has a higher 'operant rate', (Of two behaviours, that with the higher 'operant rate' is the behaviour in which the subject engages more often.) Children who, allowed to do either, eat a sweet more often than they manipulate a machine, will learn to play with the machine more often if sweet-eating is made contingent upon manipulation. This finding is in accord with theories of reinforcement which stress the function of 'reward'. But it appears also that occasional sweet-eating, if made contingent upon the more frequent behaviour of manipulation, will increase in operant rate. Findings like these seem to show, not only that *responses* can serve as reinforcers, but also that the reinforcing responses need not be consummatory, and that whether a response will serve as reinforcer depends, not upon the sort of response it is, but upon its being more frequent (in the learner's repertoire) than the behaviour to be reinforced. Irrespective of the natures of the responses, a *more* frequent response will reinforce a *less* frequent response, if the former is made contingent upon the latter. Now in the case we were considering, the to-be-reinforced response had *no* frequency at all in the situation in question, whereas the 'predicted' behaviour *was* of frequent occurrence. (That was why it was in fact predictable.) Although Premack was investigating a somewhat different problem, his conclusions would seem to support the view expressed above.

That view would appear to be able to embrace a number of contradictory theories of reinforcement and reveal them as different aspects of the same thing. To follow up this suggestion would take us beyond the limits of this book, so only two examples will be cited in illustration. When a certain cue is regularly succeeded by a certain response, the human learner comes to 'expect' that, when given that cue, he will respond in that way. Called for dinner ('Dinner's ready!') he expects to eat. If, now, some other behaviour *is* enclosed in the way we have described, the performance of that behaviour *will* fulfil his expectancy. The response-as-reinforcer view can be expressed in Tolman's terms. At the other extreme, it embraces Guthrie's view that we need not hypothesise a special agent like reward; learning can be adequately described in terms of cues and responses and the temporal relations between them.

The main point was that reinforcement consists of the *enclosing* of the to-be-reinforced response between the (prospective) cue for it and the (predicted) response which that cue already evokes. The particular item which serves as reinforcer, then, is the predicted response. In many animal-experiments this enclosure can be effected only by means of physical contingency-controls.

In much human learning, however, controls of that kind are often unnecessary. The educator, whether he be teacher or parent or even the learner himself, can often find an effective prompt for the to-be-inserted behaviour without having to make the predicted behaviour contingent upon it. A reasonably obedient child will learn to wash his hands after the dinner-warning and before he eats; it is not always necessary to impose the sanction: 'No washing, no dinner!' The crucial event is not the operation of the contingency but the *effect* of it (in those cases where contingency-control is necessary): namely the required behaviour's being made contiguous with the prospective cue, at the one end, and with the predicted behaviour at the other. The necessary effect can often be achieved by simple prompts like: 'Wash your hands now dinner's nearly ready!' and 'Read all the questions before you write down any answers!'

In human learning the required response may be fairly complex, even to the extent of incorporating what could be envisaged as a series of cue-response pairs. Washing one's hands, for example, involves responding to a tap, a plug, the soap, the towel, and so forth. The enclosed behaviour need not be, so to speak, 'pure behaviour'. On the other hand, the longer or more complex the required behaviour, the more difficult its enclosure is likely to be. There will obviously be a limit to the delay we can impose between the cue and its predicted response. Younger learners seem to need reinforcement more frequently than do older learners; but there will be limits for all. If the required behaviour is so long or so complex that he loses sight of the cue, or finds that it is taking him away from what he expects, the enclosing effect will not be achieved. It is nevertheless possible to enclose a complex behaviour if we begin with a very small part of it and gradually increase the dose.[1]

---

[1] This possibility is demonstrated by the training of the pigeon, though in that case the trainer had no option. At the outset there was no single cue which might have been used to prompt the figure-8 walk, and so the complex behaviour had to be composed little by little. My point is that, even if there is a cue for a complex response, we may still have to enclose that response by the method of ever-increasing doses. (Cf. the small doses of *cue*, described in Chapter 6).

If we now apply this view to programmed learning, the reinforcer appears, not as the confirmation of the rightness of the response to the preceding frame, but rather as some other *response* the learner makes. Taber, Glaser, and Schaefer [1] suggest that the reinforcer may be the response the learner makes to the confirmation; and further, that that response may be his 'going on' through the programme. That answer may be valid. The initial cue lies in the learner's being given the programme in the first place; and it is likely that he will in fact begin to go through it. But surely he does this in the 'expectation' that by going through it he will be able to do what the programme has promised? Surely it is this final behaviour, which he cannot as yet perform or even adequately describe, which is the basic *predicted* behaviour? He expects that by going through the programme he will be able to solve problems he cannot yet solve, or talk about something of which he knows little, or pass examinations in psychology. If it is a good programme, that expectation will be fulfilled – eventually; but in view of the point made in our previous paragraph it is reasonable to suggest that at many points throughout the programme the learner must find that he can perform recognisable parts of the ultimate task. Merely getting one's responses right, and merely getting on with the programme, are scarcely enough.

That suggestion is incorporated in some methods of teaching manual skills. The expert may have to sharpen his tools, or light his torch, clean his materials, prepare the site, arrange his materials in a vice or set of clamps, raise the metals to a certain temperature, and so forth, before he can proceed with what the beginner regards as the 'real' skill of sawing, or welding, or burning, or brick-building. Early in training, therefore, much of the preparatory, but necessary, work can be done by someone else, so that the learner can perform without having to tolerate a very long delay between the initial cue and the final response. Gradually these other tasks can be inserted.

To return to the main point: going on through the programme

[1] Op. cit. pp. 57, 58.

would qualify as a 'predicted' behaviour only in so far as it patently was a means to be expected, ultimate predicted behaviour. Further, is confirmation of every response *necessary* to ensure even the 'going on through the programme' behaviour? If the learner can and will go on through the programme, which is the hypo- thesised predicted behaviour, without perpetual confirmation, there is no logical need of confirmation. If the programme is well written, so that the responses are almost always correct, why should the learner be obliged to check them? The checking may serve only to hold him up and distract him from the main theme.[1] Also, as noted a moment ago, some of the enclosed behaviours can be envisaged as series of cue-response pairs; and it is apparently unnecessary to provide ad-hoc reinforcement for each of these. As Lumsdaine[2] has observed, within many linear programmes the frames seem to be based upon the pattern of classical rather than of operant conditioning; the writer of the programme has been much more concerned to provide prompts than to ensure immediate reinforcement.

The general conclusion would seem to be that reinforcement, in programmed learning as elsewhere, consists of the enclosing of the to-be-acquired behaviour between the cue for it and the predicted behaviour. The inserted behaviours may nevertheless be longer and more complex than those in the animal-experiments often cited in illustration. Nor, in so far as prompts for the required behaviour can be found, need the contingency-controls be so rigorous. Not every small cue-response pair within the required behaviour need be given special reinforcement. In designing the programme, however, one must have regard for the length or complexity of behaviour the learner will tolerate before he can engage in the behaviour he expects to perform.

[1] See Briggs, Goldbeck, Campbell, and Nichols, in (7), and also Lumsdaine (7), p. 143.
[2] In (7), p. 138.

Selected Bibliography on Programmed Learning

AUSTWICK, K. (ed.) *Teaching Machines and Programming*. Pergamon Press Ltd., 1964.

BRITISH BROADCASTING CORPORATION. *What is Programmed Learning?* B.B.C. 1965.

COULSON, J. E. (ed.) *Programmed Learning and Computer-based Instruction*. John Wiley & Sons, Inc. 1962.

DE CECCO, J. P. (ed.) *Educational Technology*. Holt Rinehart and Winston Inc. 1964.

DETERLINE, W. A. *An Introduction to Programmed Instruction*. Prentice-Hall, Inc 1962.

GALANTER, E. (ed.) *Automatic Teaching, the State of the Art*. John Wiley & Sons, Inc. 1959.

GOLDSMITH, M. (ed.) *Mechanisation in the Class-room*.Souvenir Press, Ltd. 1963.

GOODMAN, R. *Programmed Learning and Teaching Machines*. English Universities. Press, Ltd. 1962.

GREEN, E. J. *The Learning Process and Programmed Instruction*. Holt Rinehart and Winston, Inc. 1962.

LEITH, G. O. M. (*et al*) *A Handbook of Programmed Learning*. University of Birmingham 1964.

LUMSDAINE, A. A. & Glaser, R. (eds.) *Teaching Machines and Programmed Learning*. National Education Association 1961.

LYSAUGHT, J. P. & WILLIAMS, C. M. *A Guide to Programmed Instruction*. John Wiley & Sons, Inc. 1963.

MARGULIES, S. & EIGEN, L. D. *Applied Programmed Instruction*. John Wiley & Sons, Inc. 1962.

RICHMOND, W. K. *Teachers and Machines*. Wm. Collins Sons & Co., Ltd. 1965.

SKINNER, B. F. 'The Science of Learning and the Art of Teaching'; 'Teaching Machines'; 'Why we need Teaching Machines'.
(The three articles appear in *Cumulative Record* 45).

SMITH, W. I. & MOORE, J. W. (eds.) *Programmed Learning*. D. Van Nostrand Co., Inc. 1962.

TABER, J. I. (*et al*) *Learning and Programmed Instruction*. Addison-Wesley 1965.

THOMAS, C. A. (*et al*) *Programmed Learning in Perspective*. Lamson Technical Products, Ltd. 1963.

References

(1) ADAMS, D. K. 'A Restatement of the Problem of Learning'. *British Journal of Psychology*, XXII. 1931. See also (19).

(2) ALLPORT, G. W. *Personality*. London: Constable & Co. Ltd. 1949. See also (47).

(3) BINGHAM, H. C. 'Size and Form Perception in *Gallus domesticus*'. *J. Anim. Behav.*, **3**, 65–113. See also (6).

(4) BIRNEY, R. C. & TEEVAN, R. C. *Reinforcement*. Princeton, New Jersey: D. Van Nostrand Co., Inc. 1961.

(5) BRUCE, R. W. 'Conditions of Transfer of Training'. *J. Exp. Psychol.*, 1933, **16**, 343–61. See also (27).

(6) BUGELSKI, B. R. *The Psychology of Learning*. New York: Henry Holt & Co. 1956.

(7) COULSON, J. E. (ed.). *Programmed Learning and Computer-based Instruction*. New York: John Wiley & Sons, Inc. 1962.

(8) DE CECCO, J. P. (ed.). *Educational Technology*. New York: Holt Rinehart & Winston, Inc. 1964.

(9) DETERLINE, W. A. *An Introduction to Programmed Instruction*. Englewood Cliffs, N. J.: Prentice-Hall Inc. 1962.

(10) ELLIS, W. D. *A Source Book of Gestalt Psychology*. London: Routledge & Kegan Paul Ltd. 1938.

(11) ENGLISH, H. B. 'Learning – "They Ain't No Such Animal" '. *Journal of Educational Psychology*, XLIII. 1952. See also (19).

(12) ENGLISH, H. B. & ENGLISH, A. C. *A Comprehensive Dictionary of Psychological and Psychoanalytical Terms*. New York, London, Toronto: Longmans Green & Co. Ltd. 1958.

(13) ESTES (*et al*) *Modern Learning Theory*. New York: Appleton-Century-Crofts 1954.

(14) EYSENCK, H. J. 'Communicating with Caliban'. *Guildhall Lectures* 1960. London: University of London Press Ltd. 1961.

(15) FREEMAN, F. N. *How Children Learn*. London: Harrap & Co. Ltd. 1919. See also (39).

(16) GATES, A. I. 'Recitation as a factor in memorizing'. *Arch Psychol.*, 1917, **6**, No. 40.

(17) GUTHRIE, E. R. & EDWARDS, A. L. *Psychology: A First Course in Human Behaviour*. New York: Harper & Brothers. 1949. See also (6), (13), (21), (25), (31), (35), (36).

(18) HARLOW, H. F. 'The Formation of Learning Sets'. *Psychol. Rev.*, 1949. See also (25).

(19) HARTLEY, E. L. & HARTLEY, R. E. *Outside Readings in Psychology*. New York: Thomas Y. Crowell Co. 1958.

(20) HEBB, D. O. *The Organisation of Behaviour*. New York: John Wiley & Sons Inc. London: Chapman & Hall Ltd. 1949.

(21) HILGARD, E. R. *Theories of Learning*. New York: Appleton-Century-Crofts 1948.

(22) HULL, C. L. *Principles of Behaviour*. New York: Appleton-Century-Crofts 1943. See also (6), (13), (21), (25), (31), (35), (36), (47).

(23) HUNTER, I. M. L. *Memory: Facts and Fallacies*. London: Penguin Books Ltd. 1957.

(24) KATZ, D. *Gestalt Psychology*. London: Macmillan & Co. Ltd. 1951.

(25) KINGSLEY, H. L. & GARRY, R. *The Nature and Conditions of Learning*. Englewood Cliffs, N. J.: Prentice-Hall Inc. 1957.

(26) KOFFKA, K. *Principles of Gestalt Psychology*. New York: Harcourt, Brace & World, Inc. 1935.

(27) LAWSON, R. *Learning and Behaviour*. New York: The Macmillan Co. 1960.

(28) LEWIN, K. *A Dynamic Theory of Personality*. New York & London: McGraw-Hill Book Co. Inc. 1935.

(29) MACKINTOSH, I. 'The Resistance to Extinction of Responses Acquired under Irregular Conditions of Learning'. *J. comp. physiol. Psychol.*, 1955, **48,** 363–70. See also (27).

(30) MAIER, N. R. F. *Psychology in Industry*. London: Harrap & Co. Ltd. 1947.

(31) McGEOCH, J. A. & IRION, A. L. *The Psychology of Human Learning*. London: Longmans, Green & Co. Ltd. 1952.

(32) MELTON, A. W. (ed.). *Categories of Human Learning*. New York: Academic Press 1964.

(33) MILLER, N. E. & DOLLARD, J. *Social Learning and Imitation*. London: Kegan Paul, Trench, Trubner & Co. Ltd. 1945.

(34) MILLER, N. E. & KESSEN, M. L. 'Reward Effects of Food Via Stomach Fistula Compared with Those of Food Via Mouth'. *Journal of Comparative and Physiological Psychology*, **45,** 1952, pp. 555–63. (included in (4).)

(35) NATIONAL SOCIETY FOR THE STUDY OF EDUCATION. *Yearbook XLI Part II: The Psychology of Learning*. Illinois: University of Chicago Press 1942.

(36) OSGOOD, C. E. *Method and Theory in Experimental Psychology*. New York: Oxford University Press. 1953.

(37) OVERSTREET, H. A. *The Mature Mind*. New York: W. W. Norton & Co. Inc. 1959.

(38) PAVLOV, I. P. *Selected Works*. Moscow: Foreign Languages Publishing House. 1955. See also (6), (14), (21), (31), (36).

(39) PEAR, T. H. *Skill in Work and Play*. London: Methuen & Co. Ltd. 1924.

(40) PETERMANN, B. *The Gestalt Theory and the Problem of Configuration*. London: Kegan Paul, Trench, Trubner & Co. Ltd. 1932.

(41) PREMACK, D. 'Toward Empirical Behavior Laws. I. Positive Reinforcement.' *Psychological Review*. Vol. 66. No. 4. 1959.

(42) SANDIFORD, P. *Educational Psychology*. London: Longmans, Green & Co. Ltd. 1937.

(43) SHARP, W. L. 'The Relationship between Speed and Efficiency of Learning on the Constant Speed Finger Maze'. *J. exp. Psychol.*, 1939, **24,** 86–94, See also (25).

(44) SHEFFIELD, F. D. & ROBY, T. B. 'Reward Value of a Non-nutritive Sweet Taste'. *Journal of Comparative and Physiological Psychology*, **43,** 1950, pp. 471–81. (included in (4).)

(45) SKINNER, B. F. *Cumulative Record*. London: Methuen & Co. Ltd. 1959.

(46) SKINNER, B. F. *Verbal Behaviour*. New York: Appleton-Century-Crofts. 1957.

(47) SMITH, F. V. *The Explanation of Human Behaviour*. London: Constable & Co. Ltd. 1951.

(48) SOLLEY, W. H. 'The Effects of Verbal Instruction of Speed and Accuracy upon the Learning of a Motor Skill'. *Res. Quarterly*, 1952, **23,** pp. 231–40. See also (25).

(49) TABER, J. I., GLASER, R. & SCHAEFER, H. H. *Learning and Programmed Instruction*. Reading, Massachusetts: Addison-Wesley. 1965.

(50) THORNDIKE, E. L. *Human Learning*. New York: Appleton-Century-Crofts. 1931. See also (6), (21), (25), (35), (36).

(51) THOULESS, R. H. *General and Social Psychology*. London: University Tutorial Press Ltd. 1951.

(52) THYNE, J. M. *Patterns of Error in the Addition Number Facts*. Publications of the Scottish Council for Research in Education, XXXVII. London: University of London Press Ltd. 1954.

(53) TOLMAN, E. C. *Purposive Behaviour in Animals and Men*. New York: Appleton-Century-Crofts. 1932. See also (6), (13), (21), (25), (31), (36), (47).

(54) VOEKS, V. W. 'Acquisition of S-R connections: A Test of Hull's and Guthrie's Theories'. *J. exp. Psychol.*, 1954, **47,** 137–47. See also (27).

(55) WERTHEIMER, M. *Productive Thinking*. New York & London: Harper & Brothers. 1945.

(56) WYLIE, H. H. 'An Experimental Study of Transfer of Response in the White Rat'. *Behav. Monogr.*, 1919, **3,** No. 16. See also (27).

Index